D1532265

Television Sitcom Factbook

Television Sitcom Factbook

Over 8,700 Details from 130 Shows, 1985–2000

by
Vincent Terrace

McFarland & Company, Inc., Publishers
Jefferson, North Carolina, and London

Library of Congress Cataloguing-in-Publication Data

Terrace, Vincent, 1948–
    Television sitcom factbook : over 8,700 details from 130
shows, 1985–2000 / by Vincent Terrace.
      p.   cm.
    Includes index.
    ISBN 0-7864-0900-2 (softcover : 55# alkaline paper) ∞
    1. Television comedies — United States. I. Title.
PN1992.8.C66 T47   2000
791.45'617 — dc21   00-57865

British Library cataloguing data are available

Cover image © 2000 Dynamic Graphics

Manufactured in the United States of America

McFarland & Company, Inc., Publishers
  Box 611, Jefferson, North Carolina 28640
   www.mcfarlandpub.com

Contents

Contents

Preface

When Dana (of *Step by Step*) was a little girl, her mother (Carol) called her "Princess Bubble Buns" when it was time for her bath. Jack Stein (*Love and War*) has a dust ball under his bed that he has named Milt, and George Castanza (*Seinfeld*) accomplished only one thing in his life — scoring highest (860,000 points) on the video game "Frogger." Did you know that Dan Conner (*Roseanne*) hates it when the kids leave toast crumbs in the butter or that Salem the Cat (*Sabrina, the Teenage Witch*) likes chocolate syrup in his bowl of milk?

This is a sampling of the type of information you will find in the *TV Sitcom Factbook*, a book that covers a neglected area of television — the facts that make characters interesting and add special interest to a program. Trivia? Nostalgia? Whatever you call these tidbits of information, you'll find over 8,700 facts from 130 comedy series that began in 1985 and after, to those still current in 2000.

Coverage includes series broadcast on ABC, CBS, NBC, Fox, Nickelodeon (NIK), UPN (United Paramount Network), Disney (DIS), the WB (Warner Bros. Network) and in Syndication (listed as Syn.). All information in this book is drawn solely from the programs themselves; the series selection was based on those shows with the most interesting facts. Both long-running and here-today, gone-tomorrow series are included.

Most of the information that appears here cannot be found in any other source. If you are looking for addresses, nicknames, names of pets, character quirks, telephone numbers, license plate numbers, clothing sizes, favorite foods or jobs, to name a few, then the source to turn to is this book.

In addition to all the character facts, names of performers, networks and years of production are included. At the back there is a complete index to the performers, keyed to the entry number assigned to each show.

The
Shows

1.   Almost Home NBC, 1993

Brian Morgan (Perry King) is a lawyer with two mischievous children, Molly (Brittany Murphy) and Gregory (Jason Marsden). He runs his late wife's business, the Molly-Gregory Fine Children's Catalogue, from his home in Seattle, Washington. Millicent Torkelson (Connie Ray) is the divorced mother of three children, Dorothy Jane (Olivia Burnette), Mary Sue (Rachel Duncan) and Chuckie Lee (Lee Norris). She operates a small business, Millicent Torkelson — Custom Upholstering and Design, from her home in Pyramid Corners, Oklahoma. When her business fails and she loses her home, Millicent moves to Seattle to become the live-in nanny for Molly and Gregory.

Brian considers the Torkelsons to be the most real people he has ever met. Molly and Gregory had six prior nannies "and are known by all of Seattle as terrors" (Brian has nicknamed them Beelzebub and Mephistopheles, the Devil's children). Molly, 15, is pretty and fashion conscious, and "has a terrible snoring problem." Her secret ambition is to be a TV weather girl. She calls Dorothy Jane "Rebecca of Sunnybrook Farm." Dorothy Jane, Molly and Gregory attend Lincoln High School. Dorothy Jane loves her new environment and hopes to shed her "Oklahoma Milk Maid image." *Pride and Prejudice* is her favorite book and a picture of her favorite poet, Emily Dickinson, hangs on her bedroom wall. She works after school as a countergirl at the Chicken in a Hat fast food restaurant. Mary Sue has a doll named Martha Sue. Chuckie Lee attends Harrison Junior High School. He is a member of the Wilderness Troop and first realized what girls are when he accidentally opened the bathroom door and saw Molly nude. He plays violin, modeled for Brian's company and did a TV commercial for Snackelberry (peanut butter and jelly in one jar). When Brian takes Millicent out to dinner he puts Dorothy Jane in charge of the house (when Molly was in charge she made $300 worth of phone calls to Suzanne Somers — "I had to, I got caught in her thigh master"; when Gregory was in charge, he sold the house). See also *The Torkelsons*.

2.   Alright Already WB, 1997–1998

Carol Lerner (Carol Leifer) is a young woman looking for Mr. Right ("Only problem is I meet all the Mr. Wrongs"). She is an optometrist who runs the Collins Avenue Optical Center in Florida with her friend Renee Helke (Amy Yasbeck). Renee, a theater major in college, sells eyeglasses and contact lenses. She calls her breasts Judy and Trudy and wears provocative clothes to attract men. Carol lives in Apartment 3D at 36 Waterton Avenue and drinks Big Bear Head bottled water. Jessica Lerner (Stacy Galina), Carol's sister, lives with her parents, Alvin and Miriam (Jerry Adler, Mitzi McCall) at the Flamingo Pines Village Retirement Home. Jessica, famous for her sponge cake, shops at Bulk World and is looking for the right job. She worked as Carol's receptionist, a receptionist in a doctor's office and as a clerk at Spencer's Department Store but has a knack for annoying people and getting fired. The sets for Carol's apartment, her parents' home and the optical shop have one thing in common: an aquarium can be seen in the background.

3.   **Amen** NBC, 1986–1991

Ernest J. Frye (Sherman Hemsley) is deacon of the First Community Church of Philadelphia. He is set in his ways and refuses to accept change. Reverend Reuben Gregory (Clifton Davis) is a young minister with progressive ideas. He feels the church is behind the times and needs improvement. Hence the conflict as both men try to do what is best for the church.

Ernest, first an attorney then a judge, has an office (Room 203) on 56th Street with a shingle that reads Attorney-at-Law Ernest Frye — Where Winning Is Everything. He has A-positive blood, reads *Popular Gospel* magazine and drives a sedan with the license plate KNC 481 (his parking space has a sign that reads "Don't Even Think About Parking Here"). Each week Ernest buys one lottery ticket. When he ran for state senator, he used the slogan "Vote for Frye and Get a Piece of the Pie" (he lost against a jailed incumbent, 19,372 to 43).

In the opening theme, two girls are seen jumping rope. Ernest joins in and jumps 11 times. During the Korean War, Ernest met his late wife, Laraine Tillman, a nurse at County General Hospital. He was studying to become a lawyer and, while working for Al's Delivery Service, brought flowers to a patient, saw Laraine and fell in love. They married, had a child (Thelma) and lived happily for five years (at which time Laraine passed away). Ernest is afraid of snakes and his favorite food is meatball-topped pizza.

Reuben has a B.A. from Morehouse College, a master's degree in religious education from Yale Divinity School and a doctorate in Christian Studies from Union Theological Seminary. His career began in Cleveland where he hosted *Sunrise Semester* on TV. Reuben holds a weekly "Pastor's Pow Wow" to discuss church matters with parishioners; teaches theology at the Baxter Women's College; and oversees the church's volunteer teen hot line (295-TEEN).

Ernest's daughter, Thelma (Anna Maria Horsford), attended West Holmes High School. She was on the track team; English, science and home economics were her favorite subjects; and she had the nickname "The Undateable" (in the pilot Ernest says she was jilted 20 times in ten years; in the third episode he says 16 times in ten years). Thelma eventually found romance and married Reuben (whom she called "Sweet Potato"). She studied real estate, found a job with the firm of Underwood-Baines, did a TV commercial for Bake Rite Flour and hosted her own TV series, *Thelma's Kitchen*.

4.   American Dreamer NBC, 1990–1991

Tom Nash (Robert Urich) is a columnist for the city-based *Chicago American* (also called the *Chicago Metro*) but lives in a small Wisconsin town with his children Rachel (Chay Lentin) and Danny (Johnny Galecki). His editor, Joe Barnes (Jeffrey Tambor), visits him weekly to pick up his columns and complain about "the fresh air and general decency of the people." Tom writes about "things that worry me, things that touch my life and things I wonder about." Tom, a graduate of NYU, began his career as a stringer for a local TV news show. He later became a field reporter and married his cameraperson, Elizabeth. Fourteen years later, when they were both working for UPI, Elizabeth was killed while covering the war in Lebanon. Tom quit his job to begin a new life in Wisconsin. He was born in St. Louis (where he attended Madison High School), had a dog named Pete and wears a Green Bay Packers sweatshirt. Tom, a Pisces, had two embarrassing moments as a reporter: spilling red wine on Margaret Thatcher's dress and reporting live from the White House with an open fly.

Rachel, 15, attends Mission West High School. She is pretty, always having boy trouble and constantly bewildered by the attention she keeps getting but can't handle. She is Episcopalian (Tom and Danny are Catholic), and plans to marry a blond rock star when she turns 24. Rachel works after school at the local diner, Baker's Corner. Danny, 12, attends Wisconsin Junior High School and is a member of the Leopards, the school baseball team.

Lillian Abernathy (Carol Kane) is Tom's flaky secretary. She played a shrub in her ninth-grade presentation of *A Midsummer Night's Dream* (she received three curtain calls and a wet shoe when a dog relieved himself) and attended Mission West High School. She dreamed of attending the affluent Fairpoint Academy and spent 12 years in night school to earn her B.A. in journalism. Lillian is a Libra and has been distrustful of men since her divorce from Bill ("I even have trouble walking past the men's room"). She attended a bachelor party ("I jumped out of the cake") and knew her marriage was over when Bill said "Lily, it's over." Holly Baker (Margaret Welsh) owns the

Baker's Corner diner. Her favorite meal to serve is brussels sprout casserole. As a kid she and her sister, Drew, performed as the singing group Holly and the Pip for the Girl Scout Jamboree.

5. Ann Jillian NBC, 1989–1990

Aunt Betty's Coffee and Bean Shop is a quaint eatery in the small town of Marvel, California. Ann McNeal (Ann Jillian), the manager, is a recent widow who has relocated from Queens, New York, with her daughter, Lucy (Lisa Rieffel), to begin a new life. In Queens, Ann lived at 1027-64 South Ferry Street. She was a Radio City Music Hall Rockette; Eddie, her husband, was a fireman; and Lucy attended Saint Michael's High School. When Eddie was killed in the line of duty, Ann had to get away from it all. She and Lucy now live at 805 Etchfield Street. Ann has an account at the Fidelity Mutual Bank and is afraid of thunderstorms. She and Eddie met as teenagers and their first date was a hansom cab ride through Central Park (before a date, Ann would hang upside down to get color in her cheeks). To neck, they would go to Montague Point "to watch for Halley's Comet — which wasn't due for 30 years."

Lucy, 15, attends Marvel High School. She has a dog named Corkey (whom Ann calls "The puppy from Hell"), eats Dipples brand potato chips as a bedtime snack and goes mall shopping with Ann every Saturday. Lucy's make-out spot is Paradise Point, "where we go to watch for UFOs."

Robin Walker (Amy Lynne) is Lucy's friend and Ann's not-too-bright assistant at the coffee shop. Robin's mother has a little shrine dedicated to her and lets her go out whenever she wants "but no one ever asks me out," she says. (Lucy is jealous of this because she feels "my mother is smothering me and won't let me go out.") Robin closes the shop at 6:00 P.M. sharp; if she is even ten seconds late, she panics. She will talk to anyone on any topic "as long as I don't have to give an opinion" (she feels she may be wrong).

Melissa Santos (Chantal Rivera-Batisse), Lucy's friend, is a conceited high school bombshell (Lucy claims "she only cares about how she looks and what the guys think"). Melissa believes no girl can match her beauty and holds the beauty pageant titles "Miss Teenage Tomato" and "Miss Teen Avocado." Lucy can't dance ("I have two left feet") and Ann finds comfort in teaching Melissa to dance (she feels she is reliving her youth as a Rockette). Melissa believes she has untapped talent and wants to set it free. But, as she practices, she sobs, "I wish I could do something about this sweating, it's so icky." Melissa wants to be the next Madonna ("Who's over the hill") and has never heard of Ann's dancing idols, Ginger Rogers and Cyd Charisse.

Marvel was founded by Jacob Sweeney in 1921. While driving to San

Francisco, his Model T Ford experienced a flat tire. Rather than fix the flat, he decided to stay where he was and start a town.

6. **Babes** Fox, 1990–1991

Charlene, Marlene and Darlene Gilbert (Wendie Jo Sperber, Lesley Boone, Susan Peretz) are full-figured sisters who live together at 362 East 7th Street (Apartment 410) in Manhattan. They went to Camp Tamarack as kids and attended Edgar Allan Poe High School. They dine frequently at Stein's Restaurant and failed at a business designing clothes for full-figured women.

Charlene, the middle sister, is adjusted to the fact that she will always be heavy. She is a commercial makeup artist and has worked on Dolly Parton and other celebrities. Her boyfriend, Ronnie Underwood (Rick Overton), owns Ronnie's Take Out Food. In 1970 Charlene took tap-dancing lessons at Madame McNair's School of Dance and played the fourth dancing teapot in *Madame McNair's Winter Recital*.

Marlene, the youngest, is the prettiest and most sensitive (having a difficult time accepting the fact that she will never be thin). She was first a toll collector (called "Miss Exact Change"), then a model ("The Hefty Hose Girl") for the Merit, Barrett and Cole Ad Agency, and finally a video photographer at a dating service, Ideal Mates, Inc. As a kid Marlene dreamed of being an actress (she wanted to be Susan Dey's "Laurie Partridge" character on *The Partridge Family*) and loved to play with building blocks (her sisters called her "Block Head"). She twirled a baton and sang "You Light Up My Life" for her fourth-grade music recital and played the mother in her high school production of *Our Town*.

Darlene, fully aware that she will never be thin, is the oldest and nastiest of the sisters. She works as a dog groomer and has a puppy named Big Mike (whom she believes is a miniature Cujo). She loves impressionist art and catching snowflakes on her tongue. She had a hamster (Potsie) and is the only sister to marry and divorce.

7. **Baby Talk** ABC, 1991–1992

Mickey Campbell is an infant whose thoughts (voice of Tony Danza) relate the activities of Margaret "Maggie" Eunice Campbell (Julia Duffy), his single mother, an accountant who works out of her apartment at 46 Bleecker Street in Manhattan (next to the Goodall Rubber Company). "Mickey," Maggie says, "was born after an affair with Nick, a selfish, inconsiderate louse who wasn't fit to be a husband, a father or a human."

Second-season episodes found Maggie (now played by Mary Page Keller) moving to Brooklyn Heights (Apartment 3A) and acquiring a job with Coleman Advertising at the World Trade Center in Manhattan. She attended Penn State University and loves to shop ("I have great credit lines; it was passed down from my mother"). When she gets upset, she exclaims "The universe is expanding." She and Mickey are members of the Mommy and Me Group and Mickey's doctor has an office at the Museum West Medical Center. Mickey has type A-B blood; "Muskrat Love" is his favorite song and red Jell-O his favorite food. Maggie named him after her uncle, Mickey O'Brien, a dry cleaner. When Maggie thought Mickey was a genius at ten months, she enrolled him in the Academy for Gifted Babies (he is also on the waiting list for the Sheridan Academy). Mickey auditioned for the tropical line of Beacon Baby Foods; has a plush bear (Bo Bo) and *Mr. Duck's Jamboree* is his favorite TV show. His rubber ducky is named Ralphie.

James Halbrook (Scott Baio) is Maggie's romantic interest. He is an aspiring songwriter (wrote the "Peachy Time" gum jingle) and works as the building's janitor (he took the job to get Apartment 1A free). He attended Berkeley College and calls Mickey "The Mickster." Mickey's first word was "Daddy" (which he said when looking at James). Maggie and James married in the episode of 5/8/92.

Connie Sellecca played Mollie Campbell in the original, unaired pilot. She was replaced by Alison LaPlaca in a second, unaired pilot. All versions are based on the film *Look Who's Talking*.

8.   Between Brothers Fox, 1997; UPN, 1999

Charles Winston (Kadeem Hardison), his brother James (Dondra Whitfield) and their friends Dustin Q. "Dusty" Canyon (Kelly Perine) and Mitchell Ford (Tommy Davidson) are single men living in Chicago. The friends, who attended Northside High School, gather at the Corner Pub, a bar that serves Marv's brand beer. Charles is a sportswriter for the *Chicago Examiner* and shares Apartment 305 with James, a real estate broker for Raeburn Realty. Dusty, who attended Illinois State University, is a TV weatherman for WEBT, Channel 64. Dusty did a TV commercial for Big Head Bob's RV Land and his first job in the medium was cue card holder on the *Po Po the Clown* show (he later became Po Po because he fit the costume). Dusty has his own web site (www.dusty.com), a toll free pager number (1-800-CANYON) and shares apartment 93 with Mitchell. On Fox, Sunny Rains was Dusty's competition; on UPN it is Wendy Day. Mitchell, who is trying to kick a gambling habit, teaches at Walter Payton High School and tutors children on Saturdays.

9. Big Wave Dave's CBS, 1993

Big Wave Dave's, a surf shop on the North Shore in Oahu, Hawaii, is owned by Marshall Fisher (Adam Arkin), Dave Bell (David Morse) and Richie LaMonica (Patrick Breen), three friends who left Chicago to pursue a new life. Assisting them as their business manager is Dave's wife, Karen (Jane Kaczmarek). Their competition is Danny's Surf Shop; after one month in business each partner made $312.

Marshall and Karen were lawyers with the firm of Fisher and Fisher (run by Marshall's father); Dave was a stockbroker; and Richie, a typing teacher for the Chicago Public High School System. Marshall and Karen have been married ten years; Dave is divorced (after eight years of marriage); Richie is single.

Marshall, Dave and Richie met in high school in 1972. Every three weeks they have an argument and vow never to see each other again. Shortly after they have a make-up dinner to become friends again. Richie earned $22,500 as a teacher; when things don't go Marshall's way, he takes on various moods which Karen calls "The Six Stages of Marshall" (pouting, real pouting, sarcasm, resentment, remorse and justification).

Jack Lord (Kurtwood Smith) is an actor who played bit roles on *Hawaii Five-O* and decided to name himself after the show's star, Jack Lord. He is a Yale dropout, did a tour of Vietnam, sang backup for Bob Dylan and invented several surgical instruments that made him a fortune. Jack only surfs one day a year "because there is too much else to do." He has a cache of automatic weapons, a boat called the *Vendetta II* and a goal: to catch "Him," a giant marlin that destroyed his first boat, the *Vendetta*.

10. Billy ABC, 1992

Billy MacGregor (Billy Connolly), history teacher at Fillmore High School in New York City, moves to California to teach night school at Berkeley Community College. Billy hails from Scotland and his work permit is about to expire. At school he meets Mary Springer (Marie Marshall), a student with three children and a large mortgage. Mary is separated from her husband and looking for a tenant to rent her basement apartment. Billy and Mary solve their respective problems by agreeing to a marriage of convenience: Billy will stay in the U.S.; Mary will get a tenant and each will observe a strictly platonic relationship. Billy's passport number is K0618468 and he has a plant named Robert. Mary, a dental hygienist, lives in a house with the number 2014. She is separated from a man named Roger and has three children: Laura (Natanya Ross), Annie (Clara Bryant) and David (Johnny Galecki). Laura plays the violin and attends the Debbie Daniels Tap

Dance School. Annie, the youngest, has a security blanket (Blankey) and a plush bear (Marty). When she wants attention, she hides. David attends Berkeley High School and has an after-school job at the Chicken Pit restaurant. The kids eat Choco Puffs and Fiber Flakes cereal for breakfast. The series was originally called *Immediate Family* and is a spin-off from *Head of the Class* (see for additional information on Billy).

11.   Black Tie Affair NBC, 1993

Brodsky's Used and Hard to Find 33 1/3 Record Shop and Detective Agency at 1731 Prescott Street in San Francisco is owned by Dave Brodsky (Bradley Whitford), a wisecracking amateur private detective who doesn't like murders "because they involve blood." Dave uses a surveillance van with the name Ed's House of Hammers on it (555-NAIL). Dave had originally wanted to play ball for the San Francisco Giants "but an aggravating lack of talent stopped me." His motto is "I do insurance investigating, Polaroids and 33's. I don't do compact discs and murder." His favorite color is blue and Taft is his favorite President.

Cookie (Maggie Han), a beautiful Eurasian girl, keeps the business together. She is easily annoyed when Dave degrades women by using slang terms or street lingo for her body parts. Cookie, who lives in a fashionable apartment on Wilshire, prefers that Dave stick to records. Her habit of listening in on his phone calls upsets Dave because "she says 'don't' to all my detective cases." However, when Dave does take a case, it is Cookie who helps him solve it. The series was originally titled *Smoldering Lust*.

12.   Bless This House CBS, 1995

Burt and Alice Clayton (Andrew Dice Clay, Cathy Moriarty) are a hardworking couple who hope to one day buy a house (they currently live in Apartment 4D in Trenton, New Jersey). Burt and Alice have been married 14 years and are the parents of Danni (Raegan Kotz) and Sean (Sam Gifaldi). Burt, a post office supervisor, holds a second job as a delivery man for Sun Dairies. Alice is a cashier at Trenton Motor Cars. When Alice is fired from the car lot, she acquires a temporary job selling jeans at the Trenton Mall. She later becomes a secretary at the law firm of Richmond, Goldman and Pike. Burt drives a 1975 Chevy Citation, license plate 19C 593, with a bumper sticker that reads "My Child Beat Up Your Child."

Danni is a 12-year-old girl who wants to become a woman now, "not tomorrow." Alice is worried "because she spends too much time in the bathroom staring at her little hooters" and all Danni thinks about is becoming voluptuous. Burt is also worried because boys are starting to notice her "and what's worse — she's starting to notice boys." He is fearing "an early dating life of crime." Danni's favorite soda is root beer. On the other hand, Burt and Alice have Sean, whose only talent appears to be burping out the alphabet. He has a French poodle (Fluffy) and a turtle (Al the Turtle). He and Danni attend Trenton Elementary School.

13.   Blossom NBC, 1991–1995

The Russos are a family of four who live at 465 Hampton Drive in Southern California. Nick (Ted Wass), the father, is divorced and struggling to raise three children: Blossom (Mayim Bialik), Anthony (Michael Stoyanov) and Joey (Joey Lawrence).

Nick is a musician (attended Juilliard) and plays various clubs. He provided backup for Anita Baker, B. B. King and Chuck Berry; won Cleo Awards for commercials; and played on soundtracks for such movies as *Ghost*, *Fame* and *Dirty Dancing*. As a teenager, Nick was a member of a group called Neon Wilderness. Nick has a yellow car (painted Sunrise Surprise) and was married to Madelyn (Melissa Manchester) for 20 years; she left the family to pursue her dream of becoming a singer in Europe. The law firm of O'Hara, Schmitt, Rosetti and Bailey handled the divorce. Nick became romantically involved with Carol (Finola Hughes), a widow with a young daughter, Kennedy (Doren Fein). They married on 10/24/94.

"Blossom is the perfect combination of a little sugar and a little spice." She first attended the Crestridge School for Girls, then Tyler High School in Studio City. Blossom plays the trumpet, sleeps with her ALF doll, drinks Bailey's Diet Cola and "became a woman" in the first episode (as her friend, Six, said "Blossom blossomed"). When she was seven years old, Blossom won the National Spelling Bee in Washington, D.C. She has a scar on her chin from when she fell off the monkey bars and split open her chin. Joey calls 13-year-old Blossom "a borderline babe" ("You're in the Honor Society, you play the trumpet, but you haven't been visited by the hooter fairy yet"). As a kid Blossom had a teddy bear (Dwight) and eats ice cream and pound cake when she gets upset. Her favorite pizza is topped with green peppers and artichoke hearts. Had the series been renewed for another season, Blossom would have been attending UCLA (she was accepted to UCLA, Berkeley, Harvard and Northwestern).

Joey believes the sun is the other side of the moon and his only talent, Blossom says, "is drinking Pepsi through his nose." Sixteen-year-old Joey is not too bright, girl crazy and obsessed with breasts (which he calls "hooters," "gozangas" and "boobs"). Although Joey attends Tyler High School, he mentioned attending Grant High in one episode. Blossom believes Joey is a dork ("If the dorks had a navy, he'd be their admiral"). Joey, who dreams of becoming a professional baseball player, had a job as a delivery boy for Mario's Pizza. His catchword is "whoa" and he is a member of the Bulldogs, the Tyler High baseball team (this led to him becoming a second baseman for the Philadelphia Phillies). He was accepted by Arizona State College but his decision to play ball or attend school was not determined when the series ended.

Anthony, the eldest child, was a drug addict for four years but is now clean. He worked as a delivery boy for Fatty's Pizza and as a counter waiter at Dante's Donut Shop. He is writing a play called *Naked Chick Academy* that he hopes will make him three million dollars. When Anthony was 12 years old he attended Camp Mountain High (where he smoked his first joint). Anthony quit the donut shop to become an E.M.T. (Emergency Medical Technician). The first celebrity he helped was Justine Bateman when she fell and injured her elbow. During a trip to Las Vegas, Anthony met Shelly Lewis (Samaria Graham). They got drunk one night and married. A year later (1994), they have a baby they name Nash Metropolitan.

"I wonder what my husband will look like naked or if I'll laugh the first time I see him. I wonder what it will be like to have a mortgage, a baby or breasts" says 13-year-old Six LeMeure (Jenna Von Oy), Blossom's best friend. Six worries that "my father will go into my room and read the lyrics on my album covers" if she stays away from the house too long. Every Monday Blossom and Six (who also attends Tyler High) go to the mall after school. They eat lunch together in the school cafeteria and each saves a seat when the other is going to be late. Six, named by her father because he had six beers before making love to his wife that night, considers Blossom "a real decent person with moral values." Six and Blossom love to dance: Blossom for obvious reasons; Six "to get all sweaty and dizzy and see stars." Six is on the school's debate team and if detention were frequent flyer miles "I'd have enough miles for a free trip to Hawaii." Six, whose middle name is Dorothy, does volunteer work with Blossom at the Beacon Light Mission. Six was accepted by the following colleges: Northridge, San Diego State and West Orlando State.

The family has a pet cat (Scruffy) and the car license plate reads 629 FZQ. The Russos' living room has flower-print wallpaper and matching flower-print slipcovers on the sofa. When a TV writer friend of Nick's wanted to do a series based on his family, he produced a pilot called *Coming Up Rosie*.

14. Bob CBS, 1992–1993

Cartoonist Bob McKay (Bob Newhart), his wife Kaye (Carlene Watkins) and their daughter Trisha (Cynthia Stevenson) live at 134 Oak Street in Chicago. Bob is the creator of *Mad Dog*, a comic book published by Ace Comics. *Mad Dog* is the story of Dr. Jeffrey Austin, a mild-mannered veterinarian who acquires the glands of his Doberman pinscher, Blackie, and gains the powers of a dog when a scientific experiment backfires. Austin adopts the alias of Mad Dog and sets out to battle evil. Mad Dog, "Mankind's Best Friend," wears blue tights with an orange *M* on his chest. He is assisted by two humans: Penny (whom Bob based on Kaye) and Brad.

Bob created the strip in 1964 when he was dating Kaye. He drew the concept on a napkin and sold it to a publisher. It never caught on and was discontinued (it sold for twelve cents an issue; the first issue sold nine copies). Bob then went into the greeting card business. In 1992 Ace Comics hired Bob to revise the comic. American-Canadian Transcontinental Communications owns Ace Comics (housed in the Ace Building on Michigan Avenue). The Zamos Printing Company prints *Mad Dog* (when the first issue hit the newsstands, the last page was missing). A 70-foot balloon of Mad Dog appeared in the 1992 Macy's Thanksgiving Day Parade.

As a kid Bob had a dog named Freckles; he now has a cat named Otto who likes to watch the Disney Channel and hides when company comes. Bob hates substitute foods (for example, egg substitute "because it's too chewy") and dislikes fresh-squeezed orange juice (he prefers Tang "because the astronauts drink it"). Issue number one of *Mad Dog* is Bob's most prized possession. Bob still has one of his baby teeth ("It's a medical oddity") and won the Buster Award (comic book achievement) for "Best New Comic Creator and Artist" (*Mad Dog* won for "Best New Comic"). Bob previously won the Doilie Award for "Best Creativity" in the greeting card business. In 1993, when Ace Comics stops publishing *Mad Dog* ("The company didn't stand behind it," says Bob), Bob finds work at the Schmitt Greeting Card Company and a new boss — Sylvia Schmitt (Betty White). Sylvia lives in a swank apartment (3007) and has a pampered French poodle named Gypsy Rose Dog.

Kaye works at the Museum Shop and she and Bob attend mass at the Our Lady of Constant Sorrow Church. Bob and Kaye were married in a hospital (they were in Wisconsin when they stopped by the side of the road to pick wild flowers. Bob was stung by 100 bees, had an allergic reaction and married Kaye while recuperating).

Trisha works as Bob's colorist. She was previously a "Wench Waitress" at a pub (the Keg and Cleaver) and a waitress at the World of Pies and Cowboy Tom's Fast Food. Every December Trisha jumps rope for a charity called "The Children's Medical Benefit — Jump for Joy for Girls and Boys." As a baby Trisha slept through the night; she never experienced "the terrible twos";

she was always perky and followed the rules. "The one thing I did that was bad was to let my mind wander one Sunday while attending mass."

Bob enjoys his weekly poker game with his buddies: Jerry Fleischer (Tom Poston), creator of the comic *The Silencer*; Don Palermo (Steve Lawrence), creator of the comic *Tales from Beneath the Tomb*; Vic Victor (Bill Daily), creator of the comic *Fizzy*; and Bud Loudermilk (Dick Martin), creator of the comic *Kay Carter, Army Nurse*.

15.   Café Americain NBC, 1993–1994

Holly Aldridge (Valerie Bertinelli) is the manager of the Café Americain, a famous eatery in Paris, France, that was frequented by U.S. expatriates during the 1920s. Holly, a Scorpio, is a 30-year-old divorcée who left Minneapolis to begin a new life in Paris. She was initially a "translator of English to English" (taking the dry language and translating it into everyday American talk). She quit when her boss tried to seduce her. She wandered into the café, befriended its owner, Margaret Hunt (Lila Kaye), and became her assistant when she helped close a deal with the JuVal Soft Drink Company for mineral water. Holly's job has no actual title — "It's whatever Margaret tells me to do." Holly has a cat (Mr. Bones) and a very small apartment with a view of the Eiffel Tower ("If you hold a mirror out the window and angle it just right you see the tower"). The apartment once belonged to the famous French writer, Balzac. Holly's favorite snack cake is Hostess Sno-Balls and she is deathly afraid of heights ("It's not so much height as it is the uncontrollable urge to jump off"). In the opening theme, Holly is seen reading a copy of *USA Today*. Two patrons of the café are Fabiana Barcelli (Sofia Miles) and Madame Ubara (Jodi Long). Fabiana is "the highest paid, most sought after model in the world." She is "pushing 26" and believes there are only two kinds of poses: "starving and orgasm." She tells men she is a lesbian to avoid their advances and has a perfume named after her: Fabiana: The Fragrance. Madame Ubara is a deposed foreign First Lady who is living in Paris because she was ousted by the Vintulo government. She is at odds with Hollywood over a movie being made about her life (Delta Burke, who outweighs the rather slim Ubara by 80 pounds, is set to play her). When in office Madame Ubara used U.S. financial aid to buy clothes rather than drain the swamps to get rid of malaria. She earns money by writing an advice column for the *Weekly Globe*.

16.   California Dreams NBC, 1992–1997

The California Dreams are a soft-rock music group managed by Sly

Winkle (Michael Cade). The original members were Jenny Garrison (Heidi Noelle Lenhart), her brother Matt (Brent Gore) and their friends Tiffany Smith (Kelly Packard) and Tony Wicks (William James Jones). Jenny left to attend the music Conservatory in Rome; she was replaced by Samantha Woo (Jennie Kwan), a foreign exchange student from Hong Kong who is residing at the Garrison home (128 Ocean Drive). Samantha had attended the American High School and speaks perfect English. When Matt requires help writing songs, Jake Sommers (Jay Anthony Franke), the school "tough guy," joins the band (he also plays guitar). Shortly after, when Matt moves, Sly's cousin, Mark (Aaron Jackson), replaces him as the lead singer. The wealthy Lorena Costa (Diana Uribe) becomes the group's co-manager when she befriends Sly and allows the band to use her loft for practice (they previously used Matt's garage). Samantha, who likes to be called Sam, became a boarder at Lorena's home.

The teens attend Pacific Coast High School and hang out at Sharkey's, the local beach eatery (where Tony works as a waiter). Matt, who sings, writes songs and plays the guitar, wrote the group's first song, "California Dreams." They made a music video ("Everybody's Got Someone") and appeared on the TV show *Video '99*.

Jenny, who sings and plays keyboard, has a collection of plush animals she calls "Stuffies." A picture of James Dean is on her bedroom wall and a poster from the Dean film *Giant* is on her door. When she breaks up with a boy she locks herself in her room and watches "Thirtysomething" reruns. Tiffany, the dreamer, plays guitar and sings. She surfs, loves to wear bikinis and inevitably attracts the opposite sex: "I can't figure out why the boys stop swimming to watch me." As a kid, Tiffany would pretend to live in a fairy tale forest; realist Jenny would try but fail to convince her it wasn't the real world. Tiffany's license plate reads IM TIFFI and she works as a candy striper at Cliffside Hospital.

Sly's real name is Sylvester, but "Sly's the name; never call me Sylvester." He is somewhat sleazy and hits on any pretty girl he sees. Jenny detests Sly and smiles to torment him ("One of life's little pleasures," she says). Sly's favorite cologne is "Cashola." When Sly became program director of the school radio station (Radio PHC), he called it "Radio Sly." Jake, who sings and plays guitar and keyboard, did a show called "Shut Up and Listen." Sam, a singer, hosted "The Advice Line"; the fashion-conscious Lorena told students "What's Hot, What's Not"; and Mark became "The Campus Critic."

For a television class, the teens had to create their own shows. Tiffany did a surfing version of *Mr. Rogers' Neighborhood* called *Ms. Smith's Ocean-side* with Mark playing the mailman, Mr. McNarley. Sam and Lorena were

The Hall Monitors, high school police seeking the notorious Bubble Gum Wrapper Litterer (Jake). Sly and Tony were *The Goo-Ga-Moo Guys*, two "babe magnets" who offered advice to guys on girls.

A school aptitude test found the following job careers for the teens: Tiffany (veterinarian), Jake (floral engineer), Sam (photographer), Mark (guidance counselor), Lorena (fashion designer), Tony (musician) and Sly (fashion designer; he copied Lorena's paper). Tiffany took a job with a vet and was bitten by the animals; Jake worked at the Lady's Flower Shop (and discovered he hated flowers).

In the final episode, the teens graduate from high school and say goodbye to the group. Tiffany enrolled at the University of Hawaii; Sam is off to England to study physics; Sly and Lorena enrolled in Pacific University; Mark is going to the Juilliard School in New York; Tony is pursuing an acting career; and Jake is offered a recording contract with Stout Jam Records. "I'm So Glad I Was There" was the last song performed by the California Dreams — a dream that started when Matt and Sly heard the group Johnny Himalaya and the Wave Breakers perform at Sharkey's and were inspired to start their own band.

17. **Camp Wilder** ABC, 1992–1993

Ricky Wilder (Mary Page Keller) is an emergency room nurse whose home at 1115 Fairlawn Drive (Santa Monica, California) is affectionately called Camp Wilder by the neighborhood kids who hang out with her brother, Brody (Jerry O'Connell), and sister, Melissa (Meghann Haldeman). Ricky, 28, is divorced (from Dean), and is the mother of Sophie (Tina Majorino). She took on the responsibility of raising Brody (16) and Melissa (13) when their parents were killed in a car accident.

As a kid Ricky wanted to be a ballerina "but I didn't study, couldn't dance and I was pudgy." Ricky majored in oceanography and dreamed of working with Jacques Costeau on the *Calypso*. But she met Dean, married and moved to Albuquerque. When she realized Dean didn't love her, she divorced him and moved to California. Ricky thought of becoming a maternity nurse at age 12 and when she had doubts about her current job, she quit to become an education specialist at Sealand (leading tours and teaching marine biology). "Nursing is not what I dreamed it would be, so I quit," she says. Ricky has a recurring nightmare "about being back in high school, dressed only in my bra and panties and taking a test, then realizing I haven't been to class all year." In high school Ricky was insecure about her body and refused to take a shower with the other girls until she was the last one.

Sophie, called "Pumpkin" by Ricky, has a hamster (Barney), an invisible friend (Morty) and a pet penguin (Rusty). When Sophie thought life would be better as a boy, she started dressing like one and called herself Kurt.

Melissa, experiencing the "traumas of becoming a woman," practices kissing on fruit (peaches). She has a collection of toy horses and as a kid wore panties with characters from the *Hello Kitty* cartoon series on them. Brody, nicknamed "Spot" as a kid, runs track in high school and has a part-time job with Star View Tours.

Danielle (Hilary Swank), Beth (Margaret Langrick) and Dorfman (Jay Mohr) hang out at Camp Wilder. Danielle is partial to the blue mug with the duck on it when she's at the house. Dorfman works for a company called Roses for a Buck and has a pet snake named Ricky (Dorfman has a crush on Ricky and is obsessed with her shoes — all 12 pairs of them). Dorfman believes, at times, he is being stalked by a gorilla named Francie. As a kid Dorfman rode a stick horse he called Nugget and would only talk through a sock hand puppet he called Rosenblatt. Outside the house Ricky faces all the pressures of the world, "but inside I feel like a teenager with a really good complexion."

18. **Can't Hurry Love** CBS, 1995–1996

Annie O'Donnell (Nancy MeKeon) is a single New York girl looking for Mr. Right. She lives at 423 West 28th Street (Apartment 302) and works for the People Pleasers Employment Agency. She attends St. Catherine's Church and has a $400 limit on her Visa card. She also has "The Mystery Puddle" in her living room ("I clean it but it keeps coming back from under the floorboards"). Annie calls her breasts "Thelma and Louise" (when asked why, she responds, "That's another story"). Annie has named the two pigeons that have called her windowsill home Bill and Henry, and she dreams of a charming guy who will bring her a dozen roses and sweep her off her feet. "I know he's out there," she says, "but so far I haven't found him." Men say Annie "has teeth like sparkling porcelain stars"; "It's a curse," says Annie.

Annie's best friend, her neighbor Didi (Mariska Hargitay), lives in Apartment 303. She is a model who always keeps her hopes up "so I will not be disappointed." Didi believes her beauty is sometimes a curse when she attracts the wrong type of men. She appears to eat whatever she wants (much to Annie's regret who is struggling to maintain her figure) and never gain an ounce. She and Annie frequent a bar called Wrecks.

19. **Caroline in the City** NBC, 1995–1999

Caroline Duffy (Lea Thompson) is an artist who draws and writes the daily newspaper comic strip "Caroline in the City." She lives in Manhattan and works out of her apartment (2A). Caroline bases her strip on her own experiences as a single girl living in the big city. Caroline's favorite drink is ginger ale and she has a cat named Salty. When Caroline was ten years old she had a dog named Sparky. As a little girl, she wanted breasts so badly that "I drew boobs on everything." Caroline, born in Wisconsin, dropped out of college to take a job as a copywriter. Shortly after, she was fired for doodling; those doodles became the inspiration for her comic strip, which is syndicated in 565 newspapers. Caroline hates to miss a deadline because papers run two "Cathy" strips ("I hate that girl," says Caroline). Caroline first worked with Delbert "Del" Cassidy (Eric Lutes), the president of the Cassidy Greeting Card Company (which is owned by his father). Del later formed his own company, Eagle Greeting Cards, with Caroline as his only client. Del, a graduate of Penn State, once dated Caroline, but the affair ended "because Del had two failed marriages and can't commit to anything larger than a goldfish," says Caroline. Caroline's favorite eatery is Remo's Restaurante. The Dartland Food Company marketed a puffed wheat cereal based on the comic strip, "Sweet Carolines." Caroline cooks chicken to impress a date and when she breaks up with a guy, she goes to a museum.

Richard Karinsky (Malcolm Gets) works as Caroline's colorist. He lives at 4171 East 6th Street and is a hopeful artist who had his first public showing at the Arabia Gallery on Spring Street. He took the job "since I won't be able to make money for my art until after I'm dead." Richard doesn't come in before ten, doesn't work weekends and needs at least 90 minutes for lunch. When he gets mad, he stands in the corner of Caroline's kitchen. Richard, commissioned to paint a mural on the Reisman Building, always looks like a tortured artist. His work reflects courage and originality, but he is boring and has no sense of humor; he is working on his people skills.

Annie Spidaro (Amy Pietz) is Caroline's neighbor (Apartment 2B), a professional dancer who was born in Paissac, New Jersey (where her family owns a funeral parlor). Annie's childhood idol was Florence Henderson. Annie attended Paramus High School. Annie was a regular cast member of the Broadway play *Cats* (at the Winter Garden Theater), did a TV commercial for Dr. Furman's Foot Powder, and appeared in an unnamed and unsold pilot. When she left *Cats*, she became Princess Neptuna, the model for a cartoon character. Annie was an understudy for Julie Andrews in *Victor/Victoria* and Caroline based "the slutty next door neighbor" in her comic strip on Annie ("But my breasts are bigger," says Annie).

20.   Clarissa Explains It All NIK, 1991–1994

Clarissa Marie Darling (Melissa Joan Hart) is a very pretty 13-year-old girl who lives with her parents, Janet and Marshall (Elizabeth Hess, Joe O'Connor) and brother Ferguson (Jason Zimbler) at 464 Shadow Lane in Baxter Beach, Florida. Clarissa attends Thomas Tupper Junior High School (later Thomas Tupper High) and receives an allowance of three dollars a week. She shops at the Willow Mall and has Elvis, a "security alligator" who lives in a plastic pool (the Heartbreak Hotel) in her bedroom. Clarissa feels she was born to drive and she dreams of owning a 1976 red Gremlin. She has a collection of license plates hanging on her bedroom wall (EX5 6233; 514 097; G-85-Q; 217 CWF) and a 28-foot chain made from chewed gum ("recycled gum, please"). Clarissa wears fish earrings, likes junk food (especially Twizzlers licorice and jawbreakers) and says she hates "the kind of pixie haircuts your mom gives you at home and I hate germs everywhere." Clarissa earns extra money by walking Sarge, the neighbor's collie. She lost only $12.50 when she tried to sell Christmas cards from the Yuletide Greeting Card Company in May. At one point, when she suffered from a bad case of "E.P.S." ("That's Empty Pockets Syndrome"), Clarissa went looking for one job and found five: clerk at Bert's Bait Bucket; waitress at the Weenie Drive-Thru Hot Dog Shack; assistant at the Precious Poodle Playpen; salesgirl at Planet Fantastic 2000 Comic Books; and research assistant at the public library. Her first real job was as Kiddie Attendant (as Little Bo Peep) at the Baxter Beach Carnival. Clarissa's favorite cult movie is *Revenge of the Nerds* and she likes Tasty Taters Potato Chips ("sour cream and garlic flavor").

Clarissa's most embarrassing moment occurred when the obnoxious Ferguson brought her bra to school for "Show and Tell." Her most frightening experience occurred on her seventh birthday when she stuck her head in the sour cream dip and almost drowned. As a kid, Clarissa had a rocking horse named Trigger and "starred" in several school plays: the tail of a T-Rex in "The Prehistoric Pageant"; a wise man in "The Christmas Pageant"; and a pillar in "The Greek Day Pageant." Peanut Butter Swirl is her favorite ice cream; *The Little Mermaid* her favorite Disney movie and *21 Jump Street* her favorite TV show.

Clarissa talks directly to the audience "to explain all the things that go on around here." She talks mostly about Ferguson; "That dork boy has been a burn on my butt since he was born ... living with him is like having your hair set on fire then having it put out with a sledgehammer." *Bugs Bunny and Friends* is Ferguson's favorite TV show. Clarissa, who calls him "Ferg-Face," lives for the day when she gets even with him for taking her bra to school. Ferguson is a Republican and vice president of the Dan Quayle Fan

Club (there is no president; "you can't have an office higher than your idol").
He risks punishment by sneaking down to the living room to watch the late-
night *Spine Tingley Theater* on TV, and as a kid attended Camp Can Do.
Ferguson, born on February 13, had a public access TV show called *Boy
Thoughts* (on which he gave his opinions).

Janet and Marshall, Clarissa's parents, have been married for 15 years.
Marshall, who calls Clarissa "Sport," is an architect for the firm of Water-
son, Baker and Kleinfield. His favorite TV show is *This Old House*; he reads
Architect World magazine and a daily newspaper called *The Dispatch*. Janet,
head of the Children's Museum, won the Phineas Fiddlecarp Award for out-
standing curator. She is a vitamin freak and health food nut (Zucchini Lentil
Surprise is her favorite dinner; carob pudding cake with whipped tofu top-
ping is her favorite dessert). *Casablanca* is Janet's favorite movie; in college
she was in the Modern Ballet Dance Troupe and starred in a ballet called
"The Red Rabbits of Dawn." When she gets upset, Janet watches tapes of
the movies *The Red Shoes* and *The Turning Point*.

Sam Anders (Sean O'Neill), Clarissa's best friend, is the son of a sportswriter, and shares many of Clarissa's misadventures. He has three fish (Willie,
Mookie and Babe) and a never-seen dog named Ohio. His father, Arnold,
writes for *The Dispatch*, and his mother is the roller derby star "Dangerous
Debbie."

Clarissa wrote for the school newspaper, the *Thomas Tupper Times*. The
show's final episode was the pilot for an unrealized CBS series called *Clarissa*
(which moved Clarissa to New York City as an intern on a newspaper called
the *Daily Post*).

21.   Clueless ABC, 1996–1997; UPN, 1997–1999

Cher Horowitz (Rachel Blanchard), Dionne "Dee" Davenport (Stacey
Dash) and Amber Princess Mariens (Elisa Donovan) are three beautiful
teenage girls who attend the posh Bronson Alcott High School in fashionable Beverly Hills. Their hangout is the swank Koffee House.

Cher lives at 2232 Karma Vista Drive (zip code 90200). She, Dee and
Amber attended Rodeo Drive Pre-School and the Rodeo Drive Elementary
School; they plan to attend Stanhope College. Cher has a passion for fashion, and has a 10 P.M. weeknight and midnight Saturday curfew. As a member of the Girl Scouts Cher played Glenda, the Good Witch, in a production
of "The Wizard of Oz." Cher, Amber and Dee are "the Cool People" at
school, but Cher gets depressed "when I'm boyfriend challenged." Mel,
Cher's father (Michael Lerner, Doug Sheehan) is a wealthy lawyer and owner
of Mel Horowitz and Associates. Wheat Sprouts is his favorite restaurant and

he is writing a novel called *Hung Jury*. Cher hosts his annual pool party for new associates.

Dee, a member of the National Honors Society, is the closest to Cher, and like Cher, has a passion for fashion. When she and Cher became fascinated with muffs, they devised a combination muff-purse and began a company called Brad-Keanu Muff Purse International, Inc. (after their favorite movie stars Brad Pitt and Keanu Reeves). Dee believes that she is not only gorgeous but physically perfect. She becomes easily angered "if I hear the 'A' word" (almost). On Valentine's Day, Dee and Cher sell "Pops for Pups" (lollipops for the animal shelter). For Dee, therapy after a trying day is "shopping the retail experience." When Dee and her boyfriend, Murray Lawrence DuVal (Donald Adeosun Faison), are at odds, Dee "sinks into a bottomless pit of bumming," says Cher. Murray and Dee had their first date at To Kill a Shrimp. Murray's favorite food is chili fries. He loves animals, cries at movies "and worships the dirt Dee grinds him into." Dee and he love the movie *Wayne's World*. Murray considers himself a ladies' man, "The Rodeo Romeo," "The Bronson Bad Boy."

Amber is the most outrageous of the three (she believes people see her as "a self-centered wacko"). She flirts with male teachers to get better grades and flashes 20-dollar bills to female teachers for that A. Amber adores herself and, according to Cher, "has supermodel delusions and is in love with herself." Amber lives at 111 Jeanne Court. "If you date me," she says, "never buy me a gift from a store with barn in its name." She seeks to marry rich and be waited on hand and foot. Amber has red hair ("smoldering cherry, please, not red") and is sometimes called "Big Red." She has a dog (Tippy). After her father donated a large sum of money to the local zoo, officials named an orangutan after her. "Rose Petal," "Candy Cane" and "Buttercup" are fond nicknames Amber's father, Dr. Tripp Mariens (Dwayne Hickman) calls her.

Bronson Alcott High, named after its multi-billionaire founder, is part of the Westside Unified District. It has a tanning salon (donated by its most famous graduate, George Hamilton) and a basketball team, the Tortoises (represented by Snappy, the Fighting Tortoise).

22. **Coach** ABC, 1989–1996

Hayden Fox (Craig T. Nelson), coach of the Minnesota State University Screaming Eagles football team, appeared on the covers of *Sports Illustrated* and *Collegiate Sports Digest* magazines. He was born in Spokane, Washington, and hosts *The Hayden Fox Show*, a sports program on KCCY-TV, Channel 6. Hayden won the Curley O'Brien Award for excellence in coaching, and has his car cleaned at Helen's Car Wash. His phone number is 407-555-0199. Hayden, famous for his "five alarm chili," left Minnesota State in 1995 for a job in Orlando, Florida, coaching the Orlando Breakers, an NFL expansion team. His favorite Minnesota hangout is the Touchdown Club.

Hayden met Christine Armstrong (Shelley Fabares) at the United Charity Ball in 1986. They dated and married in 1992. Christine, born in Kentucky, attended St. Mary's High School and the University of Kentucky. She hosted a sports show on Channel 6 in Minneapolis; when this was canceled, she did a live pilot called *Magazine America*, which was not picked up because of low ratings; it was replaced by a bloopers show. She turned to morning TV and landed a co-host spot on *Wake Up, Minneapolis*. When she and Hayden moved to Florida, Christine became the host of Channel 5's *Coach's Corner*, a Breakers post-game show. Christine's license plate reads 463 BCA.

Luther Van Dam (Jerry Van Dyke) and Michael Fabian "Dauber" Dybinski (Bill Fagerbakke) assist Hayden. Luther, an assistant coach for 38 years (22 years with Hayden), fears the day he has to coach. He was born in Danville, Illinois, and earns $32,000 a year. His parrot, Sunshine, eats Acme Bird Seed, and he has a dog named Quincy. "Sweeties, the Full Sugar Cereal" is Luther's favorite breakfast cereal. Each summer during school recess, Luther gets "the summer blues" (he eats, gains weight and spends all fall working it off). He lives in a condo at Leisure Town (Florida) and had a one-week job coaching at Aberdeen College (he was fired for breaking NCAA rules).

Michael, a staff advisor to incoming freshmen, was a student at Minnesota State for eight years (majoring in forestry) before becoming Hayden's assistant. Hayden nicknamed him "Dauber" because his moves on the field reminded him of the Dauber wasp. Dauber dated Judy Watkins (Pam Stone), the women's basketball coach at Minnesota State (he called her "Sweet Stuff"; she called him "Honey"). Kelly Fox (Clare Carey), Hayden's daughter from a previous marriage, majored in liberal arts at Minnesota State. She worked as a bartender at the Touchdown Club and married a student who left her to host a TV show called *Buzzy the Beaver*. Although she had aspirations to become an actress, Kelly left the series for a job in an unnamed ad agency in New York City.

23. **The Critic** ABC, 1994; Fox, 1995

Jay Sherman (voice of Jon Lovitz) is 36 years old, divorced, balding and a much disliked TV film critic. He lives in Apartment 1202 and hosts "Coming Attractions" on Channel 67 (which is owned by the Phillips Broadcast-

ing Company and housed in a building formally occupied by the House of
Chicken and Waffles). Jay, who does his own offstage announcing as Skip
Fisher, had a small part in the film *Dances with Wolves*. Jay is proud of the
fact that he can sink a $50 million movie just by saying the word "crap."
Jay's show is dubbed into 11 languages; in Mexico Jay scares people and the
station runs a disclaimer stating that Jay is insane. Jay uses the "Shermome-
ter" to rate films; on ABC, his competition was *Humphrey the Hippo*; on Fox,
The Benedictine Monk Hour was run opposite his show. Jay panned his own
screenplay, *Ghost Chasers 3*, as the worst movie ever made. Jay attended the
New York School for the Performing Arts and wrote a book called *What I
Do in the Dark* (for which he won a Pulitzer Prize). He also won a pie eating contest when he was a kid at summer camp. When Jay temporarily lost
his job, he became the host of a low-rated cable show called *English for Cab
Drivers*. Jay was abandoned by his mother and raised at Orphan City (his
first words as a baby were "feed me"). He was adopted by the wealthy (but
senile) Franklin Sherman, the former governor of New York, and his wife,
Eleanor. Margo Sherman, Jay's sister, is a junior at Miss Hathaway's School
for Untouched Girls. She has a cat (Mittens) and reads *Mopey Teen* magazine.

24   Cybill CBS, 1995–1998

Actress Cybill Sheridan (Cybill Shepherd) lives at 11291 Moss Canyon
in Los Angeles. She has two ex-husbands, Jeff Robbins and Ira Woodbine
(Tom Wopat, Alan Rosenberg), two daughters, Zoe (Alicia Witt) and Rachel
(Deedee Pfeiffer), and a martini-drinking best friend, Maryann Thorpe
(Christine Baranski).

Cybill, "an aging actress who loses jobs to younger girls," got her first
taste of show business as a child when she entered a beauty contest in
Arkansas and was crowned "Miss Pickled Pigs Feet." She starred in the all-
nude version of "Death of a Salesman"; made her network TV debut on a
sitcom called *Family House* ("I played the husband's secretary"); portrayed
the Lizard Woman in an episode of *Star Trek*; and filmed a TV series called
Island Cop. The six episodes were so bad that *Island Cop* never aired in the
U.S.; however, it did run in Russia, where it became the number one show
for seven years. Cybill played Booty the Clown (a clown with a big butt) on
the live TV kids show *Major Milo*; co-hosted the morning talk show *Julie
in the Morning* (which soon became *Julie and Cybill*); and starred in *The X-
Files* rip-off series *Life Forms* (in which Cybill played Sara McCullum, a
woman who battles aliens. "The actual 'stars' of the show," Cybill says, "are
my breasts and legs, which receive more air time than the rest of me"). Cybill

also played Galaxy Girl on the TV series *Invincible Girl* and appeared on the "reality" TV series *Stories of the Highway Patrol* ("I was hit by a bus").

Cybill's movie career includes *Oliver Twisted* ("The worst horror film ever made"), *Punchout* and *What She Did for Love* (which contains Cybill's first nude scene). Cybill also starred in a number of TV commercials, including "The Psychic Pals Network," a feminine product called "Femgel," "Fraumeiser Beer," "Granny's Snack Cakes" and "Can-Do Supermarkets." Cybill was born in Memphis, Tennessee, and drives a 1964 Dodge Dart (license plate UPU 838). In the opening, the following names are seen on the Hollywood Walk of Fame before the camera reaches Cybill's chalked-in star: Carole Lombard, Lana Turner, Kim Novak, Lassie, and Jean Harlow.

Jeff, Cybill's first husband, is a TV and movie stuntman who owns a dog named Duke. He calls Cybill "Pumpkin" and her breasts "The Pointer Sisters." Ira, Cybill's second husband, is a lawyer turned novelist who penned *Lowenstein's Lament*. Zoe, 16 years old when the series started, first held a job as a counter girl at the Burger Barn, then as a tour guide at Universal Studios. She is Cybill's daughter by Ira. Rachel, who is married to Kevin Taylor (Peter Krause), is Cybill's daughter by Jeff.

Maryann, who uses her middle name as her first name (Theresa is her real first name), was born in Buffalo, New York, and attended St. Dominick's High School (class of '71). She is divorced from the never fully seen "Dr. Dick" (as she calls him) and is extremely angry at him for divorcing her. She has vowed to get even by spending every cent he has. She and Cybill share each other's joys and sorrows although Maryann drowns most of those sorrows in the martini she is seen holding in virtually every scene she is in.

25. Dave's World CBS, 1993–1997

Humorist Dave Barry (Harry Anderson), author of the books *Helluva Time* and *Barry Picking* (a collection of his articles), writes the daily newspaper column, "Dave's World," for the Miami *Record Dispatch*. He is married to Beth (DeLane Matthews) and is the father of Tommy and Willie (Zane Carney, Andrew Ducote). They live "West of Maple Street" in Dade County and have a female dog named Ernest. Their phone number is 555-7433; GPU 16R is their car license plate.

Dave was working as a reporter when a story came across the wire about a woman being trapped in her car by an escaped zoo elephant. Dave and a fellow reporter rushed out for the story. Dave had a banana left over from lunch in his pocket and disabled his competition's car by shoving the banana into the tailpipe. Dave got the story and began his career. In a later episode, Dave states that before he became a humorist, he wrote romance novels for

Pinafore Publishing under the pen name Letitia DeVore (his heroine was Lady Millicent).

Dave, always late with his articles, enjoys snacking on peanut butter ice cream and beer. When it comes to giving advice to the kids, Dave does what he does best — nothing. When he is alone with Tommy and Willie, he serves them soft foods "to avoid choking incidents." Dave "writes about funny things in an odd way" and is also "mechanically inclined" ("It took me only three days to master the Clapper"). As a kid, Dave had a dog (Sparky) and practiced kissing on a pillow he called Phyllis. In college, "a little experiment" caused Dave to see things — "My hairbrush became a tribe of pygmies who worshipped me." Dave grew up in the small town of Pewuckatucket and had a cat named Mr. Stubbs. In his office, Dave displays a large logo for the Sarosota Brewery.

Beth, born in Texas, is a schoolteacher. When she and Dave have to get away from the kids, they retreat to a bed and breakfast called the Spanish Moss Inn. They see movies at the Multi-Plex Cinema and order take-out food from the Crispy Hen. As a kid Beth had a pet iguana named Boris. When Beth gets upset with Dave, she over-moisturizes and her temper often gets Dave in trouble (like the time she gave the finger to a truck driver — and Dave was the one the truck driver tried to take out of the car through the tail pipe). Beth and Dave dine out at Columbo's Restaurant. Beth has a piece of their wedding cake (18 years old) in their freezer and she hides her "secret stash" ($300) in the lining of her wedding dress.

Tommy and Willie attend the Collins Street Elementary School. Dave and Beth buy the kids their pets from A Friend for Life. Willie had ants (Mr. Motto, Sloppy Joe, Bruiser), crickets (Jiminy, Gorg, Buster, Moon Unit), a turtle (Donald), a fish (Mr. Fish), a rabbit (Puffy) and a gerbil (Jerry). Tommy has a plush dinosaur (Rappie) and suffers nightmares "about the slimy creature living under my bed." Willie is allergic to mushrooms and he and Tommy eat Fruit Rings cereal for breakfast. Willie, who has a teddy bear (Barnaby), played a slice of bread in his school play, *Nutrition Is Our Friend*, and a fungus in the play *Bacteria to the Future*. He also starred in a TV commercial for Oliver Twistie Meats. Tommy starred as Ahab in the school's production of *Moby Dick*.

Mia (J. C. Wendel) is Dave's assistant. She believes she has psychic powers, and eats "Cream of Wheat, the rejuvenation food of all psychics." She doesn't take shorthand ("I write real fast"), wants to be a children's storybook writer (she wrote an unpublished book called *Dillon the Dinosaur's Really Big Day*); she also wrote an unpublished romance novel called *Walk the Plank of Passion*. Mia has a parakeet (Wesley), a plant (Vince), and a dog (Scruffy), and as a kid had a gerbil named Scooter. Mia invented the unsold board game "Circus People" and takes exotic vacations in her backyard by pretending to be somewhere. Mia is engaged to Eric (Patrick Warburton), a handyman who was a former professional wrestler named "Bongo, the Jungle Man." Eric does the repairs needed around the Barry home and is carving a living sculpture of Mia on a coconut tree he calls "Cocoa Mia." As a kid he took swimming lessons at Tommy Tadpole's Swimming Academy. He keeps his life savings in a can of Chock Full O' Nuts coffee (Mia invests her money in Triple-A-Rated municipal funds).

Kenny Beckett (Shadoe Stevens) and Sheldon "Shel" Baylor (Meshach Taylor) are Dave's best friends. They grew up together in Pewuckatucket and attended school together. Shel is a noted plastic surgeon; Kenny first worked as Dave's editor at the paper, then as a reader for Books on Tape. He is called "The Voice"; his first audio book was *The Three Musketeers*. He later became a TV weatherman for Channel 5. Kenny wears a size 10½ shoe, is allergic to peanuts and lives at 4703 El Camino Terrace. As a kid he had a plush dog (Rusty) and an imaginary friend (Too Too). His phone has three buttons: business, personal message, screening dates. Mia originally worked as Kenny's secretary; she became Dave's assistant when Kenny was downsized out of his job.

Shel, a graduate of Columbia Medical School, works with Central Hospital. In college he was a member of the SDS (Students for a Democratic Society). He is divorced and constantly has problems finding the perfect woman.

26.   Dear John NBC, 1988–1992

The 1-2-1 Club is a Manhattan-based organization for divorced, widowed, lonely and separated people who need help adjusting to the single life. Meetings, conducted by Louise Mercer (Jane Carr), are held on Friday evenings at 9 P.M. at the Rego Park Community Center. Members include John Lacey (Judd Hirsch), Kate McCarron (Isabella Hofmann), Mary Beth Sutton (Susan Walters), Kirk Morris (Jere Burns) and Ralph Drang (Harry Groener). Clancy's Bar is the after-session hangout.

John, an English teacher at the Drake Prep School (office 215), lives in Apartment 4R on Woodhaven Boulevard. He is divorced (his wife, Wendy, left him for his best friend) and teaches literacy classes each week before the club meets. He was born in Binghamton, New York, and was called "Moochie" as a kid. Pineapple strudel is his favorite dessert and he has an antique watch that has been handed down from generation to generation. John looks after Snuffy, Fluffy and Snowball, the cats of his unseen 93-year-old neighbor. At age 45 John fulfilled a lifelong dream: he took clarinet lessons at the Charles Moreloft Music School. In his spare time, John writes poetry and hopes to one day be published.

Mary Beth believes that no one appreciates her. She always expects the best to happen but it unsure how to act when something good does happen. She has been a homecoming queen, a beauty pageant winner, and works as a columnist for *Above the Clouds*, an airline magazine (she previously worked as a writer on the TV series *The Divided Heart*). As a kid, her father called her "Sunshine Girl" and "Little Honey Bun." When her father started a baby food company, he named it after Mary Beth (The Sunshine Baby Food Company) and used her baby picture on the bottles. She lives in Apartment 3.

Kate, divorced from Blake, feels closest to Louise ("She lets me see her without makeup"). She is a neat freak and owns a restaurant called Kate's Place. Kate is looking for a man who will not be attracted to her just because of her beauty and often helps Louise overcome her (and the group's) problems. She had a dog named Skipper as a kid and is always impeccably dressed.

Louise, born in Cheshire, England, lives in Apartment 5G. She became deeply depressed after her marriage broke up and spent time at Meadowbrook, a mental hospital. She is the mother of the never-seen Nigel and best friends with the Queen of England. In her youth, Louise was crowned "Miss Cheshire" in a beauty pageant (she was actually first runner-up, but when the winner's bathing suit strap broke and exposed her breasts, she ran offstage and disqualified herself). Louise struggles to take an interest in everybody's problems but often becomes depressed when she realizes that she has problems also.

Kirk, a schemer and con artist, was born in Scranton, Pennsylvania. His ex-wife, Carol, left him for another woman and he now feels he has to lie to impress women. When Kirk looks at a girl "he thinks of only one thing," says John, "does her bra unhook from the back or front." A catering service called Cuisine by Kirk, K-Buns (jeans with a K on the rear pocket), Kirkamoto Tours (a tourist service for Japanese visitors in New York) and Standby Airline Tickets (to Hawaii via Trans Universal Airlines) are cons used by Kirk to make money. He lives in Apartment 306 and claims to be a published writer (but as Kate says, "Letters to *Playboy* don't count").

Ralph, a toll taker in the Lincoln Tunnel, is single and worries about everything. He can tell how much money people throw in the toll collection bin by the sound of the coins. He lives in Apartment 3C, has *Star Trek* wallpaper in his bedroom, and is in love with Molly (Megan Mullally), the girl who works three toll booths from him. Ralph is not always sure if Molly is blowing him a kiss or is choking from car exhaust. His dream is to marry her and have two children: Penny and Buck. For breakfast, Ralph eats alphabet cereal in alphabetical order. He is later promoted to equipment supervisor and subsequently replaced by Annie Morono (Marietta DePrima), a hopeful actress seeking Mr. Right. Annie stuffs her bra to enhance her figure for auditions and is always in good spirits: "I'm a wonderful girl in a wonderful town with a wonderful life."

27. Designing Women CBS, 1986–1993

Sugarbaker and Associates — Interior Design is a company located at 1521 Sycamore Street in Atlanta, Georgia. Phone 404-599-8600 and 404-555-6787. It is owned by Julia and Suzanne Sugarbaker (Dixie Carter, Delta Burke), sisters who are as different as night and day ("Julia got the brains and Suzanne got the boobs"). Julia is well educated, outspoken and totally devoted to women's equality. She attended Chapel High School, Southern State University and studied art in Paris (the Gallery Pouzett exhibited a series of her fruit bowl paintings). "To get a vacation from being myself" (to find her spiritual self) Julia became Giselle and sang at the Blue Note night club.

Julia, who wears a size seven shoe, lives above the firm and began the company after her husband, Hayden, died. She was guardian to Randa Oliver (Lexi Randall), a very pretty, lively and precocious girl and Julia treasures a special gift from her mother — a birth certificate with no year on it. Lexi, jersey 3, pitched for the Sugarbaker Giants, a Little League team sponsored by Julia. Julia buys her goods from Fabric World.

Suzanne is the firm's saleswoman and attended the same schools as Julia (but she hates art — "I'm sick of seeing small-busted women with big butts"). She exercises with a baton to the tune of "St. Louis Blues" and flaunts her sexuality (she shows ample cleavage to get what she wants). Suzanne was crowned "Miss Georgia World of 1976"; *Sensational Breakthroughs* (a 30-minute infomercial) is her favorite TV show. She has a pet pig (Noel), wears a size 6½ shoe, and an unseen, psychotic maid (Consuella) who throws hatchets at the Good Humor man, makes necklaces out of chicken bones and howls at the moon. Suzanne's ex-husband, Dash Goff (Gerald McRaney), wrote the book *Being Belled*.

Charlene Frazier (Jean Smart), Mary Jo Shively (Annie Potts), Allison Sugarbaker (Julia Duffy), Carlene Dobber (Jan Hooks), B. J. Poteet (Judith Ivey) and Anthony Bouvier (Meshach Taylor) assist Julia.

Charlene, born in Little Rock, Arkansas, grew up in the town of Poplar Bluffs. She attended Three Rivers Secretarial School in Missouri and Claraton University in Atlanta (majoring in psychology). "I'll Be Seeing You" is Charlene's favorite song and she wears a size eight shoe. Charlene, the office manager, is a Baptist, and held a part-time job as a salesgirl for Kemper Cosmetics. She married Bill Stillfield (Douglas Barr), a U.S. Air Force colonel, at the rooftop garden of the Dunwoodie Hotel ("Ave Maria" was her wedding song). In 1990, Charlene bought the Grant Ghostly Mansion of Atlanta, a supposedly haunted house. Her pride and joy is her autographed picture of Elvis Presley.

Mary Jo is divorced and the mother of two children. She works as the firm's decorator/buyer. She has a fixation about breasts and wishes she were a 36C "because a big bust means power and respect." Mary Jo attended Franklin Elementary School and wears a size six shoe. She co-wrote (with Charlene) the children's book *Billy Bunny* and was voted parent volunteer of the year by the PTA. Mary Jo's ex-husband, Ted (Scott Bakula), is a gynecologist; her daughter, Claudia (Priscilla Weems), was a contestant in the Miss Pre-Teen Atlanta Beauty Pageant. Mary Jo is a Baptist and has a dog named Brownie.

Allison (Julia's cousin) and Carlene (Charlene's divorced sister) joined the firm in 1991 when Suzanne moved to Japan to take advantage of its economy. Allison worked previously as a seeing-eye person to a Mrs. Digby in New York (who was allergic to dogs; Allison was fired for dying her blonde hair brown), then as a secretary at the Binsford and Walker Investment Agency. Allison sobs at everything and suffers from O.P.D. (Obnoxious Personality Disorder). She works as the firm's office manager and is a member of the Common Sense self-help group.

Carlene joined the firm as the receptionist when Charlene moved to England to join Bill. She worked previously for Ray Flat's Flatbed Furniture store, and attends evening classes at college. She was born in Poplar Bluffs, is a Girl Scout troop leader (Troop 6523) and as a kid liked "Chip and Dale" cartoons.

B. J. (Bonnie Jean) became Julia's partner in 1992 when Allison withdrew her money to invest in a Victoria's Secret lingerie franchise. She is a recovering alcoholic and a former court reporter. She was married to the wealthy James Poteet (head of Poteet Industries), who died of a heart attack while dancing in a conga line. B. J. loves to shop and enjoys buying things for people.

Anthony first worked for Julia as a delivery man, then as a partner in 1990 (L-3303 is his contracting license number). He is an ex con (arrested for participating in a liquor store robbery; he served time in Cell Block D of Atlanta State Prison). He attends law school, works as a volunteer at the Home for Wayward Boys, and is director of the Atlanta Community Theater (where Julia starred in a production of "Mame"). Anthony married Etienne Toussant (Sheryl Lee Ralph), a Las Vegas entertainer (at the Follies Bergere) who likes to be called E.T. (She calls Anthony "Tony" because "he's my tiger".) E.T. believes she is one of the most beautiful women in the world and calls herself "The Ebony Princess." She has to be perfect at everything she does; if she is not, she won't do it. E.T.'s mother was one of 14 children;

Etienne is one of nine; and she wants four children with Anthony ("After four you can't get your figure back").

Alice Ghostley appeared semiregularly as Bernice Clifton, a dear friend of Julia's who lived at the Hillcrest Leisure Condominium. Bernice was also the host of *Senior Citizens Roundup* on public access cable TV.

28.   **Dharma and Greg** ABC, 1997–

Dharma Finkelstein (Jenna Elfman) and Greg Montgomery (Thomas Gibson) are complete opposites who fall in love at first sight and marry. Dharma was named so by her father, who fancied himself like the Dalai Lama. She worked as a blackjack dealer, NASCAR pit crew girl, mermaid in a Florida theme park and waitress at Jerry's Rice Bowl. Dharma now trains dogs during the day and teaches yoga classes at night. She loves organ music (the only reason she goes to a ballgame) and has her clothes cleaned at the Fluff and Fold Laundry. As a kid, Dharma had a dog named Doobie; she now has one named Stinky and Stinky has his own dog, Nunzio (whom Dharma gave to Stinky for his Bar Mitzvah). Dharma hates women who wear fur and says whatever she thinks whenever she wants. She played drums in a garage band called Snot's Army and attends Jenny Craig fitness classes. Tofu barley soup is her favorite meal. "Improve Your Karma, Vote for Dharma" was the slogan Dharma used when she ran for (but lost) a seat on the San Francisco Board of Supervisors.

Dharma's parents, Larry and Abby Finkelstein (Alan Rachins, Mimi Kennedy) are liberals who live like flower children of the 1960s. They are not married ("We're engaged," says Abby, as Larry is opposed to marriage). Larry fears the government is looking for him (for protesting the Vietnam War) and has to finish what he starts no matter how long it takes because "if I don't I forget." He worked as a rodeo clown but quit when he could no longer taunt bulls. Abby, whose hobby is painting in the nude, depends on the zodiac to guide her life. Her favorite dessert is tofu cannolis. When she moved in with Larry, Larry's mother put a curse on her. Abby calls Larry "Major Tom"; he calls her "Ground Control." They have a pet goat (Goat), drive an old ice cream truck, and attend a couples' retreat each year. Abby, a licensed Aroma Healer, serves eucalyptus snout buster tea to cure the common cold. Larry hears a constant metal hum ("Like a factory making metal shoes") but can't figure out why. He also started his own church "But nobody ever came — except the IRS," says Abby. When the lights are turned out in their kitchen, illuminated stars and planets can be seen on the walls and ceiling. Larry built Dharma's room around her bed (a trampoline) and made her a hand puppet of President Nixon.

Greg is a conservative U.S. Attorney for the Justice Department in San Francisco. He is Episcopalian (Dharma is Jewish) and attended Harvard University. At age 18 Greg was the youngest delegate ever to attend the Republican National Convention, and when Dharma ran for political office, Greg was stamp licker (a position he pulled from "The Job Hat"). He has an obsession to be right about everything.

Greg's wealthy parents, Edward and Kitty Montgomery (Mitchell Ryan, Susan Sullivan), have been married for 32 years. Kitty attended Vassar and her parents own the Standard Oil Company; Edward owns Montgomery Industries. When they were first married, Kitty opened an antique store at the airport against Edward's wishes ("I let her do it so she could fail on her own; next time she'll listen to me"). Kitty and Dharma are members of the Women's Charity Committee (where Kitty won the Evelyn Hofstedter Humanitarian Award). Kitty feels that Dharma is a "nutty diamond in the rough" and is determined to make a Montgomery out of her. To please Kitty, Dharma has changed her wardrobe slightly: she wears a bra so as not to embarrass Kitty at social functions. Kitty is amazed how Greg is able to survive on Dharma's health food menus; after eating at Dharma's, she and Edward go out for dinner. Edward's car license plate reads 3RDN 345.

29.   Dinosaurs ABC, 1991–1994

In the year 60,000,003 B.C., dinosaurs came out of the forests to marry and raise a family. A view of this society is seen through the Sinclairs — parents Earl and Fran (voices of Stuart Pankin, Jessica Walter) and their children Charlene, Robbie and Baby (Sally Struthers, Jason Willinger, Kevin Clark). Humans, portrayed as cave people, are less intelligent.

The Sinclairs live in the city of Pangaea. Earl, 43, is a Megalasaurus and works as a tree pusher (knocks down trees) for the Wesayso Development Company. He earns four dollars an hour, has a caveman alarm clock and eats Sugar Frosted Boo Boo Bears cereal for breakfast. He is a member of the YMCA (Young Men's Carnivore Association) and hangs out at the Meteor Tiki. He reads the *Tribune*; 555-3000 is his phone number and 000-00-0018 is his Social Security number. In one episode, Earl fell into the toxic waste dump at the Silent Springs Recreational Area and acquired super powers he used to battle evil as a Captain Impressive.

Fran, an Allosaurus, is 38 years old and has been married to Earl for 19 years (Earl keeps their marriage license under the TV set to balance it). Fran watches the Dinosaur Shopping Network on TV, shops at the Swamp Basket (later called the Food Chain) and held a part-time job as a TV advice host on *Just Advice with Fran*. Fran, a Pisces, frequents the Kave Mart Department Store and serves waffle meat pancakes for breakfast (her specialty is refrigerator mold pies). Fran, whose maiden name is Hinkleman, also worked for the Turf and Surf Center for Amphibians (a halfway house for amphibians seeking to make it on land).

Charlene, a material girl, attends Bob LaBrea High School. She is an average student (C grades) and strives to remain so—"So I can be average." Charlene is not the brightest kid in school and her grandmother says, "The only way Charlene will get into college is in a cake at a frat house." She purchases her cosmetics at Fifth Avenue Scales in the mall.

Robbie, a B+ student, is a precocious visionary (he believes, for example, that the caveman has a bright future) and attends Bob LaBrea High School (where he is studying "pre-history"). He has locker 38, a poster of the film *Teenage Mutant Ninja Cavemen* on his bedroom wall and was a member of the Scavengers Gang. When he turned 15, he had to observe the Ceremony of the Howling. *The Book of Dinosaurs* states that when a male dinosaur comes of age he must howl at the moon ("Only by howling do we defeat the dark spirit which turns dinosaur against dinosaur and brings an end to our days on earth").

Baby was hatched in the first episode. He knows everyone except Earl. When Earl cares for him, Baby says "Not the Mama" and hits him on the head with a Myman Frying Pan. When Fran complained to the company that their pan breaks when Baby hits Earl, the company created the unbreakable P-2000 and featured Baby and Earl (as Sir Pan) in TV commercials. Baby's first word was the gutter word "Smoo." He watches such shows as *Raptile* (a talk show), *Mr. Ugh* (a talking caveman), and the science show *Ask Mr. Lizard*. When he does something wrong, Baby remarks "I'm the Baby, gotta love me."

Ethyl Phillips (Florence Stanley) is Fran's 72-year-old, wheelchair-bound mother. She lives with the family and calls Earl "Fat Boy." Roy Hess (Sam McMurray), a T-Rex, is Earl's co-worker ("He eats like a pig and dresses like a slob," says Earl). B. P. Richfield (Sherman Hemsley) is Earl's boss, a money-hungry and vicious three-horned Triceratops.

The symbol of male supremacy in the home is possession of the TV remote control. Calendars begin with the last day of the month and end with the first day. All characters are named after oil companies. The elders rule from the Cave of Destiny, and the Job Wizard decrees what jobs dinosaurs will hold. Pistachio nuts are dinosaurs' favorite snack and their Christmas is Refrigerator Day—"A celebration of the invention of cold storage" (it ended migration to find food and allowed dinosaurs to remain in one place).

30.   **The Drew Carey Show** ABC, 1995–

Drew Carey (Himself), Oswald Harvey (Diedrich Bader), Lewis Kiniski (Ryan Stiles) and Kate O'Brien (Christa Miller) are close friends who live in Cleveland, Ohio.

Drew is the Personnel Director of the Winford-Louder Department Store. He makes $26,000 a year and lives at 720 Sedgewick Road, where he has a pool table in his backyard. Drew previously worked (for ten years) as a waiter at Antonio's, then as the Assistant Director of Personnel at Winford-Louder. Drew has cubicle 17 at the store ("The Drewbicle") and a dog named Speedy. *Xena: Warrior Princess* is Drew's favorite TV show (he writes to star Lucy Lawless under the name "Junior Warrior Drew Carey"). He believes Cher is the most beautiful woman in the world and as a kid he had a crush on Oswald's beautiful mother, Kim (Adrienne Barbeau). The accounting department at the store always misspells his name on his paycheck (for example, "Drew Fairy," "Screw Carey").

Oswald works as a delivery man for Global Deliveries; he previously worked as a rodeo clown. Lewis was originally a maintenance man at the DrugCo Chemical Company (later promoted to janitorial manager). He has a sock puppet called Professor Von Sock that he carries to help him out of tight situations. *Babylon 5* is his favorite TV show and he is allergic to strawberries and fish.

Kate first worked at the Sizzler, then in a car body shop, as a cosmetics salesgirl at Winford-Louder (fired for complaining about working on Christmas Eve), house sitter, Soup on a Stick waitress, Massage on the Job therapist and personal assistant to Mrs. Louder (Nan Martin) at Winford-Louder. Kate calls her breasts "the kids" and lives in a house near "a naked guy with binoculars who lives in a house across the alley."

The friends hang out at the Warsaw Tavern, where they invented a beer-coffee mix called Buzz Beer ("The working man's beer"). In high school, Drew, Lewis and Oswald were in a band called the Horndogs. On Wednesday nights, Lewis teaches "Beer Robics" at the tavern (do an exercise, take a drink of Buzz Beer).

Winford-Louder is "a ruthless, vindictive company that is virtually above the law," say its director, Nigel Wick (Craig Ferguson). Wick, whose secret e-mail password is "Mr. Wick," replaced the unseen Jerry Bell, the prior director who was only heard over Drew's speaker phone (voice of Kevin Pollak). To represent the unmarried employees at the store, Drew formed the Winford-Louder Singles Union.

Mimi Bobeck (Kathy Kinney) is Nigel's secretary and Drew's worst nightmare. Her desk is cluttered with troll dolls; she wears outlandish makeup and clothes and calls Drew "Pig." She is angry at Drew for getting the job she wanted and has made it her personal goal to make his life miserable. Her catchphrase is "Bite Me, Dough Boy" (referring to Drew) and she sells Sally Mae Cosmetics on the side. Her father owns a trucking company and at Christmastime, she starts a business called Mimi's Door-to-Door Christmas Tree Service.

Mimi lives in Apartment 234 and the neighborhood kids think she is a clown ("Do you have numbers on your skin so you know what colors go where" say kids). Mimi is also the landlord for the Winford-Louder real estate holdings and when people see her home, they remark, "Now I know what you do with your makeup when you take it off—you throw it against the walls."

31. Ellen ABC, 1994–1998

Apartment 7 on North Sweeter in Los Angeles is occupied by Ellen Inez Morgan (Ellen DeGeneres), a lesbian who has just declared her sexuality. She is a graduate of Edgemont High School (Class of '79), shops at the Buy and Bag and has an account at the Interstate Bank. She has two goldfish (Lyle and Eric) and as a kid had a goldfish named Goldie. In one episode Ellen became a hero when she rescued (stole) a 65-year-old lobster (Scout) from a restaurant and set it free. Ellen, born in Louisiana, first worked as a waitress at Burger World, then as the owner of a store called Buy the Book (which she sold to the Tom and Larry Corporation to buy a house; she remained at the bookstore as the assistant manager). As a follow-up to her previous ballet school training, Ellen performed the lead in "Giselle" for the Edward Dru Hollywood Dance Studio.

Paige Clark (Joely Fisher) is Ellen's best friend. She works for Tri Global Pictures, first as a secretary, then producer's assistant and finally as a development executive (her first film project was *The Long Engagement*). Paige and Ellen met at Camp Pineridge at age ten; when Ellen admitted she was a lesbian ("Ellen: The Episode"), Paige was the first girl she kissed.

Audrey Penney (Clea Lewis) works as a salesgirl at Buy the Book. Her favorite color is pink, a color she became addicted to when she was working at Santoni's Fish Market in 1989. She was carrying a 20-pound Alaska salmon, saw her reflection in the lobster tank and was hooked on pink. Audrey also names her cars; Rapture is her current one; Princess, Sheri and Rosebud were her prior cars. Her hero is Florence Henderson (for her role on *The Brady Bunch* as Carol Brady) and won the Westminster Science Fair as a kid with her project "Sea Horses—The Cute Fishes."

Joe Farrell (David Anthony Higgins) runs the coffee shop area of Buy the Book. When Ellen sold the store, he opened his own business — Hot Cup of Joe. He originally worked at Cafe London. The series originally aired as *These Friends of Mine.*

32. Empty Nest NBC, 1988–1995

Harry Weston (Richard Mulligan), a widowed pediatrician, lives at 1755 Fairview Road in Miami Beach, Florida, with his daughters Carol (Dinah Manoff), Barbara (Kristy McNichol) and, later, Emily (Lisa Rieffel).

Harry, a graduate of the Bedford Medical School (1959), has a tenth-floor office at the Community Medical Center (later a second-floor office when the Greykirk Corporation purchases the building). He buys his supplies from the Radacine Supplies Company and uses Starbright Bandages for his patients. His parking space is J-25 and "Dr. Harry" is printed on his coffee mug. "The Sword of Weston" is the family crest and Harry hosted "Ask Dr. Weston," a call-in radio program on WWEN (990 AM). On 9/25/93, Harry sells his practice and becomes partners with Dr. Maxene Douglas (Marsha Warfield) in the Canal Street Clinic (a poor people's clinic next to Ernie's Garage). Harry has a dog named Dreyfuss. His phone number is 555-3630.

Carol Olivia, Harry's eldest daughter (mid-thirties), is divorced and had ten jobs before the series began. Her first series job was the assistant director of the University of Miami Rare Books Library. She quit in 1991 to begin her own catering business, Elegant Epicure. When that failed (1994), she became a reporter for the Dade County *Crier* (at 1111 Blight Street). Carol has fat attacks each spring and is a member of the support group Adult Children of Perfectly Fine Parents. She has a difficult time finding boyfriends and by 1993 had had 37 bad relationships. After an affair with a broke sculptor (Patrick Arcola), Carol gave birth to a baby she named F. Scott Weston (after her favorite author, F. Scott Fitzgerald).

Barbara, the middle child, is a police officer, then a sergeant with the Miami Police Department. She is perky and upbeat, terrible with money and plunges into the unknown. She and Harry co-wrote a children's book (*Jumpy Goes to the Hospital*) and "Beetle Bailey" is her favorite comic strip. Barbara collects back scratchers and uses Zesty, "the official antiperspirant of the Miss Junior Teen USA Pageant." As kids Barbara and Carol attended Camp Weemawalk; Carol was called "Stay in Tent"; Barbara was "Swim Like Fish." Carol calls Barbara "Barbie Barb."

Kristy McNichol left the series (10/17/92) due to manic depression. Her absence was explained as being on various undercover assignments. Emily, Harry's mentioned but previously unseen daughter, returned home (1/2/93) to work out boyfriend problems. Emily had been attending the Hollyoak Girls School when she heard about a program offering work in a clinic in Vietnam. She left to pursue it. When that bored her she went to Japan, where she worked as a karaoke waitress, then to Italy, where she was a hand model. Emily, 23, calls her father Harry and left the series after a year to return to school.

Laverne Todd (Park Overall), Harry's nurse, is from Hickory, Arkansas, and is married to Nick Todd (a baseball player who left her and moved to Japan to become a member of the Osaka Hens team). Laverne, whose maiden name is Higbee, reads the *National Inquisitor*, and wears Passion Pink lipstick. Her license plate reads BGF 5N7.

Charlie Dietz (David Leisure) is Harry's obnoxious, food-pilfering neighbor. He works as the fifth assistant purser on the luxury liner *Ocean Queen* and is a member of the Stallion Club. He considers himself to be a ladies' man. The Weiner Shack is his favorite eatery.

33. Evening Shade CBS, 1990–1994

Woodrow "Wood" Newton (Burt Reynolds), his wife, Ava (Marilu Henner), and their children, Molly, Will and Taylor (Candace Huston, Jacob Parker, Jay R. Ferguson) live at 2102 Willow Lane in Evening Shade, a small town in Arkansas. The family dog is named Brownie.

Wood played football for Evening Shade High School (he was called "Thumper" and wore jersey 37). He attended the University of Arkansas, then became a quarterback for the Pittsburgh Steelers (he was called "Clutch" and wore jersey 22). He was Honorable Mention, All-American one year; All-American the next. He then became the Southwest Conference Most Valuable Player, runner-up for the Heisman Trophy and NFL rookie quarterback (he is fourth in completed passes). He single-handedly won the Eastern Division playoff game, completing six passes with a minute and 53 seconds left on the clock; and with ten seconds left and no time outs, he scored the winning touchdown with a broken collarbone. Although he had a fantastic football career, Wood holds the record for the most fumbles and most yardage lost.

Wood is now the P.E. teacher and coach of the Mules, a losing football team at Evening Shade High School (the team's mascot is Carl the mule). Wood's favorite song is "Blueberry Hill" (selection B-5 on the jukebox at Blue's Barbecue Villa, the local diner). Wood's good-luck charm is a towel he dyed black when he was with the Steelers; and he recalled that his first sexual experience was with Big Ruthie Ralston at the Purple Dawn Whorehouse in Hot Springs, Arkansas. He also played the role of Colonel Rodney Stone in the TV miniseries, *The Blue and the Gray II*.

Ava, 33, has been married to Wood for 15 years. She is a prosecuting attorney (graduated second in her class) and on their thirteenth wedding anniversary, she gave Wood a jukebox that plays "Blueberry Hill" and announced she was pregnant (she gave birth to Emily Frieda on 5/6/91). When Ava was 12, she was overweight and called "Chubby Evans" (Evans is her maiden name); it took her two years to lose the weight. Ava's most prized possession is her antique bathroom window. She and Wood honeymooned at Harrison Point (they stayed in the Peach Blossom Suite of the hotel).

Taylor, 15, attends Evening Shade High and is a member of the Mules — but he would prefer not to play (he wants to become an actor and fears hurting his face). Eleven-year-old Molly attends Evening Shade Grammar School. Wood and Ava think of her as nine ("so she can always be our little girl"; Molly wishes "they would stop treating me like a baby"). Molly wears a Littlest Angel Bra and a size 5½ shoe. *The Wizard of Oz* is her favorite movie. She entered the Little Miss Evening Shade Beauty Pageant but lost when she attempted to walk in high heels and fell. Her hangout is Doug and Herman's Ice Cream Parlor.

Evan Evans (Hal Holbrook) is Ava's stern father, the publisher of the town's newspaper, the *Argus*. His beeper number is 555-1011, and he feels Wood ruined his life by marrying Ava when she was only 18. Evan married Fontana Beausoleil (Linda Gehringer), a stripper who is famous for running naked across the football field and causing the Mules to lose a championship game. On 3/15/93, Fontana gave birth to a boy, Scout.

Harlan Eldridge (Charles Durning), the town physician, works at City Hospital (called also Evening Shade Hospital). He and his sexy wife, Merleen (Ann Wedgeworth) live on an estate they call Tara. Harlan is a member of the Civil War Society and is most proud of his trophy room, where his collection of stuffed fish is displayed on the walls. He has a boat called *Tara of the Sea*. Merleen believes she exudes sexuality and is thus a magnet for perverts. She is proud of three pictures that hang on the wall: an American Indian, Billy Graham and Tom Selleck. For Christmas 1990, Merleen prepared a pamphlet called "A Styrofoam Christmas" (how to make reindeer out of styrofoam). Merleen reads *Southern Pride* magazine and had a singing group with her sisters, Joleen and Lerleen, called the Frazier Sisters.

34. **Family Album** CBS, 1993

Denise and Jonathan Lerner (Pamela Reed, Peter Scolari) and their children Nicki and Jeffrey (Alicia Levitch, Philip Van Dyke) live at 8461 Bedford Street in Philadelphia. Their phone number is 555-6938. Denise is an architect and earns $65 an hour; Jonathan works with his father in an unidentified business. The family's favorite meal is pot roast with baby carrots. Denise believes that Jonathan's mother, Lillian (Doris Belack), is "Hitler, the other woman in our marriage." Nicole, who prefers to be called Nicki, is "a 14-year-old budding bombshell" whose sleeping habits mean money for Jeffrey. Nicole sleeps in her bra and panties and Jeffrey charges his friends a dollar "for a peek at Nicki asleep — but only for a few seconds." Jeffrey's most prized possession is his videotape of the last episode of *The Tonight Show Starring Johnny Carson*. Lillian calls Jonathan "Gum Drop"; Sheila (Nancy Cassaro), Denise's sister, has a tattoo on her butt that reads "Gus"; and Elvis (Giovanni Ribisi), Sheila's son, is a mischievous rascal "who is auditioning for *America's Most Wanted*." Ruby (Rhoda Gemignani), Denise's mother, owns Ruby's Beauty Salon.

35.   Family Matters ABC, 1989–1997; CBS, 1997–1998

Carl Otis Winslow (Reginald VelJohnson) is a sergeant (later lieutenant) with the Chicago Police Department. He is married to Harriette (Jo Marie Payton France, Judyann Elder) and is the father of Eddie (Darius McCrary), Laura (Kellie Shanygne Williams) and Judy (Jaimee Foxworth). Also living with them at 263 Pinehurst Street is Rachel (Telma Hopkins), Harriette's widowed sister, and Carl's mother, Estelle (Rosetta LeNoire). Living next door is Steven Quincy Urkel (Jaleel White), a nerd with an unrelenting crush on Laura, who plagues Carl's life.

Carl is with the Metro Division of the 8th Precinct (his car code is 2-Adam-12) and held a temporary job as the WNTW-TV, Channel 13 traffic reporter. In high school (mentioned as both Kennedy High and Vanderbilt High) Carl was in a singing group called the Darnells and was called "Rack and Roll Winslow" at the Corner Pocket Pool Hall. Carl has an account at the Investors Bank; 555-6278 (later 555-0139) is his phone number and his license plate reads L95 541. When Carl was a street cop, he was partnered with a dog named Rex.

Harriette met Carl at Vanderbilt High. She originally worked as the elevator operator at the *Chicago Chronicle*; she is now the paper's security director and has keys to 300 offices. Chocolate chip cookies are her favorite snack and she has a scar on her left knee from a tricycle accident as a kid. She and Carl dine at the Chez Josephine Restaurant.

Eddie, Laura and Steve attend Vanderbilt High. Edward James Arthur Winslow is the oldest (born 1/28/74) and believes that when it comes to good looks, God smiled on the men in his family. He isn't too bright, is known as "Fast Eddie Winslow" at the pool hall, and is a member of the Muskrats basketball team (jersey 33). Eddie, who will not sleep without his Scooby-

Doo night light, was a waiter at the Mighty Weenie and later became a police officer.

Laura, the middle child, was voted the 1992 Vanderbilt High Homecoming Queen. She is pretty, fashion conscious, bright and frightened by the fact that Steve Urkel loves her. Rainbow Cloud is her favorite perfume and she is a cheerleader for the Muskrats basketball team at school. She attempted a business called the Winslow Babysitting Service that failed due to a lack of employees.

Judy, the youngest child, was dropped from the show without explanation; she was there — and then she was gone. She was bright and pretty and held the record for selling 232 boxes of Girl Scout cookies. Valerie Jones played Judy in the pilot.

Steve first met Laura in kindergarten. She made him eat Play-Doh and took an instant dislike to him; he felt it was love at first sight. Steve eats his lunch on a Laura placemat. He has a photo of her on his desk and pictures of her on his locker door. He calls her "Laura, My Love" and must walk 20 feet behind her at school. Steve is equipment manager of the golf club at school and says "I'm 98 percent brain, two percent brawn." Steve has a stay-away fund (relatives send him money so he will not visit) and after people see Steve they remark "I thank God I never had children." He plays the accordion and was said to have eaten a mouse. "Did I do that?" is his catchphrase; anchovy paste on a dog biscuit is his favorite snack. Steve is a stringer for the school newspaper, the *Muskrat Times* and created a robot in his own image he called the Urkelbot (for the National Robotics Contest; he later made one in Laura's image he called the Laurabot). He is a straight A student and got only one C (in home economics when the yeast didn't rise in the bread he was making). Steve won the *Amateur Weekly* magazine contest with the Transformation Machine (which changes him into the suave Stefan Urquette). Steve's car is the ultra compact Isetta 300 (two wheels in the back; one centered in the front). The license plate was originally P27-128, then URK MAN. When Steve realized he could never have Laura, the gorgeous Myra Monkhouse (Michelle Thomas) found him. However, in the last episode, Laura returns to Steve and they become engaged. Steve is then chosen by the ISP (International Space Program) to test his invention, the AGF 5000 (Artificial Gravity Field). During the flight, dubbed "Nerd Watch '98," Steve's lifeline becomes detached from the ship (*Explorer*) and Steve is last seen drifting into endless space.

Rachel is a stunning 34-year-old freelance writer and the mother of Richie. In first-season episodes, her last name is Cochran and Richie is an infant. When the second season began, Richie was advanced to three years of age (Bryton McClure) and Rachel's last name was Crawford. When

LeRoy's, the afterschool hangout, burns down, Rachel buys the property and rebuilds it as Rachel's Place, a diner that employs Laura and Steve as wait staff. Rachel and Harriette were born at Regis Memorial Hospital.

36.   Family Rules UPN, 1999

At 34 Beck Street (city unnamed) reside Nate Harrison (Greg Evigan), a widower, and his four daughters, Hope (Maggie Lawson), Anne (Shawna Waldron), C.J. (Andi Eystad) and Lucy (Brooke Garrett).

Nate, whose late wife was named Jan, coaches basketball at Morgan College. Hope, the oldest girl (17), considers herself to be cool and had a pet guinea pig named Steve. Anne, 16, shares a bedroom with Hope and is the responsible, brainy child. She had a pet bird (Tweedles), cooks, cleans and does things Hope calls "the mom's gone martyr thing." Anne has a piggy bank where she keeps her money — at least she thinks so; the bank is full of IOU's from family members who constantly borrow from it. C.J., 14, has a happy outlook on life. She is a bit kooky, a bit irresponsible and a bit dim-witted. She had a pet rabbit (Mr. Hoppy) and, like her sisters, attends P.S. 31.

Lucy, called "Luce" by Nate, is the youngest (10) and more like the boy Nate wanted (she is interested in "guy things" like sports and camping). She is a Girl Scout and closest to Nate's friend, Phil (Markus Redmond), whom she calls Uncle Phil (who has a French poodle named Cha Cha).

37.   Ferris Bueller NBC, 1990

Ferris Bueller (Charles Schlatter) is a 17-year-old "who gets away with murder and everywhere he goes fun happens." He lives at 164 North Dutton Place in Santa Monica, California, with his parents, Bill and Barbara (Sam Freed, Cristine Rose), and his sister, Jeannie (Jennifer Aniston).

Ferris, a junior at Ocean Park High School, drives a 1962 Corvette with the license plate ASB 589. His birthstone is the opal; he hangs out at Danny's Pizza Palace and he claims "high school is the best way to keep track of friends."

Jeannie, 18, is a senior at Ocean Park High. She is beautiful, vicious and nasty and lives for the day Ferris will get caught and be punished by her parents (she feels her life was perfect until he was born). Jeannie loves to wear bikinis to the beach — but her mother refuses to let her ("what is the point of having a great body if I can't show it off," she sobs). While she may not be able to wear what she wants to the beach, her mother doesn't seem to mind the tight, short skirts and low-cut blouses Jeannie wears to school

("My dress-to-kill clothes"). If Jeannie sees a boy she likes, she dresses as Pippi Longstocking (long dress and pigtails) to attract him "with my innocent look." If Jeannie breaks up with a boy, she goes on an ice cream and chocolate sauce binge ("boys bad, ice cream good," she says). Jeannie, called "Princess" by her father, has one great fear: that her friends will discover she had her nose fixed and she is not perfect. Her license plate reads 2PEK 635 (later 2RNT 672).

Sloane Peterson (Ami Dolenz), the junior-class beauty, is Ferris's girlfriend. She attended Saint Catherine's School for Girls as a kid and hopes to become a ballet dancer. Barbara is a realtor with Koenig and Strey Realtors; Bill, an accountant, reads a magazine called *Outlook*.

Edward Rooney (Richard Richle) is the school's stern principal. He is determined to catch Ferris in a misdeed because he feels Ferris is a bad influence on good students "and a ticket to nowhere." Rooney had high hopes of becoming a pilot, but he had a fear of high places and tight spaces "and a fear of throwing up at mach two." He has been principal for nine years and has a fruit cocktail every day at 2:15 P.M.

Ocean Park High, part of the Unified School District, was called Palisades High in the pilot episode. The series is based on the film *Ferris Bueller's Day Off*.

38.   First Time Out WB, 1995

Jackie Guerra (Herself), Dominique Costalano (Leah Remini) and Susan Gardner (Mia Cottet) are best friends who live in Beverly Hills. Jackie is the manager of a trendy hair salon called Tudor; she and Dominique, an assistant at Ventura Records; and Susan, a psychotherapist, share an apartment at 48 Beverly Boulevard. Jackie graduated from Yale; Susan is upset that she is getting older; and Dominique has a tough exterior (she is the fifth of five girls; her father was hoping for a boy he wanted to call Dominick). The girls hang out at Tio's Cafe. Jackie's friend, Nathan Fisk (Craig Anton), thinks he is a ladies' man (but the ladies don't). He publishes a monthly magazine called *Nahtan* (Nathan spelled backward), "The Prestigious Magazine for People Who Think Like Me."

39.   The Five Mrs. Buchanans CBS, 1994–1995

The small town of Mercy, Indiana, is home to "Mother" Emma Buchanan (Eileen Heckart), her three daughters-in-law, Alexandra (Judith Ivey), Delilah (Beth Broderick) and Vivian (Harriet Sansom Harris), and Bree Larson (Charlotte Ross), a soon-to-become Mrs. Buchanan.

Emma is a 70-year-old meddling mother-in-law. When her sons (Ed, Jessie, Roy and Charles) were young, their father ran off with another woman, leaving Emma to raise them alone. She did what it took to keep the family going. She put her sons through college and never complained. "The woman would qualify for sainthood if it were not for one little thing" says Alexandra, "she's a bitch." Emma's pride and joy is her hand painted nativity-scene figurines.

Alexandra (Alex) is Jewish and originally from New York City (where, in 1974, she was arrested and spent a weekend in jail for streaking in Central Park). Alex's house number is 4349. She has been married to Roy (John Getz) for 19 years. Alex claims "a Buchanan marriage is not easy — especially when you're married to a Buchanan boy and his mother." Alex's maiden name is Isackson and she attended the all-male Parkins College (in 1974 she protested the admission policy and was allowed to attend). She and Delilah own Buchanan's Antiques and Collectibles.

Delilah is a blonde, busty bombshell who developed in the fourth grade and has always been popular with boys. She posed nude for *Playpen* magazine and worked as a stripper in Corpus Christi, Texas. When she met her Buchanan — Charles, a minister on a crusade to close strip joints — he said "Repent sinner" and fell in love with Delilah; they have been married for six years.

Vivian is straight-laced and has been married to Ed for eight years (he runs the Buchanan Used Car Lot). She is rich, doesn't work and is the assistant beverage lady of the Ladies' Auxiliary. She has two extremely mischievous but never-seen children, twins Leonard and P.J.

Bree attended Louisiana High School and is engaged to Jessie (who works for Ed at the car lot). As a kid Bree had a teddy bear named Waddles; her pride and joy was a Malibu Missy doll and her friend Skip. Bree met Jessie (Paul Johannsson) at Disneyland (where she worked as Cinderella in the Flights of Fantasy Parade, the Minnie Mouse Parade and the Go Go Goofy Parade). Bree's mother, Frances "Tink" Larson (Jean Kasem), played Tinkerbell in Disney parades for 19 years until she got "fairy burnout" and now works in a shed behind Space Mountain sewing name tags on Mickey Mouse ears.

40. Flying Blind Fox, 1992–1993

Alicia Smith (Tea Leoni), a freelance artist and fashion model, lives at 386 Bleecker Street in New York's Greenwich Village. She is beautiful, wild, and unpredictable; her friends say "she should be committed." When she first began modeling, Alicia called herself "Kero"; when she tired of that she became "Chloe" for several months. Alicia loves to wear clothes that reveal her breasts in sexy bras and claims that her most embarrassing moment occurred when she was dating a UN dignitary "who stole a pair of my panties and sold them to a Third World country as their flag." Alicia first realized she had extreme sex appeal when she was 14 years old (on hot summer days she would run through the sprinklers in a see-through sundress and drive her neighbor, an elderly doctor, crazy. He begged for just 15 minutes of her time. Alicia's repeated refusals led him to develop the artificial aorta). Alicia attended the Zurich Academy for Girls in Switzerland and she seems to have an adventure every day. She describes a typical day: "I accidentally assisted a refugee escaping from an FBI stakeout while I adjusted my panty-hose in front of the surveillance van." Alicia also claims that "men make fools of themselves around me — like the time I was at the beach and the lifeguard left a woman in an undertow to ask me to brunch; or the venetian blind salesman who fell for me and was later found to have a collection of mannequins dressed like me seated around a dinner table." When jobs were scarce, Alicia went to Mexico to star in the movie *Bride of the Marsh Monster*. It became such a hit in the Philippines that the government issued an air mail stamp with Alicia's picture on it.

Alicia has an uneasy relationship with her somewhat psychotic father (Peter Boyle), a man of mystery who claims that "if I tell you what I do for a living I'll have to kill you." He has no name, and works for some ultra-secret government agency. When Alicia wants to visit him, she has to be blindfolded and stuffed in the trunk of a car (a Fiat).

Neil Barash (Corey Parker) is the man who dates Alicia. He met her at a restaurant (the Madison Bistro) and is her complete opposite. He was born in Hartsdale and works with his father in the advertising department of Hockman Foods (a snack food company). He later works for Dennis Lake (Charles Rocket), the sleazy owner of a B-horror movie company called Scepter Films, producers of such "classics" as *Revenge of the Ozone Mutant Mermaids, Panic at Three Mile Island, Massacre at Cleavage Farm, Frosty the Maniac* and *Beverly Hills 9021-Dead*. As a kid Neil attended Camp Tomahawk and won the Most Improved Camper award. He had a parakeet named Mickey and his mother calls him "Mo Bo."

Megan (Clea Lewis), heiress to a laxative-company fortune, is Alicia's best friend, an artist's model who falls for men she thinks hate women. She is not as glamorous as Alicia and was the inspiration for a famous painting called "Depression Ascending a Staircase." Megan also posed topless for two lithographs of her nipples: "One is on tour in Paris; the other is on display at Milt DeLeon's Steak House in Oceanside." Megan later found a steady job as a subject in psychology experiments at a local junior college.

41. **Frasier** NBC, 1993–

Frasier Crane (Kelsey Grammer) is a 41-year-old psychiatrist who hosts "The Frasier Crane Show," a daily 2 P.M.–5 P.M. advice program on radio station KACL (780 AM; 555-KACL) in Seattle. He lives at the Eliot Bay Towers (Apartment 1901) with his father, Martin (John Mahoney) and Martin's live-in home care specialist, Daphne Moon (Jane Leeves).

Frasier attended Brice Academy High School and Harvard University (where his minor was music). If Frasier had been born a girl, his parents would have named him Laura. He is divorced from the stern Lilith (Bebe Neuwirth) and is the father of Frederick (Luke Tarsitano). Frasier has a low high fiber breakfast "so I can start my day off right" and enjoys coffee with his brother, Niles (David Hyde Pierce) at the Cafe Nervosa. Bartok's classic "Concerto in C" is Frasier's talk show theme song; his license plate reads 330 WPT.

Niles, a psychiatrist in private practice, has an I.Q. of 156 (Frasier's is 129). Niles was married to the neurotic, well dressed, very thin and never-seen Maris. His license plate reads SHRINK and he has a pet parrot named Baby. Niles first lived at the luxurious Montana Hotel, then at the not-so-posh Shangri La Apartments (at 52 Elm Street) while he was divorcing Maris. When the divorce was granted, he returned to the Montana; at the Shangri La, he was called "The Coyote." Niles is allergic to parchment (his ear itches, he sneezes "and I have a tough time at the library") and when he attends a theater performance, he brings his own seat cushion. When they were married, Niles and Maris would spend romantic weekends at their lakeside cottage, Shady Glen. Niles and Frasier play squash for relaxation and eat at McGinty's Diner. When their favorite restaurant, Orsini's, was closing, they purchased it and reopened it as the Happy Brothers Restaurant.

Martin, a retired police officer, has a dog named Eddie (whom Frasier dislikes for his constant habit of staring at him) and an eyesore of a recliner that clashes with Frasier's decor. Martin is obsessed with solving a 20-year-old murder case, "The Weeping Lotus Murder" (someone killed a hooker and tried to stuff her body into a bowling ball bag). He feels he is overlooking a crucial clue but can't figure out what it is. In his youth, Martin was a mounted policeman and rode a horse named Agadies. Each year Martin embarks on a fishing trip to Lake Noomeheegen and has a secret shoebox that contains 30-year-old songs he wrote for Frank Sinatra (but never sent).

Daphne was born in Manchester, England, and as a child was the star of the British TV series *Mind Your Knickers* (about a 12-year-old girl in a private boarding school; she played Emma). Daphne is psychic and gets "psychic headaches" when there is negative energy around her. She is also a pool shark (she learned her skills from her brothers when she was six years old). Roz Doyle (Peri Gilpin) assists Frasier at the radio station (producer/call screener/engineer). She is from Wisconsin (where her mother is the attorney general) and is a law school dropout. The character of Frasier first appeared on the series *Cheers* (where he was a bar regular).

42. The Fresh Prince of Bel Air NBC, 1990–1996

Will Smith (Himself), born in West Philadelphia on July 3, 1973, attended West Philly High and carried his books in a pizza box so no one would know he was studying. Fearing that her son was hanging out with the wrong crowd, Will's mother, Viola, sends him to Bel Air, California, to live with his rich relatives, Philip (James Avery) and Vivian Banks (Janet Hubert-Whitten, Daphne Maxwell Reid) in the hope they will teach him values.

Will first attended the Bel Air Academy, then the University of Los Angeles (ULA). He plays ball at the L.A. Recreational Center and held jobs as a car salesman at Mulholland Motors; waiter at the Brawny Deep (where he dressed as a pirate); waiter at the college hangout, the Peacock Stop; waiter at the off-campus sportsbar, Chesler's Touchdown; and finally as the assistant talent coordinator (books guests) for the TV show *Hilary*. When Will returned to Philadelphia at the end of the 1994 season, he took a job as a cook-waiter at Duke's House of Cheese Steaks. When NBC brass "realized" the title of the show is *The Fresh Prince of Bel Air*, the NBC Retrieval Team went to Philly and returned him to Bel Air.

Philip proposed to Vivian on the air on *Soul Train* (they were at the unscramble board and Philip used the letters intended to identify a celebrity to ask Vivian to marry him). He lives two houses from Ron and Nancy Reagan ("We even share the same pool man") and is a lawyer with the firm of Furth and Meyer (he is later a judge). Philip, middle name Zeke, grew up on a farm in Yamacrow, Nebraska. He had a pet pig (Melvin) and won the Young Farmers of America Pig Passing Contest four years in a row; he was also the first black president of the Young Farmers of America. He attended Princeton University and Harvard Law School, and won the Urban Spirit Award for his community work. He is a Capricorn (born 1/30), has a pool stick he calls Lucille and is part owner of a record store called the Sound Explosion.

Vivian is a college professor who does substitute teaching at the Bel Air Academy, USC, ULA and UCLA. Vanilla Swiss Almond is her favorite ice cream flavor and she gave birth to her and Philip's fourth child, Nicholas Andrew, on 2/22/93. Their other children are Hilary (Karyn Parsons), Carlton (Alfonso Riberio) and Ashley (Tatyana M. Ali).

Hilary, 21, is beautiful, extremely feminine and conceited. She attended UCLA (quit when she found it too difficult) and dreams of a glamorous job so when people ask what she does she can see them turn green with envy. She first worked in the Bel Air Mall, then as the personal assistant to a has-been movie star (Marissa Redmond). When Philip took Hilary's credit cards away ("You spend more money on clothes than some small nations spend on grain") Hilary found a job with Delectable Eats Catering. When this dissatisfied her, she found work as the weather girl on KFPB, Channel 8's *News in Action* (a paper called "The I Hate Hilary Newsletter" was published criticizing her skimpy wardrobe and lack of weather knowledge). This led to her hosting her own talk show, *Hilary*.

Hilary has her hair done at a salon called Black Beauty and posed nude for a *Playboy* layout on weather girls called "Warm Fronts" (Hilary's breasts were covered by clouds). Hilary reads *17* and *She* magazines and will never wear the same clothes twice. She has a knack for losing her house keys (she has 30 copies made each month and hopes someone will return the ones she has lost; her address is on each key). At age nine Hilary played the violin, but gave it up ("It irritated my chin"); she later tried ballet, but had to stop ("I thought I would get feet like Fred Flintstone"); and in high school, she was a cheerleader, but gave that up "because they wanted me to cheer at away games and travel by bus."

Carlton, born 8/4/74, first attended the Bel Air Academy (3.9½ grade-point average; member of the poetry and glee clubs) and ULA with Will. Here Carlton worked as manager of the bookstore, the Peacock Stop. Carlton's favorite cereal is Fruity Pebbles and he is majoring in pre-law (he hopes to attend Harvard Law School). He had his first crush on Tootie (*The Facts of Life*) and still hopes to meet her. He believes the world has gone crazy "since M&M's introduced the blue ones"; Will believes he is an idiot for all the crazy things he does. As a kid Carlton had a dog named Scruffy.

Ashley, born in 1979, first attended the Hollywood Preparatory Institute, then the Bel Air Academy (which she left to attend Morris High School). Hilary is proud that Ashley is dating right and becoming as beautiful as she is. Ashley plays the violin and her favorite video game is Tetris. Her most embarrassing moment occurred at an honor awards ceremony, where she was sitting with her legs crossed. When she was called for an English award, she got up — but her leg had fallen asleep and she fell on her face. When she wrote a song called "Make Up Your Mind," Will tried to launch her on a music career (which failed when Will had radio stations constantly play the song and kids got sick of hearing it). When her parents are away, Ashley throws parties.

Geoffrey (Joseph Marcell), the prim and proper English butler, started his career with a Lord Fowler. He enjoys "loosening up" at the Circle M Dude Ranch on his weekends off and calls Will "Master William" (Will calls him "G").

43. Friends NBC, 1994–

Monica Geller (Courteney Cox), Rachel Greene (Jennifer Aniston), Phoebe Buffay (Lisa Kudrow), Ross Geller (David Schwimmer), Joey Tribiana (Matt LeBlanc) and Chandler Bing (Matthew Perry) are six close friends who attended Lincoln High School and now live in Manhattan. "The ugly naked guy" lives in the building across the street from Monica's apartment.

Monica shares Apartment 20 with Rachel. She is a chef and first became interested in cooking "when I got my first Easy Bake Oven and opened Easy Monica's Bakery." While she won't admit it, her love of cooking was also responsible for her being overweight in high school. Monica is head chef at Alesandro's Restaurant and the food critic for the *Chelsea Reporter* (where she receives a penny a word for her reviews). She also worked as a roller skating waitress (with blonde wig and stuffed bra) at the Moondance Diner and with Phoebe in a short-lived catering business (Monica did the cooking; Phoebe drove the van). Ross claims that Monica makes the best turkey sandwich in the world (her secret is "the moist maker"—a gravy-soaked slice of bread in the middle of two slices of turkey and the outer bread). One night after an affair, Monica became a little wild: she took off her bra and placed it on the telephone pole next to her building to remind her that she is always attracted "to guys who are either too old or too young." Monica numbers the bottoms of her coffee mugs "so I can keep track of them."

Rachel, middle name Karen, originally worked as a waitress at the group's favorite hangout, a coffee shop called Central Perk. Possessing a flair for fashion design, Rachel quit the waitress job and found employment at Fortunato Fashions, then at Bloomingdale's as a Junior Miss (assistant) (she was later promoted to assistant buyer). When the store eliminated her job, she became a Bloomingdale's Personal Shopper (helps people shop). When a better opportunity came her way, she quit for a job as fashion consultant at Ralph Lauren. Rachel's favorite movie is *Weekend at Bernie's*—but she won't admit it; if asked, she'll tell you it's *Dangerous Liaisons*. She sleeps in a T-shirt that reads "Frankie Says Relax" and is not allowed to borrow Monica's clothes or jewelry "because I lose her stuff."

Phoebe, called "Pheebs," is a masseuse at Healing Hands, Inc. She has a dim-witted twin sister named Ursula (also played by Lisa Kudrow) who works as a waitress at Riff's Bar (she appears occasionally on the series *Mad About You*). Phoebe, a vegetarian, was born on February 16, is somewhat of a psychic, and enjoys playing and writing folk songs (she performs at Central Perk and has recorded the "hit" song "Smelly Cat"). "I also have a deep, dark secret," Phoebe says, "I married a gay Canadian [Duncan] so he could get his green card." Phoebe claims to make the best oatmeal raisin cookies in the world but doesn't make them often "because it would be unfair to the other cookies." When her business venture with Monica failed, Phoebe tried to turn her van into a taxi and begin Relax-a-Taxi (a cab with a massage table in the back). Phoebe keeps her grandmother's ashes in her car (under the front seat in a wooden box) and when she found a police badge on the street, she pretended to be a vice cop with the 57th Precinct "who worked as an undercover whore."

Ross is Monica's brother. He is a paleontologist with the Museum of Natural History (also mentioned as the Museum of Prehistoric History). As kids he and Monica would compete against each other for "The Geller Award" (a troll doll nailed to a piece of wood). In college, Ross played the keyboard and composed "wordless sound poems" (music with sound effects; each song ended with an explosion). Ross's beeper number is 555-JIMBO and he had a pet monkey, rescued from a lab, named Marcel (who was given to the San Diego Zoo when he matured). Ross was married to Carol (Jane Sibbett) but lost her to her lesbian lover, Susan Bunch (Jessica Hecht). Carol gave birth to Ross's son, Ben, shortly before leaving him.

Joey is the dim-witted member of the group. He is a hopeful actor with the Estelle Leonard Talent Agency. His big break came "when I got the part of the butt double for Al Pacino" (in an unnamed movie). Joey appeared in a porn movie (title not given) when he first started acting and was a regular on the TV soap opera *Days of Our Lives* (playing Dr. Drake Ramore. The character, named "The most dateable neurosurgeon" by *Teen Beat* magazine, was killed off when he fell down an elevator shaft). Joey guest-starred on an episode of *Law and Order*, made an infomercial (for the milk carton spout) and played Victor, the husband in an unnamed Broadway play at the Lucille Cortel Theater. His favorite foods are sandwiches. As a kid he had an imaginary friend named Maurice, who was a space cowboy.

Chandler, a data processor, shares Apartment 19 with Joey (across the hall from Monica). Chandler hides the fact that "I have a third nipple" and has *TV Guide* delivered to him under the name Chandler Bong. His favorite TV shows are *Baywatch*, *Wonder Woman* and *Xena: Warrior Princess*. When Chandler breaks up with a girl, he goes through three phases: the sweatpants phase, the strip club phase, and the envisioning himself with other girls phase (as Joey calls them). When Joey and Chandler order a bucket of crispy fried chicken, Joey eats the skin "and the chicken is up for grabs." While Chandler has to live with Joey, he also contends with Joey's two pets —

a duck and a chicken (the duck is called Duck and the chicken, Chicken; Chandler has also called the chicken "Our Chick" and "Little Yasmine"— "after a real chick"—Yasmine Bleeth of *Baywatch*). Chandler is afraid of bras ("can't work them") and was called "Sir Limpsalot" in high school after Monica accidentally dropped a knife that cut off the tip of his pinky toe.

44.   Full House ABC, 1987–1995

The house at 1882 Gerard Street in San Francisco is home to Danny Tanner (Bob Saget), a widower with three daughters: D.J. (Candace Cameron), Stephanie (Jodie Sweetin) and Michelle (Mary Kate and Ashley Olsen). Also living with them are Jesse (John Stamos), Danny's brother-in-law, and their friend, Joey (David Coulier).

Danny, Jesse and Joey attended Golden Bay Union High School (where Danny was called "Dan Dan"). Danny, originally a sportscaster on KTMB-TV, Channel 8's *Newsbeat*, now co-hosts *Wake Up, San Francisco* with Rebecca Donaldson (Lori Loughlin). In college, Danny had a TV show called *College Pop* and as a kid had a "friend" named Terry, the Talking Wash Cloth. Danny, a neat freak, attributes his condition to his fifth birthday when his mother gave him, her "special helper," a set of vacuum cleaner attachments. Danny buys his special low-salt gherkins at Pickle Town and has a car (license plate 4E11449) called Bullet. His late wife, Pam (Jesse's sister) was killed in a car accident.

Jesse, whose heritage is Greek, has the real first name Hermes. Because he was teased and called "Zorba the Geek," his mother changed it to Jesse. Jesse's last name was first Cochran then Katsopolis. He is a partner with Joey as a commercial jingle writer in J.J. Creative Services (later called Double J. Creative Services). They also worked as deejays ("The Rush Hour Renegades") on KFLH radio. Jesse, who had a band in high school (called both Disciplinary Action and Disciplinary Problem), is now with a group called Jesse and the Rippers (who play at the Smash Club; Jesse has a contract with Fat Fish Records). At one point he was with a band called Feedback. Jesse later inherits the Smash Club and turns it into the family-oriented New Smash Club. Jesse was dropped by the Rippers (for spending more time moussing his hair than playing the guitar) and formed a new band called Hot Daddy and the Monkey Puppets. Jesse's idol is Elvis Presley. He has a Mustang (plate RDV 913) called Sally. "Have mercy" is his favorite expression. He buys Elvis Peanut Butter (Hunka Hunka type) and was known as Dr. Dare when he rode his motorcycle (he would take on any dare). Prior to working with Joey, Jesse was a "pest control specialist" (bug exterminator). He fell in love with and married Rebecca. They honeymooned in Bora

Bora and moved into the converted attic in Danny's home. Rebecca's engagement ring is inscribed with the words "Love Me Tender"; Rebecca gave birth to twins Nicholas and Alexander (Blake and Dylan Tuomy-Wilhoit) on 11/12/91. Rebecca was born on a farm in Valentine, Nebraska, and had a pet cow named Janice.

Joey Gladstone is a stand-up comic and cartoon voice impersonator looking for his big break. He appeared on *Star Search* and did a pilot called *Surf's Up* (he was Flip, the surfer-dude mailman. When the live-action format didn't work, it was turned into a cartoon with Joey as Flip, the surfing kangaroo). He made another pilot, *The Mr. Egghead Show* with Jesse as the Music Professor. Joey next became the host of Channel 8's *The Ranger Joe Show* (where he entertained kids from the Enchanted Forest with his hand-puppet assistant, Mr. Woodchuck; Jesse was a regular as Lumberjack Jesse). He and Jesse were also members of the Chi Sigma fraternity in college. Joey has a 1963 Rambler (license plate JJE 805) he calls Rosie. His favorite expression is "cut it out."

D.J. (Donna Jo), the oldest of the girls, attended the Frasier Street Elementary School, Beaumont Junior High, Van Allen Junior High and Van Allen High School. She loves to shop, is editor of the school newspaper and has her own phone (555-8722). As a kid she had a favorite pillow called "Pillow Person." She wears Passion Plumb eye shadow and had a job as the Happy Helper at Tot Shots (a mall photographer). D.J.'s dream is to own a horse (she briefly had one named Rocket in sixth grade).

Stephanie Judith, the middle child, attends Frasier Street Elementary, then DaMaggio Jr. High School. She carries a Jetsons lunchbox; Mr. Bear is her favorite plush animal and Emily is her favorite doll. When the kids made fun of her name and called her "Step on Me," she temporarily called herself Dawn. During the taking of the class picture Stephanie sneezed and was nicknamed "Sneeze Burger." Stephanie (jersey 8) was a member of the Giants Little League team (coached by Danny) and threw "The Tanner Twister" ("A curve ball like no other girl"). Stephanie is a Capricorn and her catchphrase is "how rude." She did a commercial for Oat Boats Cereal and was a member of the Honeybees Scout Troop. *Charlotte's Web* is her favorite book. Pizza and strawberry yogurt are her favorite foods.

Michelle Elizabeth is the baby of the family. She attended Meadowcrest Preschool, then Frasier Elementary. On her first day at Meadowcrest, Michelle let Dave, the class bird, out of his cage and he flew away. In her first-grade production of *Yankee Doodle Dandy*, Michelle played the Statue of Liberty. She had an invisible friend (Glen) and eats Honey Coated Fiber Bears breakfast cereal. She was Officer Michelle of the Polite Police at school; has two goldfish (Martin and Frankie) and "you got it, dude," is her catchphrase. *The Little Mermaid* is her favorite movie and she was called "Trail Mix" when she, D.J. and Stephanie attended Camp Lakota in 1993. Jesse calls Michelle "Munchkin."

Kimmy Louise Gibler (Andrea Barber) is D.J.'s best friend. She is very pretty and tends to get D.J. into trouble with her antics. Kimmy writes the column "Madame Kimmy's Horoscope" for the school newspaper and she and D.J. frequent the Food Court at the mall. Kimmy cuts economics classes "because I'm going to marry a doctor and hire a maid" and *Dirty Dancing* is her favorite movie (which she fast-forwards to the kissing scenes). Kimmy calls Danny "Mr. T" and worked with D.J. as a waitress at the New Smash Club. She had a dog named Cocoa (later called Sinbad).

The Tanners have a dog named Comet; Friday is "mop the floors till you drop day" at the Tanner house; Hill Top Cable provides cable service; and Danny hosted *The We Love Our Children Telethon* on Channel 8.

45.   The George Carlin Show Fox, 1994–1995

George O'Grady (George Carlin) is a nasty New York cab driver. He lives in Apartment 4C and drives taxi number 397193 (later 3G09) for the New York City Cab Company. He has been exposed for bilking customers on the TV show *You've Been Busted* and his cab has been called "The Taxi of Terror." He previously appeared on TV when he became intoxicated at Shea Stadium and streaked across the playing field ("I got to third base before they threw the tarp over me"). George's pride and joy is his collection of jazz records. He has a dog named Miles (after musician Miles Davis).

"Broadway" Harry Rosetti (Alex Rocco) is George's bookie. Before George became Harry's best customer, Harry robbed cigarette trucks for a living—"but I was always caught and arrested, so I went into a different line—bookmaking." Harry has been married to the ultra-sexy Barbara (Adrienne Barbeau) for 31 years but has only known her for 24 years (he doesn't count separations and the two years he spent in Italy waiting for things to cool down when he was a suspect in the unsolved shooting of a mobster).

Jack Donahue (Anthony Starke) owns the Molin Tavern, the bar hangout. He was thrown out of bartender school for drinking and sells Molin Tavern T-shirts for $12.98. Sydney Paris (Paige French) is the Molin's busty barmaid. She is a model waiting for her big break and is a former Miss Texas; she is now with the Pinnacle Modeling Agency.

Kathleen Racowski (Susan Sullivan) is George's girlfriend. She owns the To Fur with Love pet shop and graduated from Hofstra University in 1970. Neil Bick (Christopher Rich) is the rich plastic surgeon who frequents the Molin and whom George finds to be the perfect patsy. He attended

Georgetown University. The Ravenswood Restaurant in Connecticut is his favorite eatery.

46.   **Get a Life** Fox, 1990–1992

Chris Peterson (Chris Elliott) is a 30-year-old who never forgot what it is like to be a kid. He lives at home with his parents, Fred and Gladys (Bob Elliott, Elinor Donahue), at 1341 Meadow Brooke Lane in Greenville, Minnesota. Chris's phone number is 555-9034.

In 1971, Chris saw an ad in the back of a comic book for a Neptune 2000 submarine that operates on 54 "D" batteries. To pay for it, he took a job as a paperboy for the *Pioneer Press*. Twenty years later, he has the same job. Chris is a failure at everything, but he is the last one to realize it. His male ancestors dressed as women to get off the *Titantic*; he likes turkey ("but only the dark meat"), and the proudest moment of his life occurred when he had his picture taken with TV's Batman (Adam West) at an auto show.

Chris watches *Fraggle Rock* every morning, believes Darryl Hannah is the world's greatest actress, and worries that the local video store will discontinue its X-rated section ("I can't tell you how many nights' sleep I lost over that"). He has a ventriloquist's dummy (Mr. Poppy), his favorite color is peach and "The Family Circus" is his favorite comic strip. His favorite TV show is *Sandy's Laff and Song Jackpot*.

Chris believes that he was meant to be many things but was dealt a cruel hand by fate. He tried to become a model, enrolled in the Handsome Boy Modeling School, and took the name "Sparkles" Peterson — but couldn't find a job. Thinking he was meant to be an actor, he landed the role of a wildebeest in *Zoo Animals on Wheels* at the Greenville Musical Theater. Bad reviews ended that career. When Chris turned 31 (11/19/91) he moved into the garage of Gus Borden (Brian Doyle-Murray), an embittered ex-cop with a drinking problem. Gus lives at 1804 York Avenue and reads the girlie magazine *Thigh World*. Chris pays him $150 a month in rent.

Fred and Gladys believe Chris "is like a diamond in the rough that needs polishing" (or, as Fred also puts it, "an idiot"). Chris believes he has a happy-go-lucky outlook on life — "I'm happy being an idiot." Fred was born in Chicago; Gladys is an army brat. Their wardrobe consists mainly of bathrobes (which they wear almost everywhere) and they eat breakfast off presidential commemorative plates. They use Mrs. Butterworth's pancake syrup. Fred's license plate reads IRG 522.

Larry and Sharon Potter (Sam Robards, Robin Riker) are Chris's neighbors (at 1343 Meadow Brooke Lane). Larry believes Chris is "a gas-headed idiot who gets on everyone's nerves." He is an accountant for the firm of

Bushman and Simon, hems Sharon's dresses and makes homemade taffy. Sharon considers Chris to be her worst enemy in life and has "idiot proofed" the house to keep "Chris and his disgusting Chris microbes" out of her home. Each year Sharon bakes chocolate divinity squares and distributes them to the neighbors.

47. **Going Places** ABC, 1990–1991

Alexandra "Alex" Burton (Heather Locklear), Kate Griffin (Hallie Todd), and brothers Jack and Charles Davis (Jerry Levine, Alan Ruck) are writers for a *Candid Camera*-like TV show called *Here's Looking at You*. It is produced in Los Angeles by Dawn St. Claire (Holland Taylor) for National Studios. The writers share a three-bedroom home at 1800 Beach Road.

Alexandra was the former producer of an early-morning show called *Wake Up, Denver*. She loves to cook and is "the glue" that holds the argumentative group together. She has an impressive answer for everything and often fools people — but says "I'm only kidding" when they start to believe her. Although she did not reveal her weight, Alex "blew up to 103 pounds" when she stopped smoking. Her good luck charm is her plush rabbit, Mr. Fluffy.

Kate, born in New York City, is the sharp-tongued one of the group. She has proclaimed herself as the group's boss and previously wrote for stand-up comics in Manhattan. Rocky road is her favorite ice cream and she wears Colonial Red nail polish.

Jack and Charles are from Chicago. They believed they were the only writers and balked at working with Alex — until they saw her bent over a desk in a short, tight skirt — "No problem." Charles is the creative one; he has a 32-inch waist and wears a 40 regular suit. Jack, the joker, wears a 38 regular suit.

Lindsay Brown (Staci Keanan) is the pretty teenage girl who lives next door. Her parents are rarely home (always traveling) and she has made the team her substitute family. Lindsay attends Hollywood High School, loves horror movies and is closest to Alex.

When the competition, *In Your Face*, beats *Here's Looking at You* in the ratings, the show is canceled (replaced by the reality show *America's Funniest Most Wanted*). Alex, Kate, Jack and Charles find jobs as writers on *The Dick Roberts Show*, a daily talk fest hosted by Dick Roberts (Steve Vinovich). Dick is an egomaniac who is difficult, arrogant, pompous, and abrasive, and who has little respect for anyone. Arnie Ross (Philip Charles MacKenzie) is the show's new producer. Dick's antics have given him ulcers and he lives on Maalox and Pepto Bismol. In the opening theme, the regulars are seen on the Hollywood Walk of Fame. Alex places her hands in the imprints of Betty Grable; Kate in the hands of Bette Davis; Jack in the hands of Al Jolson; and Charlie places his foot in the footprints of Jack Benny.

48.   The Golden Girls NBC, 1985–1992

Blanche Elizabeth Devereaux (Rue McClanahan), Rose Nylund (Betty White), Dorothy Zbornak (Bea Arthur) and Sophia Petrillo (Estelle Getty) are senior citizens who share a home at 6151 Richmond Street in Miami Beach, Florida.

Blanche proudly boasts that her initials spell BED. She is totally liberated and flaunts her sexuality to get what she wants from men. She was born in Atlanta, Georgia, and now works in an unnamed museum. She enjoys drinks at the Rusty Anchor Bar. Blanche, a Baptist, was chosen Citrus Festival Queen, and appeared on the cover of the *Greater Miami Penny Saver* in an ad for Ponce de Leon Itching Cream. In college Blanche, whose maiden name is Hollingsworth, was a member of the Alpha Gams sorority and each year on her anniversary, she tries on her wedding gown. If she has gained weight, she drastically diets to keep her figure. She is divorced from George Devereaux.

Rose was born in the strange little town of St. Olaf, Minnesota, "The Broken Hip Capital of the Midwest" ("We revere our old people and put them on pedestals — but they fall off and break bones"). Rose attended St. Olaf's grammar and high schools, then Rockport Community College (where she joined the farmer's sorority, the Alpha Yams), and finally St. Paul's Business School. Her hobbies are cheese making, Viking history and stamp collecting.

Rose, a Lutheran, mentioned her maiden name as both Lindstrom and Gierkleckibiken. She was married to the late Charlie Nylund, the owner of a tile grouting business. Rose listens to all-talk WXBC radio and works as the production assistant for *The Enrique Ross Show*, a consumer affairs program on WSF-TV, Channel 8. She is later associate producer of *Wake Up, Miami*. (Rose first worked as a waitress at the Fountain Rock Coffee House; she is also a Sunshine volunteer at the Community Medical Center.)

As a kid Rose had a pet mouse (Larry), two dogs (Rusty and Jake), a cat (Scruffy), teddy bears (Fernando and Mr. Longfellow), a nickname (Twinkle Toes) and a pet pig (Lester, who could predict Oscar winners by wagging his tail). Rose was struck by lightning ("But only once") and always tells the truth. She now has a cat (Mr. Peepers) and is a Sunshine Girls Cadet Troop leader. Twelve is her favorite number and she wrote her high school fight song, "Onward St. Olaf." Rose lost "The Little Miss Olaf Beauty Pageant" 23 years in a row (her talent was rat smelling) but her biggest disappointment was losing the title "Miss Butter Queen of St. Olaf" (after 16 years of training she became a finalist but lost when her churn jammed).

Dorothy, born in Brooklyn, New York, is a substitute English teacher for the Florida public school system. Her favorite TV show is *Jeopardy* and she was the first one in the Petrillo family (her maiden name) to attend college (where she majored in history). Dorothy was married to Stan Zbornak (Herb Edelman) for 38 years before they divorced. In the final first-run episode (5/9/92) Dorothy marries Blanche's uncle, Lucas Hollingsworth (Leslie Nielsen) and moves to Atlanta, Georgia, to begin a new life.

Sophia, Dorothy's mother, was born in Sicily and works part time at the Pecos Pete Chow Wagon Diner (later, for Meals on Wheels, then as activities director at the Cypress Grove Retirement Home). Sophia previously lived at the Shady Pines Retirement Home. She calls Dorothy "Pussycat" and "Big Foot." She plays bingo at St. Dominick's church, buys her shoes at Shim Shacks and has an uncle named Nunzio who lives with a goat. She and Dorothy are Catholic. See also *The Golden Palace*.

49.   The Golden Palace CBS, 1992–1993

Golden Girls spinoff that finds Blanche Devereaux (Rue McClanahan), Rose Nylund (Betty White) and Sophia Petrillo (Estelle Getty) pooling their resources and purchasing the Golden Palace, a 42-room Miami hotel, to help them through their golden years. Blanche becomes the manager; Rose, the housekeeper; and Sophia, the kitchen manager. Chuy Castillos (Cheech Marin) is the hotel's Mexican chef. He attended the Fashion Institute of Technology and wanted to make a statement in men's fashion, but drew number seven in the 1969 lottery draft and went into the army—where he learned how to cook. Roland Wilson (Don Cheadle), Blanche's assistant, worked previously at Disney World as one of the Seven Dwarfs—Sneezy.

50.   Good Morning, Miss Bliss DIS, 1988–1989

Carrie Bliss (Hayley Mills) is an eighth-grade schoolteacher at J.F.K. Junior High School in Indianapolis, Indiana. Richard Belding (Dennis Haskins) is the principal; featured students are Zack Morris (Mark-Paul Gosselaar), Lisa Turtle (Lark Voorhies), Samuel "Screech" Powers (Dustin Diamond) and Nicole "Nikki" Coleman (Heather Hopper).

Carrie, a widow, has been teaching history for 11 years. She cares about her students ("Their problems are my problems") and uses innovative teaching methods that sometimes backfire. Her classes are held in Room 103. She was voted Indiana Teacher of the Year by *School Days* magazine. Zack is the schemer and always trying to impress girls. Lisa is the fashion-conscious student who wears makeup to school without her parents' knowledge. Nikki, the crusader of the group, stands up for what she believes in, and is also a pitcher on the school's baseball team. Lisa is trying to bring out Nikki's feminine side and make her into a girl ("But it isn't an easy job"). Screech, the nerd, is glue monitor ("Believe me, it's not as glamorous as it sounds") and has two pet mice (Spin and Marty). The Cosmos is the after-school hangout. Signs posted around the school read: "Do Not Remove Food from the Cafeteria," "Take Steps One at a Time," "No Running in the Hallways," "Do Not Slam Lockers While Classes Are in Session" and "This School Says No to Drugs."

The episodes have been retitled *Saved by the Bell* for syndication and feature an older Zack telling viewers that "this episode is from our junior high days." See also *Saved by the Bell*.

51. **Good Sports** CBS, 1991

Gayle Roberts (Farrah Fawcett) and Bobby Tannen (Ryan O'Neal) co-host *Sports Central*, an information program for the Rappaport Broadcasting System's ASCN (All Sports Cable Network). They also host *Sports Chat* (interviews) and *Sports Brief* (updates).

Gayle, 40, was a model who dreamt of becoming a sports journalist. She appeared on the cover of *Sports Illustrated* and was given a chance to host a show by ASCN's owner. Gayle, called "The Doris Day of the Sports World" for her wholesome image and perky outlook, has the birth name Gayle Gordon (she changed her last name to Roberts to avoid confusion with Gale Gordon, Lucille Ball's longtime sidekick; Mr. Mooney, for example, on *Here's Lucy*). Gayle does charity work for the Los Angeles Mission, has a goldfish (Frankie) and can't stand hearing the word *bitch*. Gayle is allergic to goat cheese and can't eat baby back ribs. "Fog" by Carl Sandburg is her favorite poem by her favorite poet.

Bobby, 42, had a brief career as the recording star "Downtown" Bobby Tannen (his only album was *Downtown Sings "Downtown" and Other Chart Busters — Including the Hit Single, "Wichita Lineman"*). He was also the number-one draft pick from the University of Miami (jersey 12) but quit football two years later to manage the career of his new wife, singer-stripper Yvonne Pomplona (Sheri Rose). Three weeks later, following his divorce, he made a comeback with the L.A. Rams (jersey 13). He next became an Oakland Raider and wrote the tell-all book, *Panty Raiders*. When team member Lyle Alazado read the book "he broke Bobby's body and tore his face off." Bobby appeared in bandages on the cover of *Look* magazine with the headline "Bye Bye Bobby." He worked as a delivery boy for the Friends of Pizza before being teamed with Gayle (whom he dated 20 years earlier when he was with the New York Jets).

Bobby and Gayle live in separate apartments at the Landmark Building (Gayle considers him "a self-destructive punk who never grew up"). Bobby has a goldfish (Valley), collects beer cans (he has 147 unopened brands from 98 countries) and when he scored a touchdown, the organist at Shea Stadium would play the song "Downtown."

R. J. Rappaport (Lane Smith), the station owner, runs the company like a military general (he attended Culver Military Academy and Amherst College). R.J. also operates Rap-Ha-Port (a 24-hour comedy channel) and calls his assistant, John McKinney (Brian Doyle-Murray) his "yes man." He and R.J. had a morning radio show called "Mac and Rap in the Morning."

R.J.'s hobby is taking television sets apart even though they are not broken. Rappaport Airlines sponsors *Sports Brief* ("The airline with fewer fatalities than any bicoastal airline").

Local 107 handles the electrical work at the station. In the episode "Electricity" (6/3/91), Farrah is seen reading the book, *The Burning Bed*, and Ryan is reading *Love Story* (both starred in film adaptations of the books they were reading). Michael Cole appeared in "Moody Blue Swings" (6/8/91) as Dr. M'odsquad (pronounced "Mod Squad," from his series of the same title), a vet Bobby sought for his sick fish.

52.   Grace Under Fire ABC, 1993–1998

Grace Kelly (Brett Butler) and her children Libby (Kaitlin Cullum), Quentin (Noah Segan, Jon Paul Steuer, Sam Horrigan) and infant Patrick (Dylan and Cole Sprouse) live at 445 Washington Avenue in Victory, Missouri. Grace, 36, is divorced from Jimmy (Geoff Pierson) and first worked as a waitress at Stevie Ray's Bar, then as a field worker in Section 7 of the CBD Oil Refinery, a volunteer for the Crisis Center (where she was known as Chris) and finally as office manager for the Reliance Construction Company. Before leaving the oil company to attend Missouri State College (to get her BA in English), Grace was promoted to crew chief; between classes, Grace frequents the Equator Coffee House.

Grace was born in Huntsville, Alabama (attended Huntsville High School). Her maiden name is Burdette. She had a serious drinking problem that she has now overcome ("I stopped when I saw a big red dog jump out of my lingerie drawer"). Strawberry is Grace's favorite ice cream flavor; Canadian bacon her favorite food for breakfast. She buys her lingerie at a store called Bras, Bras, Bras and enjoys Little Debbie Swiss Cake Rolls. Her license plate reads FXB 352 (later AEH 497). Grace rents movies at Video World and 555-0159 is her phone number. When Grace's landlord sold the house she was renting, she moved across the street to house number 446 (formerly owned by the elderly Mrs. Walker).

Grace first dated Russell Norton (Dave Thomas), the owner of Smiley's Pharmacy on 3rd and Lakesburg (when he took over the business, he never changed the store's name). He has a dog (Phil) and uses a cologne "that's cheap, chicks dig and kills bugs dead." His favorite restaurant "is where girls stopped dancing on the tables five minutes before." He has a 1984 LeBaron that he babies and he and Grace sometimes dine on the *Delta Queen*, the gambling riverboat docked offshore. Grace then dated Rick Bradshaw (Alan Autry), head of the oil company. He had a dog (Ralph), lived in a house with the number 1261 and left Grace for a high-paying job in Alaska.

Elizabeth Louise, nicknamed Libby, is a *Star Trek* fanatic. She has a doll (Helen), a pet squirrel (Spot), a goldfish (Fishy Fisherman), is a member of the girls' soccer team at Glenview Elementary School and winner of the fourth-grade "Why I Like Our State" contest. She is learning to play the trumpet, and keeps her Barbie doll in the refrigerator's butter dish "because Ken likes his Barbie cold." Libby also entered the Little Miss Muppet Pageant (she sang "Tomorrow" and came in next to last).

Quentin, the troublesome member of the family (he rebels against Grace's authority) finds serenity on the roof outside his window. In grade school, Quentin took the empty beer cans his father crushed against his head for Show and Tell and was first in trouble with the law for trespassing on property owned by the Victory Country Club.

Wade and Nadine Swaboda (Casey Sander, Julie White) are Grace's neighbors. Wade, a Marine (called "Wade the Impaler") during the Vietnam War, was originally a telephone lineman; then traffic reporter for KPLG radio; helicopter reporter for KQMO-TV, Channel 6; and finally an officer with the 6th District of the Victory Police Department. As a kid he had a treehouse with the sign "No girls or Communists allowed" and as a baby won the title "Little Mr. Man." Wade enjoys making pottery and believes that digital clocks will be the end of safe driving ("Kids will not know what ten and two o'clock are").

Nadine, Grace's best friend, is a waitress at Stevie Ray's Bar. When Grace had each of her children, Nadine was there for her ("Jimmy always had an excuse"). Nadine has been married four times and has never had anything consistent in her life — except for Grace, who is always there for her. When Nadine gave birth to a girl she and Wade named Rose, she had to have her Boo Boo Bear (her focal point) when she went into labor. Nadine left Wade during the show's final season and moved to Colorado, leaving Wade to fend for himself. The series ended before anything was resolved.

53.   Growing Pains ABC, 1985–1992

Jason Roland Seaver (Alan Thicke), his wife Maggie (Joanna Kerns) and their children Mike, Carol , Ben and Chrissy (Kirk Cameron, Tracey Gold, Jeremy Miller, Ashley Johnson) live at 15 Robin Hood Lane in Huntington, Long Island, New York. The Municipal Removal Service picks up garbage on Tuesdays and Fridays; FEM 412 is the license plate of the family's station wagon.

Jason, who operates a private psychology practice from his home, was originally a doctor of psychology at Long Island General Hospital; he later does volunteer work for the Free Clinic to help the poor people of his community. Maggie originally worked as a researcher for *Newsweek* magazine, then as a reporter for the Long Island *Daily Herald,* reporter for *Action News* on Channel 19 (using her maiden name of Malone) and a columnist for *The Sentinel* ("Maggie Malone, Consumer Watchdog").

Jason and Maggie, who is 13 months older than Jason, met at Boston College. (He was a psychology major. Maggie originally majored in child psychology but switched to journalism in her junior year.) Jason was a member of the rock group the Wild Hots and as a child his imaginary friend was 1950s TV game show host Bud Collyer ("who would come over to my house and play games"). Maggie won the 1989 Working Mother of the Year award.

Michael Aaron, the oldest child, attended Dewey High School, Alf Landon Junior College and Boynton State College. He had aspirations to act, and starred in the Dewey High production of *Our Town.* Mike's first professional acting job was on the TV series *New York Heat* as Officer Bukarski (who was killed off; Mike's name was misspelled in the credits as Michael Weaver). He next landed a role on the TV soap opera *Big City Secrets* before he developed an interest in teaching (remedial studies at the Learning Annex of the Community Health Center for $100 a week). Mike's previous jobs: paperboy for the *Herald* (200 customers on his route), waiter at the World of Burgers, salesman at Stereo Village, car wash attendant, night man at the Stop and Shop, and singing waiter at Sullivan's Tavern. Mike's license plate reads BLA 592 (later 236R DKS).

Carol Ann is pretty, sensitive, smart and wishes she could shed her brainy image and be thought of as "dangerous, provocative and sexy." Carol attended Dewey High then Columbia University in Manhattan (which she left in 1990 for a job as a computer page breaker at GSM Publishing; she returned the following year as a law student). At age seven Carol was a member of the Happy Campers; she was voted 1988 Dewey High Homecoming Queen and was president of the school's Future Nuclear Physicists Club. Portraits of W. C. Fields, Laurel and Hardy and the Marx Brothers adorn her bedroom walls. When Tracey Gold suffered from anorexia nervosa (an eating disorder) and took a leave of absence (1991-92) her character was said to be in London attending school. Elizabeth Ward played Carol in the unaired pilot.

Benjamin "Ben" Hubert Humphrey Seaver attended Wendell Willkie Elementary School then Dewey High — where he showed potential for surpassing Mike as the worst problem student ever. As a kid he had an imaginary friend named Pirate Sam. Christine, affectionately called Chrissy, is six years old and attends the Parkway Preschool; in later episodes she attended Greenway Elementary. Her favorite bedtime story is "Mr. Mouse" and she has an imaginary mouse "friend" she called Ike. Her plush toys: Bertha Big Jeans (a bear), Papa Pig and Mr. Blow Hole (a whale). Chrissy was originally an infant (twins Kristen and Kelsey Dohring) but on 9/19/90 the character was advanced to age six and played by Ashley Johnson.

The last episode (4/25/92) finds Jason, Maggie, Chrissy and Ben moving to Washington, D.C., when Maggie becomes the executive director of media relations for an unseen senator. Carol moves into a dorm at Columbia; Mike remains in the apartment over the Seavers' garage (he mentions that he "has to break in new landlords").

54.   Hanging with Mr. Cooper ABC, 1992–1996

Mark Cooper (Mark Curry), a substitute teacher at Oakridge High School, lives at 653 Hamilton Street in Oakland, California. He shares the house with Vanessa Russell (Holly Robinson) and Robin Dumars (Dawn Lewis). Mark is a former Oakridge High basketball star (jersey 15) who failed to make the NBA. He teaches science and history and relates basketball stories to make his points. He drives a 1967 Dodge Dart (license plate MR COOPER), teaches driver's ed and is called "Coop" by his students. During the summer he coaches the Oakland Peanut League basketball team and is also cheerleading coach for Oakridge's Penguinettes. Mark wears a size 13EEE shoe; had a tryout with the Golden State Warriors basketball team and did a commercial for Skylords Athletic Shoes. His license plate originally read 583 BVD.

Vanessa was originally an executive secretary at the investment firm of Toplin and Toplin. She had hoped to become a stockbroker but developed an interest in the medical profession and worked as assistant to an orthopedic surgeon; nurse at the Sweetwater Retirement Home; EMT (emergency medical technician) trainee; and finally an EMT with an ambulance crew. Prior to this, Vanessa worked as a waitress at a Japanese restaurant, then in a soul food eatery called Loretta's. Vanessa, born in Washington, D.C., loves salmon mousse garnished with mandarin orange sauce and Russellnog (her own special Christmas eggnog with a touch of cinnamon). Her license plate reads 011 JJE (later 3AGU 906). As a kid she had a dog named Dino.

"Vanessa," Robin says, "is thin, beautiful and never lifts a finger; she eats like a horse and never gains an ounce." Robin diets, exercises two hours a day and would kill for Vanessa's body. Robin and Vanessa were college roommates (members of the Alpha Delta Rho sorority) and moved in with Mark to save on expenses. Robin, the music teacher at Oakridge High, believes that she is mechanically inclined "but isn't" says Mark ("Like the time she fixed the toaster and Vanessa's hair caught fire; or the time she fixed the car and had three parts left over").

When Robin moves (second season), Mark and Vanessa buy the house; Mark's cousin, Geneva Lee (Saundra Quarterman), a single mom, and her daughter, Nicole (Raven-Samone), become their new tenants. Geneva is initially the music teacher at Oakridge, then acting principal, and finally principal. She buys her clothes at the Bargain Ranch and moved in with Mark so Nicole could have a male influence in her life.

Nicole, who has a plush pony named Linda, is "ruthless" at the board game Candy Land. She attends Oakland Elementary School, is a member of Brownie Troop 2 and a member of the Fireflies, an all-girl pre-teen baseball team (coached by Mark). Nicole's favorite TV show is *Lester the Lizard and the Crocodile Kids*.

Before Geneva's job as acting principal, P. J. Moore (Nell Carter) was Oakridge's principal. She and Mark grew up together and Mark called her "Peaches." P.J. left for a better job in Chicago. She had a dog named Monster.

55. Harry and the Hendersons Syn., 1991–1993

The quaint 2,000 square-foot home with 100 feet of copper plumbing at 410 Forest Drive in Seattle is home to George and Nancy Henderson (Bruce Davison, Molly Cheek), their children Sarah and Ernie (Carol-Ann Plante, Zachary Bostrom) and Harry (Kevin Peter Hall, Dawan Scott, Brian Steele), a legendary Big Foot (the sociable Harry adopted the Hendersons as his family after he was struck by George's van on Interstate 5; he now lives in their loft). Harry's voice was provided by Patrick Pinney.

George was initially a marketing executive for the People's Sporting Goods Store, then publisher of a magazine called *A Better Life*. His childhood dream was to meet Annette Funicello and sing on *The Mickey Mouse Club*. George's license plate reads 608 GHR.

Nancy, middle name Gwen, works with the Student Exchange Council. As a kid Nancy had a pet frog (Slimey) and played triangle in her high school marching band. The most risqué thing Nancy did "was not wear a bra between 1972 and 1975." She was arrested (civil disobedience) for protesting without clothes on a nude beach. When she gets upset, she eats Breyer's Rocky Road ice cream. When Nancy gets angry at Harry she calls him "Mister" (for example, "Go to your loft, Mister").

Sarah attended Madison High School, then Northern College of the Arts. She is on the track team, wrote the song "Somewhere Out There" for the Homecoming Dance and hopes to one day write a book about Harry and her family—"But I'm going to use a pen name. I don't want anyone to think I'm nuts." Sarah, middle name Nicole, had a hamster (Melissa) and worked at Photo Quickie. She calls her white lace bra "my lucky bra" and has aspirations to be an actress (she starred in the community theater production of *Beauty and the Beast*—with Harry as the Beast). She also played saxophone in her high school orchestra.

Ernie attends Madison Jr. High. He is the closest to Harry; "Ernie" was the first word Harry spoke. Although Ernie dislikes girls, he became friendly with Darcy Farg (Courtney Peldon), the pretty, rich and feminine girl who lives next door. (Darcy's last name was initially given as Payne.) She and Ernie were members of the Padres Pee Wee League baseball team (they play at Mercer Field). She had a cat (Damian "the bird killer") and a sidewalk mineral water stand (Chez Darcy).

Brett Douglas (Noah Blake), Nancy's brother, assists George on the magazine. He considers himself a ladies' man and was previously a steward on a cruise ship (where he met and married Michele; she left him after 25 days to star in the film *Babes from Venus*. He refers to it as "The day she disembarked without me"). Brett, whose favorite hangout is Club 700, calls George "G-Man," Nancy "Nance," Ernie "E-Man" and Harry "Hair Monger."

Samantha Glick (Gigi Rice) and her daughter, Tiffany (Cassie Cole) were the Hendersons' original neighbors. Samantha works for Channel 10 and reports on *The News at 5*. She also hosts *Crime Time with Samantha Glick* and *Seattle Celebrities*. She wishes the Hendersons "would get a pet duck like a normal family." When Tiffany, called "Tiffy" by her mother, first saw the Big Foot she called him "Hairy Guy"; this prompted George to call him Harry. Without explanation Samantha and Tiffy were dropped and replaced by Darcy.

Harry is eight feet one inch tall and weighs 680 pounds. He has a Barry Manilow tape collection and loves granola bars (which he calls "Num Num" and "Numie Numie"). In final-season episodes, Harry's existence becomes known when he is exposed by a tabloid TV show. To protect Harry, George writes to the president requesting that the Big Foot be declared a national park. The request is granted, giving Harry the freedom to live anywhere he wishes. He chooses to live with the Hendersons. George and Nancy wrote the book Sarah wanted to do called *My Life with Big Foot* (originally called *Harry and Me*).

56.   **Head of the Class** ABC, 1986–1991

Charlie Moore (Howard Hesseman) is an I.H.P. (Individual Honors Program) history teacher at Fillmore High School in Manhattan. He was born in Idaho and attended Weesur High School (where he wrote the play *Goodbye Weesur, Hello Broadway*) then Idaho State College. Following graduation he moved to New York but his dream to direct on Broadway never happened. He staged *Hamlet* at the Playhouse in New Jersey and directed the off–Broadway play *Little Shop of Horrors*. He appeared in plays by Chekhov and Ibsen, and his most embarrassing moment occurred when he appeared in *Hair* and did the nude scene in the wrong act. Charlie reads the *Times*, dislikes anchovies and wears a size 16½-35 shirt. He lives next door to the Plant Store and appeared as "The King of Discount Appliances" for Veemer Appliances in TV commercials. He left Fillmore to become an actor when he accepted the lead in a road company production of *Death of a Salesman*.

Charlie was replaced (1990-91) by Billy MacGregor (Billy Connolly), a Scottish teacher (born in Glasgow) who attended Oxford University in England. He has a second job at the Mother Hubbard Day Care Center and interweaves his life experiences with his lessons. He has a Rand McNally world map (number 429) on his classroom wall. See also *Billy*, the spinoff series.

Dr. Harold Samuels (William G. Schilling), the principal, proposed the I.H.P. to the school as a means of letting students monitor their own studies. Harold attended Canarsie High School in Brooklyn and relaxes by taking folk-dance lessons on Wednesday nights. He calls the I.H.P. class "a well-oiled machine; they know the answers to everything." Bernadette Meara (Jeanetta Arnette), the vice principal, is from North Carolina. She reads the *Post* and her saddest Christmas occurred at age seven, when she didn't get a Susie Q Easy Bake Oven.

Simone Foster (Khrystyne Haje), Darlene Merriman (Robin Givens), Maria Borges (Leslie Bega), Janice Lazarotto (Tannis Vallely), Viki Amory (Lara Piper) and Sarah Nevins (Kimberly Russell) are the main female students. Simone, sweet, shy and sensitive, is a straight A student. Her greatest gift is her romantic vision of life. Simone's specialty is English and her spare time is occupied by charity work. The fictional Robert T. Lasker is her favorite poet and, as a member of the chess club, she is called "Mister." Darlene, the child of a wealthy family, lives on Park Avenue. She is a descendant of Sally Hemmings, the black woman by whom Thomas Jefferson had children. Her specialty is speech and debate and she believes she is very attractive to men ("I represent the physical and intellectual ideals men want"). Darlene puts herself on a pedestal and is editor of the school newspaper, the *Spartan*.

Maria is dedicated to learning. If she gets anything less than an A she grounds herself ("It's the only way I can learn"). Her greatest gift is her understanding of the human condition. She left to further her singing career at the High School for the Performing Arts. Janice, gifted in all areas of study, has a photographic memory. She is a child genius and entered the I.H.P. at age ten — "She knows everything; she's spooky." Janice plays the cello (second chair) in the school orchestra and "dreams of colonizing another planet entirely out of Legos." She left to attend Harvard.

Viki is adopted and has a knack for falling in and out of love with her teachers ("It's something I can't control. It comes, poof; it goes, poof"). She is from Florida and her family is always on the move. Sarah, president of the Student Council, works after school at City General Hospital.

Dennis Clarence Blunden (Dan Schneider), Arvid Engen (Dan Frischman), Eric Mardian (Brian Robbins), Alan Packard (Tony O'Dell) and Jawaharlal Choudhury (Jory Husain) are the main male students. Dennis, the practical joker, is skilled in chemistry and physics. His second home is the principal's office (where he stares at a picture of George Washington on the wall). His locker combination is 27-14-5. He borrowed $326.92 and a John Travolta lunchbox from Darlene since the first grade. Dennis loves to eat, but not the cafeteria food (he orders from Izzy's, a fast food store). He also held a job at Casa Falafel, Mr. Moore's favorite eatery.

Arvid, a math major, has a perfect attendance record (2,252 days as of 10/2/90). He has not missed one day of school since he first started — nothing has stopped him "not subway strikes, blizzards, hurricanes or illness." He runs the school radio station (WFHS, 410 AM), plays triangle in the school orchestra and is a member of the glee club. Arvid wears a size nine shoe (usually brown) and had the nickname "Badges" (he has a 4.0 grade average and won many awards). Carl Sagan is his favorite writer and the accordion is his favorite musical instrument. He was a Boy Scout (Troop 645) and is also the lunchroom monitor. When he gets upset, he speaks to the picture of Albert Einstein he carries in his wallet.

Eric, the son of an alcoholic father, has learned the harsh realities of life at an early age. He is gifted; when he was four his father read *Treasure Island* to him; a year later, Eric read it back to his dad. When the I.H.P. challenges other schools in a competition, Eric calls the meets "Nerd Bowls."

Alan, a member of the Young Americans for Freedom, has set his goal to become president of the U.S. He is gifted in the natural sciences, and *Cattle Queen of Montana* (co-starring Ronald Reagan) is his favorite movie. Jawaharlah is gifted in the political sciences (he left the series when his family moved to California for business reasons).

I.H.P. classes are held in Room 19 and begin at 8:50 A.M. The class computers are called Fred and Wilma and the class starred in a production of *Grease*, directed by Charlie. In the final episode, graduation is held at the same time the school is to be demolished. The students chose the following colleges: Sarah Lawrence (Simone), Stanford (Darlene), Cal Tech (Arvid), MIT (Viki and Dennis) and Columbia (Sarah).

57. Head Over Heels UPN, 1997–1998

Head Over Heels is a Miami-based dating service owned by brothers Jack and Warren Baldwin (Peter Dobson, Mitchell Whitfield). As a kid Warren watched *The Dating Game* (Jim Lange, the host, was his hero) and because of that show, he went into the dating business. His dream is to become a TV game show host. Warren and Jack attended Lincoln High School. Warren is straight laced and all business; he hopes to find true love for his clients. Jack, the footloose younger brother, is a playboy and sees the agency as a means by which to meet beautiful women. Jack, an Elvis fan, has a VIP card at his favorite strip club, the Booty Bar, and has a crush on Carmen Montalvo (Eva LaRue), the agency's pretty office manager. Carmen, who likes picnics and mambo music, is studying to become a psychologist. She detests Jack's advances and longs for Warren to notice her. Valentina (Cindy Ambuehl), the receptionist, was a former stripper at the Booty Bar. Her favorite pastime is shopping at the South Beach Fashion Mall. Jack and Warren have drinks at the Banana Bar. The San Troupe Modeling Agency is next door to Head Over Heels.

58. Hearts Afire CBS, 1992–1994

Georgie Ann Lahti (Markie Post) is a liberal journalist. She wrote questions for *Jeopardy* (she created the "Potent Potables" category) and an episode of *Rhoda*. She worked for the *Chicago Tribune* then the *Chicago Post*. She left the *Post* to pen the book *My Year with Fidel* (she had an affair with Castro and thought it should be told). When that failed, she went to work as "a cultural liaison in Paris" ("I worked at Euro Disney helping people on and off the teacup ride"). She then moved to Georgetown and found a job as speechwriter for Strobe Smithers (George Gaynes), a senile, conservative senator. When John Hartman (John Ritter), Strobe's senatorial aide, learns that Georgie is broke, he offers to let her stay at his spacious home (1184 Arlington Drive). John is divorced (from Diandra, who left him for another woman) and the father of Ben and Eliot (Justin Burnette, Clark Duke). Ben and Eliot attend the Overland Elementary school. Eliot has a pet snake (Sam) and his first word as a baby was "moon." Georgie calls John "Hartman"; he calls her "Miss Lahti."

Georgie, a Pulitzer Prize nominee and winner of the Peabody Award for excellence in journalism, is trying to quit smoking but can't ("I smoke when I get upset and I get upset a lot"). "My credit line is not enough to buy a Vivien Leigh commemorative plate and I have a problem being taken seriously because of my good looks." Georgie has done outrageous things ("I ran around the Trevi Fountain in Rome in my bra and panties") and when she took the SAT test, she was singled out for writing the longest answers ever given on a multiple choice test ("I wasn't satisfied with E — none of the above"). As a kid Georgie had a snow-cone stand, won the Davy Crockett Bravery Award and wanted to wear her Halloween costume (a devil) to school every day. Georgie eats Kix breakfast cereal, plays the trumpet and, as time progressed, she and John fell in love and married. They moved to Clay County, John's hometown, to find a better family life. Here, John, Georgie and their friend, Billy Bob Davis (Billy Bob Thornton), take over the weekly newspaper, the *Courier* (located on Main Street) with John as the editor, Georgie the reporter, and Billy Bob, the society editor. Madeline Sossinger (Conchata Ferrell), a psychologist who rents space in the paper's building, writes the advice column, "Dear Madeline." John has a dog (Rugboy); 555-8663 is his phone number. In final-season episodes, the paper's name is changed to the *Daily Beacon*. At this time, Georgie gives birth to a girl (8 pounds, 10 ounces) she and John name Amelia Rose.

Strobe has been married to Mary Fran (Mary Ann Mobley) for 30 years. Strobe plays the piano and had his own band during the 1940s. Mary Fran was born in Sparta, Georgia, and took the beauty pageant route to get out of town. She won the Miss Tennessee and the Miss USA crown. Strobe met her when he was a beauty contest judge. She sang "As Time Goes By" and he could see no one but her. Mary Fran wants Strobe to retire so she can take his seat in the Senate ("It's my turn now after putting up with him for 30 years"). If Strobe doesn't quit, Mary Fran is threatening to air their dirty laundry in public. Strobe is in bed by 8:30 P.M. He and John have monthly meetings at Harry's Bar.

Dee Dee Star (Beth Broderick) is the office receptionist and carries on a secret affair with Strobe. She was born in Amarillo, Texas, and worked as a beautician at the Beauty Pit Salon. She worked previously at Foto Mat.

Dee Dee believes other women feel threatened by her good looks. To show them that she is as intelligent as she is beautiful, she began a business called "Mail Order Bikini Bra and Panties."

Mavis Davis (Wendie Jo Sperber), the office secretary, is married to Billy Bob (John's assistant). She believes Dee Dee is "the last bimbo on the hill" and left Billy Bob (when the series switched locales) to get her Masters Degree at NYU. Their daughter, Carson Lee (Doren Fein) lives with Billy Bob.

Miss Lula (Beah Richards) has cared for Georgie since she was three years old (her mother died shortly after her birth). Georgie's father, George Lahti (Edward Asner), is a disbarred attorney (he spent two years in prison and was the former president of the American Trial Lawyers Association). George took up ceramics in prison and is an excellent cook. He is staying with John and works as the housekeeper (first season episodes). To pay for her father's legal fees, Georgie wrote several romance novels: *Flamingo Summer*, *Naked Spring* and *Lust Beyond Tomorrow* (all under the pen name Dusty Silver).

59.　High Society CBS, 1995–1996

Eleanor "Ellie" Walker (Jean Smart), a New York socialite and novelist (known for her trashy love stories), lives at 511 Sutton Place in Manhattan. Ellie, whose real name is Eleanor Antoinette Worshorsky, was born in Pittsburgh. She is sassy, chases men and drinks a bit too much. In fourth and fifth grades Ellie was voted "best French kisser" and had a dog named Goochie. She frequents restaurants but doesn't like corner tables "because no one can see me." Ellie has written the following books: *Swedish Meat Boys*, *Hermephrodite*, *High Sierra Streetwalker*, *Hung Jury*, *Pool Boys Plunge*, *Stiletto Summer*, *Submissive Samurai* and *The Naked and the Deadline*.

Dorothy "Dot" Emerson (Mary McDonnell) owns Emerson Publishing, the company that produces Ellie's books. Dot's company is number one in travel and leisure books; her hairdresser is John Michael John John. Valerie "Val" Brumberg (Faith Prince) is the bland, uninteresting, non-wealthy friend. Val was hostess at Le Petit Burger (fired for arguing with the chef over the size of a burger) and was born in New Jersey.

60.　The Hogan Family NBC, 1987–1990; CBS, 1990–1991

A reworked version of *Valerie* (see entry) which begins six months after Valerie's death in an automobile accident. The Hogans — Michael (Josh Taylor) and his sons David, Mark and Willie (Jason Bateman, Jeremy Licht, Danny Ponce) — still live at 840 Crescent Drive in Oak Park, Illinois (555-

4192 is their phone number). New to the cast is Sandy Hogan (Sandy Duncan), Mike's divorced sister, who has relocated from Minneapolis to help Mike raise his sons. Sandy, David's godmother, works first as a guidance counselor, then as vice principal at the local high school (called Colfax High then Oak Park High School). She majored in psychology in college and was called "Queen of the All-Nighters" for her ability to stay awake all night and study. Sandy likes old movies, detective novels and working out with Jane Fonda's video exercise tapes. As a kid, Sandy had a dog named Sparky.

David, the eldest son, attended Colfax High then Northwestern University. He was a member of the Bulls basketball team in high school and held a job as a waiter at the Four Corners Restaurant.

Fraternal twins Mark and Willie attend Oak Park Junior High then Colfax/Oak Park High School. Mark is a member of the rock and mineral club, the chess club and recipient of the Good Citizenship Award at school. He has a lizard (Chuck), two fish (Plato and Socrates) and sees school as "another day, another A." Willie, the less studious brother, is forever in trouble and held a job (with Mark) at Bossy Burger and Hi Tops (a shoe store). When he was 14, Willie rented an X-rated video called *Bimbo Mania* starring Denise DeJour that also got Mark into trouble when Sandy caught them with it.

Lloyd Hogan (John Hillerman) appeared in final-season episodes as Sandy and Michael's father. He is rather bossy, set in his ways and came to live with the family (he previously lived in California). He has a yacht called the *Bounty*, frequents Sergio's restaurant, and can't read paperback books ("It makes the story seem so disturbing"). He calls Sandy "Princess."

"Hi-dee-ho" is the shrill greeting the Hogans receive from their neighbor, Patty Poole (Edie McClurg). Mrs. Poole (as she is called), won the 1973 Iowa casserole contest with her tuna casserole, is a member of the Bowlerina's bowling team, and is happily married to Peter (Willard Scott), whom she calls "the Mister" (he calls her "Pussycat," "Minx" and "Patty Cake"). Mrs. Poole collects snowglobes, loves square dancing and lives in a house Peter calls Poole Manor. Peter's favorite musician is Mitch Miller; Patty has a parrot (Mr. Tweeters) and a dog (Casey) who has his own room.

61. Home Free ABC, 1993

Vanessa Bailey (Diana Canova), is the divorced mother of two children (Abby and Lucas) who, at age 37, is starting law school. She lives with her brother, Matthew Bailey (Matthew Perry) and her mother Grace Bailey (Marian Mercer) at 1273 Ashbury Drive in Ocean View, California. Vanessa won "The Miss Penmanship Award of 1967" and for her sixteenth birthday, her father hired the Rolling Stones to follow her around "so I could have music wherever I go." Her favorite punishment for Abby (Anndi McAfee) and Lucas (Scott McAfee) is potato peeling. Abby practices kissing on her pillow while Lucas, afraid of the dark, sleeps with a Tinkerbell night light.

Matt is a reporter for the *Beach Cities News Advertisers*, a local newspaper. Matt tried television by becoming the weekend Lifestyle Reporter for Channel 6 News ("If It's Important to You, It's News to Us"). He quit when they would not allow him to do hard news stories (only fluffy news). Matt also writes "Chat with Matt" for his elementary school newsletter and covers stories like the new scorpion at the Insect Museum. Vanessa and Matt own a cabin in the woods, built by their father, with a moose head named Bullwinkle on the wall.

62. Home Improvement ABC, 1991–1999

Tim Taylor (Tim Allen), nicknamed "The Tool Man," is the host of *Tool Time*, a comical Detroit cable TV home improvement show. Tim is married to Jill (Patricia Richardson) and is the father of Randy, Mark and Brad (Jonathan Taylor Thomas, Taran Noah Smith, Zachery Ty Bryan). They live at 508 Glenview Road. Tim worked as a salesman for Binford Tools when owner John Binford selected him to host *Tool Time*. Tim appears to be a master of any project on TV, but is a klutz at home when it comes to fixing things. He has blown up a washing machine, five toasters and two blenders; his remedy, "it needs more power," rarely works (he has, for example, a blender than can puree a brick). Binford Tools sponsors the program, and can be reached at P.O. Box 32732, Minneapolis, Minnesota, 48252 (later P.O. Box 32733, Detroit, Michigan; or by phone at 801-555-Tool). *Tool Time* airs Saturdays on Channel 122 (also given as Channel 112); it is simulcast on Channel 88 in Spanish. The motto of Binford Tools is "If it doesn't say Binford on it, somebody else makes it." A claw hammer was the first tool manufactured by Binford.

"Blood, Sweat and Gears" is the *Tool Time* truck (a Chevy) and Bob Vila is Tim's favorite guest. A frequent guest is Pete Bilker (Mickey Rose) of the K and B Construction Company.

Tim's hobby is restoring classic cars. He spent three years building a 1933 Blue Goose Roadster hot rod (plate 2L TIME); he later worked on a 1946 Ford.

Tim won the "Car Guy of the Year Award" for his devotion to classic automobiles and wrote the book *How to Maintain Your Bench Grinder*. He takes five sugars in his coffee and trout almondine is his favorite dinner. His sacred, "no women allowed" area at home is the garage, where he maintains a workshop. When Jill gets angry at Tim, she slams the workshop door; the vibration knocks his Binford tools off their pegboard hooks. Tim can't resist the Sears catalogue home improvement sale and is the youngest person to ever join the Triple A. "Monkey Town" is his favorite video game. In the show's opening theme, Tim wears a Detroit Lions jersey.

As a teenager, Jill had a dog named Puddles, wore Tinker Bell perfume, and was called "Jilly Dilly" by her father. She was an army brat, attended Adams High School and met Tim in college (on their first date, they danced a slow dance to the song "Without You" at the Glitter Ballroom). Jill, a song expert, considers herself "The High Priestess of Pop Songs." Jill was a researcher for *Inside Detroit* magazine; when she was laid off, she went back to school to get her master's degree in psychology. Jill's maiden name is Patterson. Her kitchen rules are "the blue sponge for the sink; the green sponge for the counter." Jill later mentions she attended the Huntley School for Girls and the Hockaday School for Girls (where she played Juliet in *Romeo and Juliet*).

Al Borland (Richard Karn) assists Tim on "Tool Time." He was a Navy man and spent a year as a heavy crane operator (local 324) before co-hosting *Tool Time*. Al, constantly teased by Tim for wearing flannel shirts, invented the "Tool Time" board game and made a video called "How to Assemble Your Tool Box" (directed by Tim). Al's superior knowledge of tools and construction actually saves the show when Tim's antics foul up projects (Tim has become a regular at the hospital's emergency room). Al lives in Apartment 505 with his supposedly (never seen) overweight mother (who has a pet turtle named Scooter). He takes the correspondence course "Getting in Touch with the Square Dancer in You."

Al and Tim hang out at Harry's Hardware Store (originally called Kelly's Hardware Store; Al later owns 20 percent of the store, located at 3rd and Main in Royal Oak); their favorite eatery is Big Mike's. As a kid, Al had a business called "Little Al's Lemonade Stand" ("When it comes to lemons, I'm your main squeeze" was Al's slogan). He later attended Gilmore High School. He named his first sawhorse Lily and complains when Tim leaves the cap off the epoxy tube. Al was also the host of *Cooking with Irma*, the show that follows *Tool Time*. He plays miniature golf at Putt Putt Panorama.

"Hi-dee-ho, Neighbor" is the greeting Tim gets from his neighbor, Wilson Wilson, Jr. (Earl Hindman). Wilson lives at 510 Glenview Road and his face is never fully seen (always obstructed by something, usually the picket fence that divides their property). Wilson gives Tim advice on how to solve his problems and calls him "Good Neighbor." He has a scarecrow (Oliver) and a mynah bird (Mozart). His late wife was named Kathryn. Wilson celebrates unusual "holidays" (like the end of the Punic Wars), raises spiders, sings to his plants when he cross-pollinates them, and plays the Alpine Horn (used for herding sheep) in the Alpine Horn and Yodel Festival. Wilson has had dinner with Albert Einstein, knows world leaders and can talk brilliantly about anything. He is interested in insect mating, hangs ancient Crete bells in his backyard to attract friendly spirits, and is a trained midwife. Wilson sculpts shrines out of yak butter and his idea of a romantic dinner is haggis (sheep's liver served dumpling style). He attended the Greenville School for Boys (where he played Juliet in *Romeo and Juliet*) and wrote the column "Rock Beat" (about rocks) for the Wichita *Star*. He greets Jill with "Hi ho, neighborette." His father, a scientist, was Wilson Wilson, Sr.

Lisa (Pamela Anderson) was the first "Tool Time Girl" (announces the show, shows a bit of cleavage and leg, brings in needed props). Heidi (Debbe Dunning) replaced her when Lisa left to attend medical school (later becoming a paramedic at Detroit Hospital). Heidi opens each show with "Does everybody know what time it is?" (The audience responds with "Tool Time").

63.   Hope and Gloria NBC, 1995

Hope Davidson (Cynthia Stevenson) and Gloria Utz (Jessica Lundy) are friends who share adjoining apartments (Hope, 3-C; Gloria, 3-B) in Pittsburgh. Hope, divorced after ten years of marriage, is the producer of *The Dennis Dupree Show* (which airs on WPNN, Channel 5). Hope makes her own candles and potato chips ("you can control the salt count"); she previously worked for CNN and is a member of the Third Street Presbyterian Church. She is sweet, vulnerable and shy, and has B-positive blood.

Gloria, divorced and the mother of five-year-old Sonny (Robert Garrova) is a hair stylist at Cookie's Salon. She is brash and sassy and calls Hope "Gushy Gush" (Gloria is trying to make Hope more aggressive). Gloria's favorite cereal is Lucky Charms. Her ex-husband, Louis (Enrico Colantoni) works for Bud Greene's Carpetorium.

Dennis Dupree (Alan Thicke) is the obnoxious star of the talk show (which airs daily at 4 P.M.). Dennis has been in TV for 23 years and his mentor is Merv Griffin (who called him "The Kid"). He began his career on radio (WNYW in New York) with Regis Philbin as co-hosts of "The Morning Zoo Program." Dennis has also written a black musical called *Man and Woman* ("I may be white, but I'm black on the inside").

64.   I Married Dora ABC, 1987–1988

Peter Farrell (Daniel Hugh Kelly), an architect with the firm of Hughes, Whitney and Lennox, lives at 46 LaPaloma Drive in Los Angeles with his children Kate (Juliette Lewis) and Will (Jason Horst). When his wife leaves him, Peter hires Dora Calderon (Elizabeth Pena), a young woman from El Salvador, as his housekeeper. Several months later, when Dora's visa is about to expire, Peter marries her to keep her in the country and with his family. Their phone number is 555-3636.

As a kid, Peter's mother called him "Bunny" (because his favorite bedtime story was "The Runaway Rabbit") and his mother's homemade cookies would change him "from a pouty puppy to a happy hippo." In high school, Peter was a letterman. He was a running back for the football team and set a record for most touchdowns in one game. Peter claims he and Dora are not really married and are free agents when it comes to dating. Dora agrees that they have a marriage of convenience (although she secretly loves him) and asks simply "If our marriage is going to work you can't sneak around with other women. You have to bring them home to meet your wife and children." Dora calls Peter "Mr. Peter" and functions only as his housekeeper (had the series been renewed, the focus would have changed to Peter and Dora falling in love with each other, based on the last episode). Dora's pride and joy is her kitchen junk drawer where she stores and can find "all the stuff you don't know what to do with, but you don't want to throw away, because one day you are going to need that thing you don't know what to do with right now." Dora was a cheerleader in her high school; Peter was at Woodstock in 1969.

Kate, Peter's 13-year-old daughter, considers her best assets to be her gorgeous thick hair and her love of the Beastie Boys' music. She is a bit dense, believes going around the world "is like going from here to the mall a lot of times" and straightens her blonde hair by clamping it in a vise. She plays saxophone in her unnamed school band (but worries how her makeup looks) and plays golf with Peter at Putter World. Kate, a member of a Brownie troop as a kid, claims she possesses the three P's to be popular: "positive, pretty and perky." She hates public speaking class "because you have to give a three minute speech and I hate giving speeches. There's so many words to choose from and you actually have to know what you're talking about. Is that pressure or what?"

When Kate auditioned for the school's cheerleading team and was found to be too stiff in her movements, she was offered the opportunity to wear the team mascot costume, the Badger. She turned it down and joined the school band "because a guy would like to see a girl who plays the sax rather than a girl dressed as an animal." When Kate, who wears a perfume called Sensual, and her friends dress in short skirts and tight blouses and "feel sexy," they go to the mall "so other people can see how hot we are." Peter worries about Kate; Dora tells him "she's a 13-year-old girl. Her job is to whine and complain and be moody. If she is not making your life miserable, you're doing something wrong." It was when Peter opened Kate's bedroom closet door and saw a poster of Bon Jovi he knew "my little girl is growing up" (she previously had a poster of Strawberry Shortcake).

Other than being there when he is needed, no information is given about Will, Peter's younger and smarter child. Kate calls him a jerk "but he's a nice jerk." His only interest appears to be snooping in Kate's room when she is not home.

65. The Jackie Thomas Show ABC, 1992–1993

Jackie Thomas (Tom Arnold) is the star of *The Jackie Thomas Show*, a hit comedy series about a wacky father and his family. Jackie is conceited, demanding and obnoxious; his mere presence strikes fear in the hearts of his costars, writing staff and network executives. He was born in Ottumwa, Iowa (in Wapello County), and previously worked in a slaughterhouse (his TV character is a butcher). Jackie can't think and act at the same time. His favorite TV show and theme song is *Green Acres*. He started his own charity, Jackie Thomas Save Our Universe, and lives in a house on the beach, but nobody knows where ("And I'd like to keep it that way," he says). He enjoys owl hunting ("in Iowa, where it's legal") and becomes angry when a co-star becomes too popular, gets too much fan mail or too much air time. Jackie is hoping to win the Oscar for his show (not realizing that TV shows win the Emmy) and works to get Arnold (the pig from *Green Acres*), a star on the Hollywood Walk of Fame ("He's a pig among pigs" says Jackie).

Jerry Harper (Dennis Boutsikaris), the head writer (office 26), previously wrote for *Barney Miller, Cheers* and *Taxi*. He has a picture of his idol, Dick Van Dyke, on his desk, and when he first came to work, he was greeted by a bonfire made from the scripts of previous head writers. His ex-wife called him "Mr. Snippy" (he would always answer a question she asked with a joke).

Laura Miller (Alison LaPlaca), Jerry's assistant, says simply "Jackie is insane. I'm not talking wacky, funny insane; I'm talking clinical, dangerously insane." She longs to be a writer and is the only one "who can unjam the copy machine." Dustin Hoffman is her favorite performer; she worked for UNICEF and was the Senior Vice President of Charities and Stuff when Jackie went on a charity kick.

Nancy Mincher (Maryedith Burrell), a staff writer, previously wrote for *The Brady Bunch* and *Who's the Boss?* She was fired from *The Brady Bunch* for trying to seduce Greg. She claims, "I'm the one responsible for giving Marcia depth."

Grant Watson (Michael Boatman) and Bobby Wynn (Paul Feig) are the remaining staff writers. Bobby is Jackie's drinking buddy from Iowa. He performs standup comedy at various clubs and Jackie keeps him around as the writer's joke man. Grant wrote a screenplay called *Throwing Stones at the Moon* (about the domineering son of a troubled college professor who falls in with the wrong crowd).

Sophia Ford (Jeannetta Arnette) and Chas Walker (Breckin Meyer) are Jackie's co-stars. Sophia plays Jackie's TV wife, Helen; Chas is their teenage son, Timmy. Sophia appeared nude in *Playboy* magazine ten years ago and dreads the thought of kissing Jackie on the show (she does so only to keep her job).

Doug Talbot (Martin Mull) is the network's flunkie. He was vice president of NBC and worked there at the same time as Jerry. Doug was fired for trying to cancel *Cheers*.

66.   Jenny NBC, 1997–1998

"We were obnoxious little brats. We cut classes, broke curfew and snuck into 'R' rated movies," says Margaret "Maggie" Marino (Heather Paige Kent) about her and her best friend, Jennifer "Jenny" McMillan (Jenny McCarthy). "But now we're poised, composed and no longer kids as we start a new beginning." Maggie is referring their move from Utica, New York, to the Playpen, a mansion in the Hollywood Hills that was owned by Jenny's late father, movie star Guy Hathaway. (While filming *It Happened in Paris* in Utica, Guy met Jenny's mother. They had an affair and he left after the wrap party. A year later Jenny was born but Guy distanced himself. He never forgot Jenny and willed her his mansion.) Guy (George Hamilton) was a "big" star whose glory years were 1970–1971. He made a disco album (*Me, Myself and Guy*), an exercise tape ("Guy-Zercise") and a six-episode TV series called *The Adventures of Dickie* (about a father and his young son).

Jenny and Maggie work at Inky Pete's High Speed Copying and Offset Printing (copies are three cents each) and sell Skin So Nice skin care products on the side. In Utica, Jenny and Maggie worked at Chubby Boy Burger. They were on the girls' basketball team at Utica High (Jenny wore jersey 22; Maggie, 11) and Jenny's favorite sport is volleyball. Jenny gets the hiccups when she is nervous. She and Maggie have to control their coffee intake or they become edgy and hyper. Maggie, whose idea of culture is shopping at the mall, is afraid to watch the film *Ghost* with Jenny ("Jenny cries and it becomes a two hour weep-a-paloosa"). When Jenny plays sports she gets caught up in the competition "and becomes a monster and forgets her friends." Jenny's phone number is 555-0127 and her neighborhood is secured by the Crime Tech Prevention Patrol. Looking at guys and making up stories about who they are and what they do is a childhood game the girls still play wherever they go. "We may have our quarrels, we may go our separate ways, but we'll be there for each other. We're friends," says Maggie.

67. Jesse NBC, 1998–2000

Jesse Warner (Christina Applegate) is a young woman trying to reorganize her life following her divorce from Roy (who she caught in bed "with that chick" from the video store. "And what's worse," Jesse says, "that shank still charges me if I don't rewind"). Jesse is the mother of "Little" John (Eric Lloyd) and works as a waitress at her father's pub, Der Biergarten, in Buffalo, New York (where the waitresses wear Bavarian-style dresses).

Jesse, a Sagittarian, is always the boot when she plays Monopoly. She drinks Chock Full O' Nuts coffee and when she has a cheese sandwich, it has to be ham, cheese, ham "because if the cheese is on top it means it will touch the mustard — and two yellows can't touch." Jesse paid $300 for her orange Volkswagen (plate AQN 249) and lives at 346 McCord Avenue with her father, John Warner (George Dzundza) and brothers Darren (David DeLuise) and John Junior (John Lehr). Jesse and her brothers attended Fledgemore High School. Although she dropped out of school to get married, she has now returned to get her diploma and become a nurse (she later receives a scholarship to the Rochester Nursing School). Jesse becomes manager of the pub whenever her father leaves town or there is something unpleasant to be done.

Junior worked as a gas station attendant, then stopped talking for a time; he now washes dishes at the pub. He has a talent for holiday cheese sculptors (Santa Claus cheese for Christmas; a Mayflower ship cheese for Thanksgiving). Darren is a hopeful actor whose only credit appears to be a TV commercial as pitchman for Freddie's Electronics Store. He uses the TV remote control to switch from channel to channel to watch commercials. John Sr. is divorced from Susan (Lesley Ann Warren). Jesse is dating Diego Vasquez (Bruno Campos), her next door neighbor, a college art teacher and hopeful artist (he had his first public showing at the Bergen Gallery). Linda (Liza Snyder) and Carrie (Jennifer Milmore) are the pub's waitresses. Linda calls the uniforms "Franken Head costumes"; Carrie, who is bad at making change, sometimes lets customers make their own change.

Second-season episodes changed the premise somewhat. The bar, Jesse's brothers and father are gone (as if they never existed). Jesse, a single mother, attends nursing school and works part time at the Student Health Center. Carrie is now a keeper at the Buffalo Zoological Society;

Linda, who lives next door to Jesse in Diego's house, is a bartender (later a security officer) at the Buffalo Airport.

68.   Joe's Life ABC, 1993

Joe Gennaro (Peter Onorati) is a househusband living in Manhattan. When the Cold War ended, his job at an aircraft manufacturing plant was terminated. His wife, Sandy (Mary Page Keller), has found employment at Temp Jobs and Joe, able to work nights as a chef at Gennaro's Restaurant (owned by his brother Stan), cares for their children, Amy (Morgan Nagler), Paulie (Robert Gorman) and Scotty (Spencer Klein). Joe, a N.Y. Giants football fan, hates to shop (on his twelfth birthday, he was given ten dollars by an uncle. He went to Macy's passed up footballs, basketballs and baseballs and bought a Susie Q Easy Bake Oven). Joe and Sandy see movies at the Sunset 5 Cinema. In 1984, Joe gave Sandy a lime green vest that glowed in the dark; since then he gives Sandy money to buy her own birthday gift from him.

Amy, 14, hangs out at the Pizza Place after school. Her dream car is a white K-80 convertible. Twelve-year-old Paulie is interested in astronomy. When he was five, Amy dared him to eat the Yellow Pages. He was up to "air conditioning" when his parents walked in and stopped him. Scotty, five years old, has three plush animals: Petey (the talking dinosaur), Quacky Duck and Puff Puff.

69.   The John Larroquette Show NBC, 1993–1994

The Crossroads Bus Terminal in St. Louis, Missouri, provides the setting. John Hemingway (John Larroquette), the manager, is an alcoholic who is trying to quit "but everybody keeps offering me a drink." He has a master's degree in English lit and got the bus-terminal job because he was the only one who applied for it. He has a sign in his office that reads, "This Is a Dark Ride" (which he found in an amusement park as a kid) and frequents the Raincheck Room Bar (where he typically orders a club soda). John, who says, "I've been a drunk for 20 years," lives in Apartment 3 of a building with the number 1138 on it (when John lived in Chicago, Clancy's Bar was his hangout). When John moves into a new apartment (2B, second season), he acquires a romantic interest — Catherine Merrick (Alison LaPlaca), a nurse at the County General Emergency Room, who lives in Apartment 2C. John has an account at the National Fidelity Bank.

Mahalia Sanchez (Liz Torres) is John's assistant. Her husband ran off with a 17-year-old girl and left her to raise their four children. Carlie Watkins

(Gigi Rice) is a gorgeous prostitute who charges $300 a night. She has a pet crow (Phoenix) and gave up her profession to buy the Rainbow Room Bar. Dexter Wilson (Daryl "Chill" Mitchell) is a tough black youth who runs the food counter in the terminal.

70.   **Just Shoot Me** NBC, 1997–

Jack Gallo (George Segal) is the owner of *Blush*, a fashion magazine based in Manhattan. Jack claims *Blush* was the first magazine to encourage women to express their sexuality; to encourage them to "drop their mops and pick up a briefcase" and the first magazine to give a voice to female politicians. Most women, however, believe *Blush* treats women like trophies.

Jack began *Blush* in 1967 and runs it like his blood type — B-positive. He is married to Allie, a woman 30 years his junior, and is the father of Hannah (neither are seen). He is divorced from Eve (Jessica Walter), the mother of his daughter, Maya (Laura San Giacoma). Jack is a big kid at heart, loves electronic gadgets and has a racehorse named Tax Dodge. He has lunch at the Carnegie Deli, and Meadow After a Rainstorm is his favorite aftershave lotion.

Maya is the articles editor for *Blush* (she previously worked as a writer for Channel 8 news). She lives in Apartment 803, tutors children in her spare time, finds video games exciting and believes people see her as "a straight-laced, uptight school teacher." "But I'm not," she says, "I like to have fun." Maya was born on January 1 and as a kid was called "Crisco" by schoolmates "because I was fat in the can." She attended the Westbridge School and majored in Shakespeare in college. She appeared in 10 productions and named the family cat Othello. Earlier, when Maya had an interest in flying, she named her pet turtle Amelia Earhart (she also had a dog named Rags). Maya has B-negative blood and in the fourth grade entered a spelling bee. She spelled chipmunk as chipmonk and refused to leave the stage until the judges checked a special dictionary. It was discovered that chipmunk can be spelled with an "o."

Assisting Jack is Dennis Finch (David Spade), a schemer who sees his job as an opportunity to meet beautiful models. Dennis, born in Albany, New York, is a yuppie whose favorite song is "Time in a Bottle." Jack sees his magazine as his castle and Dennis as his gargoyle. Dennis writes the advice column "Dear Miss Pretty," collects old TV action figures (for the money he can get for them) and ceramic kittens (which he loves and saves). He previously worked as a gift wrapper at Bloomingdale's and spends his spare time "thinking of women's breasts and bottoms." He has "a gift" for hearing certain words (like "nude" and "sex") from great distances. Dennis believes he works hard, gets little pay, and is given no respect.

Nina Van Horn (Wendie Malick) is the fashion editor for *Blush*. Her real name is Claire Noodleman and she was a top model of the 1970s and '80s (her big break came when she was discovered modeling hats in Boston). She reads *Vogue* and has appeared on the covers of such magazines as *Vogue, Redbook, Blush* and *Mademoiselle*. She appeared on *Jeopardy* (celebrity week), *The Bionic Woman* (as a Fembot), *Wake Up, New York* (giving makeup advice) and *Cops* ("but you can't see me; they pushed my face in the grass"). She was the spokesperson for Noxema Skin Creme and auditioned for a TV commercial for Simple Time Stuffing (as a homemaker; she was rejected for not being motherly enough). Nina is allergic to peanut butter ("my lips swell up") and grew up on a farm where she was called "The Horse Calmer Downer" (she calmed horses during storms). Nina, voted Model of the Year in 1974, bases her entire life on her looks (which she fears losing) and believes casual wear is ruining society ("adults should wear sophisticated clothes").

Elliott DeMoreau (Enrico Colantoni) is the head photographer for *Blush*. He attended Hawthorne High School in New Jersey and was working as a street photographer when Jack hired him. He and Nina are constantly at odds and seem to have only one thing in common — an old blues singer named Cholera Joe Hopper (who had such hits as "A Pebble in My One Good Shoe," "Chin Hair Mama" and "Swollen Glands").

71. Just the Ten of Us ABC, 1988–1990

Graham Lubbock (Bill Kirchenbauer), athletic director at Saint Augustine's, a Catholic high school for boys, and his wife, Elizabeth (Deborah Harmon), a homemaker, live in Eureka, California. They have a dog (Hooter), a milk cow (Diane) and eight children: Marie (Heather Langenkamp), Wendy (Brooke Theiss), Cindy (Jamie Luner), Connie (Jo Ann Willette), Sherry (Heidi Zeigler), J.R. (Matt Shakman) and infant twins Harvey and Michelle. Their phone number is 555-3273.

Graham, a former coach at Dewey High School on Long Island (New York), also coaches the Hippos, Saint Augustine's football team. He met Elizabeth, a deeply religious Catholic, at a CYO (Catholic Youth Organization) mixer and they married in 1970. Graham, who enjoys Ho-Ho's and Ovaltine, is overweight and constantly nagged by Elizabeth to go on a diet. He held a second job as a counter boy at the Burger Barn (he used the name "Mitch" so no one would know he worked there) and the first thing he looks for in the refrigerator is a beer. Elizabeth does volunteer work at the Food Bank and as a girl wanted to become a nun, but her mother talked her out of it — "You should find a husband while you still have your looks." Her mother ruled with an iron fist and Elizabeth abandoned her dream.

Marie, the eldest at 18, feels she is one of God's chosen and wants to become a nun "because I love God and deep down I know this is the best way to serve Him." Marie is attractive, but hides her beauty behind glasses and loose-fitting clothes. She wears a size five dress, a 34C bra and held a job serving food at the Eureka Mission. Saturday is Marie's day to buy groceries and cook, and she believes people think she is a little insane because "I don't always phrase things properly."

Wendy, 17, is boy crazy and totally self-absorbed. She wears a size five dress, a 34B bra, a size 7½ shoe and the lipstick shades Midnight Passion and Dawn at His Place. Wendy enjoys shopping at the mall and has the ability to take a beautiful moment of one of her sisters "and drag it into the gutter." She doesn't understand big words (they confuse her) and says "attitude gets me men. I think I'm beautiful. I fool people, but I'm not as perfect as you think I am. I've got fat ankles" (which she calls "my shame"). Wendy also claims that girls like her are a tease: "Show a little cleavage, some thigh and maybe even a glimpse of our bikini line." While Marie would like to know "how much bikini line," she calls Wendy "wicked and evil" for saying such things.

Cindy, 16, knows she is beautiful and never doubts it, but she has no common sense and is not too bright. She wears a size eight dress and a 36C bra. Cheese is her favorite food. Cindy has a slight weight problem and is a member of the Diet Control Clinic. Her first job was receptionist at the Eureka Fitness Center (at $8 an hour) and was host of her own radio program ("What's Happening, Saint Augie's") over the school radio station, KHPO. Cindy's middle name is Anne, but for years she thought it was Diane. Cindy is as boy crazy as Wendy and doesn't realize she is a tease. She is sometimes afraid that she leads boys on until she realizes "what am I thinking, I can't lead myself." Wendy believes Cindy's body is like a flashing neon sign — "Open all night, no waiting, we deliver." Wendy and Cindy say "Hi-eee" and "By-eee" for hello and goodbye.

Connie, 15, is pretty, bright, and the most sensitive of the girls. She hopes to become a journalist and writes for her school newspaper, the *Herald-Gazette*. Connie wears a size five dress, a 34A bra and is jealous of girls with large breasts (she believes girls with big chests get all the attention; she wore falsies in one episode — and found she was right; but she felt uncomfortable and discarded them). Connie (jersey 83) loves to play basketball with her father (who is determined to beat her) and considers Marie and herself "the two Lubbock sisters who are not man crazy." She feels Marie is the one person she can talk to on boy matters. Connie's first job was to sweep animal entrails at the MacGregor Slaughterhouse at $4 an hour.

Marie, Wendy, Cindy and Connie formed the ultra-sexy singing group

The Lubbock Babes in second-season episodes (they performed regularly at Danny's Pizza Parlor). When the girls tried to make their own clothes to cut expenses, some "of the ugliest clothing" Graham had ever seen emerged. "I may not know how to sew a sweater," Cindy said, "but I sure know how to wear one."

Sherry, 11, is the most intelligent family member. She strives for excellent grades and although she should be in grammar school, she attends Saint Augie's (an exception was made to the all-male rule to allow the Lubbock girls to attend). Sherry believes Marie "is our wacko sister" and is constantly amazed by the antics of Wendy and Cindy.

J.R. (Graham Lubbock, Jr.) is a freshman at Saint Augie's. He loves horror movies, peanut butter and playing practical jokes on his sisters. J.R. is not athletic and Graham fears he will not follow in his footsteps. The series is a spinoff from *Growing Pains*.

72. Kirk WB, 1995–1997

Kirk Hartman (Kirk Cameron), a recent college graduate living in New York City, cares for his siblings, Phoebe, Corey and Russell (Taylor Fry, Will Estes, Courtland Mead), after their parents are killed in a car accident. Kirk lives in Apartment 202 and first worked as a graphic artist for Graphics, a company that paints billboards, then as a penciler for Wham Comics, and finally an executive vice president of creative affairs for Shotz Comics, a hole-in-the-wall company that produces "Barney the Badger" comic books. Kirk's idol is Stan Lee (writer-creator of Spider-Man) and has created a comic book character called "Magno Man," who has all the powers of Earth's magnetic forces. At Shotz, Kirk later draws the revised version of an old comic called *Mercury Man*.

Kirk shops at the West Village Market. He fell in love with and married Elizabeth Waters (Chelsea Noble), a nurse at St. Bernard's Hospital. She first lived across the hall from Kirk (Apartment 201) then in Apartment 4-B when she, Kirk, and the kids needed a bigger place. Schools for the kids are not named.

Seven-year-old Russell has a plush duck (Mr. Quacky); Phoebe is having a difficult time "becoming a woman"; she wore a "Hello Kitty" undershirt before getting her first bra, which an embarrassed Kirk bought for her. Corey, Kirk feels, will follow in the footsteps of his carefree friend, Eddie Verducci (Louis Vanaria), a clown at the local car wash (he later works at the Parker Health Club).

73.   A League of Their Own CBS, 1993

During World War II, candy bar king Walter Harvey (Garry Marshall), creator of the Harvey Bar, hires washed up ex-ballplayer Jimmy Dugan (Sam McMurray) to manage the Rockford Peaches, an Illinois team in the first All American Girls Professional Baseball League (AAGPBL) to save the game (and make money) when baseball's biggest stars go off to war.

Jimmy was with the 1929 Cubs and was called "The kid on the team." He had 151 RBIs and went on to a great career. In his youth Jimmy was called "The Carpenter" ("because I nailed all the girls"). He took the job because the money was good. Benny the chimp (whom Jimmy won in a poker game) is the team's mascot; when Jimmy enters the girls' locker room he says, "man on the floor."

Evelyn Gardner (Tracy Nelson), Betty Horne (Tracy Reiner), Dottie Hanson (Carey Lowell), Kit Keeler (Christine Eilse), Mae Mortibito (Wendy Makkena) and Marla Hooch (Megan Cavanaugh) are the Rockford Peaches. Evelyn, jersey 15, plays right field; she is married to Frank. Betty, the catcher, wears jersey 1. She is a widow (late husband, George) and the quiet one on the team. Betty is a former Miss Georgia and cares for the other girls when they get hurt. Dottie, jersey 8, plays first base. She is from Oregon and her husband, Bob, is in the army. Dottie is the only girl Jimmy feels he can talk to "man to man" (he considers her to be like one of the players from his old ball club). Kit, the pitcher, wears jersey 23; Mae, jersey 15, plays centerfield; and Marla, a powerful hitter, plays second base (jersey 32).

Jimmy earns $80 a week; Dottie, considered to be the best player, makes $90; Mae, $75; Marla, Kit and Betty, $45. The Suds Bucket is the local watering hole. Based on the 1992 feature film.

74.   Life ... and Stuff CBS, 1997

Ronnie (Pam Dawber) and Rick (Rick Reynolds) have been married for ten years and are the parents of Shawn (Tanner Lee Prairie) and Jerry (Brandon Allen). Ronnie is a housewife who fears Rick will leave her for a 17-year-old cheerleader; she also becomes upset if Rick looks at another woman's chest ("that means he's ignoring me"). When she's hungry, Ronnie orders out from Jackpot Chicken.

Rick met Ronnie in college and began his career in advertising in Portland, Oregon; he is now a creative director but feels his career is unfulfilled, the kids don't appreciate him and he has a troubled marriage. His only pleasure is "my 70-inch projection screen TV with wraparound sound and satellite dish." Rick's dream of married life was like the family on *Leave It to Beaver* and he wonders why his married friends with children didn't talk him out of having children. After sex with Ronnie (which Rick marks on the calendar in the kitchen) he drinks a Yoo Hoo. The kids attend the Putnam (New Jersey) Pre-School. Jerry has a teddy bear named Mr. Teddy.

Adding to Rick's misery is his brother Andy (David Bowe) who has no goals, no plans, no money and is always having fun. He lives in the driveway in an old, beat-up Winnebago he calls Casa Del Andy. He calls Ronnie "Mrs. Bro."

75. Living Dolls ABC, 1989

Trish Carlin (Michael Learned) is a former high fashion model who now runs The Carlin Modeling Agency from her home at 68th Street and Madison Avenue in Manhattan. Trish appeared on the covers of such magazines as *Vanity Fair, Harper's Bazaar, Ladies' Home Journal, Redbook* and *Vogue*, and has opened her home to four beautiful teenage girls she feels have "the look" needed to become models: Charlene "Charlie" Briscoe (Leah Remini), Emily Franklin (Halle Berry), Martha Lambert (Alison Elliott) and Caroline Weldon (Deborah Tucker).

The girls attend Lexy High School and share two rooms in Trish's home. Charlene, born in Brooklyn, is streetwise and doesn't believe she is as beautiful as people tell her she is. She appears to have a tough exterior, but is a softie on the inside. Charlie helps Trish with the cooking and takes charge of situations when Martha, Caroline or Emily get into a bind. Charlie likes to be herself ("what you see is what you get") and is rarely impressed by anything — even when she is told she is special ("a good burger is special," she says, "not me").

Martha, nicknamed "Pooch," loves the attention modeling gives her. She enjoys dressing up for any occasion and is teased by Charlie for constantly talking about her home state (Idaho). Caroline enjoys shopping at Bloomingdale's and faces a crisis each morning: "What should I wear today?" She is a C student at school and has joined the Book on Tape Club to avoid reading books. She relates aspects of life based on episodes of her favorite TV show (*Star Trek*) and believes in "Model Unity" ("we have to stick together when things get tough for one of us"). She is a bit dense and tries to be bright, but her efforts always fail (especially since she has to write notes on the palms of her hands to remember what she has to say to appear smart).

Emily, called "M" by Caroline, is the smartest one of the girls (a straight A student) and hopes to become a doctor ("being a doctor is all I dream about"). She gets very upset if she scores badly on a test and fears that if her grades slip "the closest I will ever get to being a doctor is modeling lab coats." She plays racquetball to relax and gives the girls advice they don't always understand (for example, "follow what your heart says no matter what your heart says").

Rick Carlin (David Moscow), Trish's teenage son, can't explain to his friends what it is like living with four beautiful models, but he is determined to make a profit from it (he sells model souvenirs and offers "Real Model Tours" for $1.50). Charlie calls him a "Twerp."

Although the girls strive to do their best at school, their teachers consider them "Human Hangers" ("Girls who are so pretty that they can't be smart"). The girls made a music video for rock star Nick Austin; Trish has a houseplant (Amadeus) and after exercising, Trish heads straight to the kitchen.

76.   Living Single Fox, 1993–1997

Flavor is a contemporary monthly black magazine owned by Khadjah James (Queen Latifah), a single woman living in Prospect Heights, Brooklyn, New York, with her cousin Synclaire James (Kim Coles) and friend Regine Hunter (Kim Fields). Their apartment is variously A, 1A and 3A.

Khadjah attended Howard University (where she held a job after classes in a rat costume for Chuckie Cheese). She was editor of her high school and college newspapers and calls her magazine *Flavor* "because we've got taste." The one thing you don't do is lend Khadjah money (she can't eat or sleep until she pays it back). Khadjah's competition is the tacky *Savor* magazine; *Flavor* is located above the Chemical Bank Building in Manhattan.

Snyclaire is from Missouri and works as the magazine's perky receptionist. As a kid Synclaire had a turtle (Fred) and a plush cow (Mr. Jammers); she now has a hamster named Robespierre. At Howard University, Synclaire wanted to work at Chuckie Cheese "but my head was too big for the rat head." Synclaire has a desk full of good luck troll dolls "to spread joy and happiness in the office" and uses an "emotional filing system. Things that make Khadjah happy are in front; the things that make her weary are in back; and the things that upset her are not within her reach." Before acquiring the job at Flavor, Synclaire worked as a cashier, telephone solicitor, babysitter and order taker at Turkey Burger Hut. Synclaire makes Christmas ornaments out of the plastic eggs that contain Leggs pantyhose and feels sad at the end of the day "because I have to say goodbye to the makeup that got me through the day." When she feels blue, Synclaire wears wind chime earrings.

Regine is a buyer for the Boutique. She can't bear to be without a man by her side. She dresses sexily and shows ample cleavage to attract men. She is self-centered, self-absorbed and wants kids — "These genes are too good to waste." Khadjah calls her "loud and busty" (Kim Fields' real-life breast reduction surgery was incorporated into the series, changing the Regine character somewhat. She became less obnoxious and more caring). Regine, real name Regina, is a woman on a mission to marry a man "who knows that fine wine doesn't come with a twist off cap." She believes that she is irresistible to men and that "sometimes life is not fair to me. That's why bras come in different sizes." She believes her breasts ("my double d's") got her into M.I.T. and made her homecoming queen. Regine also lives by her code, "the three c's of men" ("catch, control and conquer"). She also believes that if she is in a room and a man does not look at her "then he must be gay"; the downside: if Regine is without a man, she goes on a chocolate-eating binge.

Maxene "Max" Shaw (Erika Alexander) is a lawyer for the firm of Evans, Bell and Associates in Manhattan. She was born in Philadelphia and later became an attorney for the Public Defenders Office. She has her own apartment, but has made Khadjah's her second home.

Overton Wakefield Jones (John Henton) is the building's maintenance man. He is dating Synclaire and lives by the handyman's code "I won't rest until it's fixed." He has a dog (Sanford; named after his favorite TV show, *Sanford and Son*) and three fish (Cocoa, Maurice and Kyle). Overton, called "Obie" by Synclaire, shops at the Hardware Hacienda. Sundays are special for him and Synclaire — "It's flea market shopping day." He was born in Cleveland and has "a secret shame" (a childhood fear of clowns that has followed him into adulthood). When he gets upset, he quotes lines from the Disney film *Pinocchio*. Kyle Barker (T. C. Carson) is Obie's roommate (they share apartment C). He is a stockbroker and believes that he is irresistible to women. Kyle was in a band called Water ("the missing element in Earth, Wind and Fire") and had a love-hate relationship with Max.

77. Love and War CBS, 1992–1995

Wallis "Wally" Porter (Susan Dey) is a beautiful 35-year-old businesswoman and famous chef who owns the trendy Chez Wally Restaurant on Manhattan's 72nd Street. After five years, her marriage to Kip Zakaris (Michael Nouri), a conceited actor, breaks up. When Wally loses the restaurant in the divorce settlement, she walks out of the courtroom and wanders into the Blue Shamrock, a quaint 1940s-style bar, located between a bail bondsman and a credit dentist. After several double vodkas, Wally becomes intoxicated and buys 80 percent of the bar from owner Ike Johnson (John

Hancock) for $70,000. Ike's brother, Abe (Charlie Robinson), becomes the new bartender when Ike passes away and leaves his 20 percent share to him.

Wally lives at 1016 East 74th Street (Apartment C). She attended the Cordon Bleu School in Paris and can debone a chicken in 20 seconds. She can serve 12 dinners in 21 minutes and once received a letter from Julia Child saying that her *coq au vin* was the best she ever tasted. Wally, born in Connecticut, is an Episcopalian and was named the most promising chef in New York City. She has a hard time serving lobster ("I name them and get attached to them"). When Wally needed to find herself, she left suddenly for Paris and gave Abe ownership of the bar. Abe hired Dana Palladino (Annie Potts), a former chef at the Le Petite Bateau who was fired for standing up for her rights (she was passed over for an executive position by a man). She is the daughter of a famous artist (Dante), worked as a chef for Mick Jagger during his Steel Wheels Tour, and spent a year on the Alaska Pipeline just to learn how to cook salmon. She was raised in Europe and at age ten had her own table at Harry's Bar in Paris. She now lives in a loft in Manhattan with the name "Schaefer Sewing Machine Company" on it. Her cat is named James and she uses Morton brand salt in her salt shakers. Dana's favorite movie is *Casablanca*.

Wally first met Kip in an off–Broadway production of *Westside Story* (he was Jet number 2). Kip also appeared in *The Front Page* (off–Broadway); the deranged typesetter on an episode of *Lou Grant*; Ozzie the Terrorist in the TV movie *Victory at Entebbe*; a vampire in the film *Vampire from Hell*; the insane crossing guard in an episode of *Sweating Bullets*; the star of a pilot called *Turf and Surf* (about a meat inspector who drives a Ferrari); Stone, the bartender on *The Bold and the Beautiful*; Mr. York, the psychopathic math teacher on *Jake and the Fatman*; the voice of the liquid that corrodes the Enterprise on *Star Trek: The Next Generation* and Lt. Gil Lombardi on *The New Kojak*. When Kip appeared in *Richard III*, the newspapers called him "a nightmare in tights."

Jack Stein (Jay Thomas), Mary Margaret "Meg" Tynan (Suzie Plakson) and Ray Litvak (Joel Murray) are the bar regulars. Jack, 42, writes the opinion column, "The Stein Way" for the New York *Register*. He was born in Brooklyn and as a kid attended Camp Olympus; in college he was a member of the Sigma Chi Fraternity. He loves jazz music, lives in Apartment 4C and has named the dust ball under his bed Milt. Jack won the Algonquin Award for his story on illiteracy and frequents Maurice's House of Steaks and Waffles. For a charity event, he and columnist Jimmy Breslin ran naked across the Brooklyn Bridge. He dated Wally and the first movie they saw together was *Betty and Helen* at the Clairmont Theater. He buys his shoes at Sears and uses Old Spice cologne.

Meg is a sportswriter for the *Register*. She attended Our Lady of Grace elementary school, Our Lady of Hope High School, and New York University. She is brash and tends to poke her nose into other people's business. Ray works as a "sanitation engineer" (garbageman) for the New York City Department of Sanitation. He calls the bar's lone pinball machine "Line Drive" and lives in an apartment on Staten Island with items he found in the city dump.

Nadine Berkus (Joanna Gleason) is the Shamrock's waitress. She lives in Westchester, drives a minivan with the license plate SUPER MOM and is afraid to be sexy (the most outrageous thing she ever did was to wear an off-the-shoulder sweater when she took her car to Jiffy Lube). Her kids are in college and her husband, Charles, is in prison for insider trading.

In the original unaired pilot, *Love Is Hell*, Jay Thomas played columnist Jack Simon and Joel Murray was Joe, the garbageman.

78.   **Mad About You** NBC, 1992–1999

Paul and Jamie Buchman (Paul Reiser, Helen Hunt) are marrieds who live at 142 West 81st Street (Apartment 11D) in New York City. Paul, born in Manhattan (4/19) attended the N.Y.U. Film School and now owns his own documentary company, Buchman Films. He later works for the Explorer Channel. Paul was influenced by the first movie he saw as a child, *Attack of the 50-Foot-Woman*. *A Day in the Life of a Button* was the first film he made and he also directed the "classic" film, *Hooter Vacation*. Paul has a dog (Murray) and *Spy Lady* was his favorite TV show as a kid.

Jamie is 30 years old and works as the regional vice president of the Ferrah-Ganz Public Relations Firm on Madison Avenue. When she is laid off, she first works as a press agent for the mayor of New York. She later starts the Buchman and Devanow PR Firm with her friend Fran Devanow (Leila Kenzle). Fran is married to Mark (Richard Kind), a doctor at Lennox Hill Hospital.

Jamie was born in New Haven, Connecticut, and attended Yale University. Her middle name is Eunice and Stemple is her maiden name. Her father calls her "Peanut" and she likes to be liked by other people; she gets upset if people don't like her and goes out of her way to impress them so they will like her (in high school, Jamie was known as "the Stemple sister who showed a boy her boobs to be liked"). As a teenager, Jamie was a counselor at Camp Winnewog and her image appears in the comic book, *Mega Void*, as the evil Queen Talin. In 1997, Jamie gave birth to a girl she and Paul name Mabel. Paul and Jamie's favorite eatery is Riff's and they rent movies from the Village Video store.

79.   Maggie Winters CBS, 1998–1999

Margaret "Maggie" Elaine Winters (Faith Ford) is the assistant to the women's apparel buyer at Hendley's, a department store in the town of Shelbyville. Maggie, who has a college degree in design, has recently returned to her home town after leaving her husband (for cheating on her). She and her employer, store manager Rachel Tomlinson (Clea Lewis) frequent Sonny's, the local bar-diner. Rachel and Maggie grew up together and attended the same schools (Shelbyville Elementary; Hull High). Rachel feels she is not as pretty as Maggie and was jealous of her "because you got breasts before me." She delights in getting even with Maggie by becoming boss of "the small town girl who moved away and came crawling back." At Hull High Maggie was known as "Maggie the Lion-Heart" (she would use her "mom voice" to call the school so supposedly sick kids could cut class). As a three year old, Maggie would embarrass her mother by stripping when company arrived.

80.   Major Dad CBS, 1989–1993

John D. "Mac" MacGillis (Gerald McRaney) is a major with the U.S. Marines. He is married to Polly (Shanna Reed), a widow with three daughters, Elizabeth, Robin and Casey Cooper (Marisa Ryan, Nicole Dubuc, Chelsea Herford). The girls carry their father's last name until the episode of 5/13/91 when John adopts them (and their last name changes to MacGillis).

John, a history major at Vanderbilt College, joined the Marines in 1967 (another episode mentions 1969). He did his basic training on Parris Island and served three tours of duty as a corporal in Vietnam. He was born in Snake River, Mississippi, where his parents owned a farm on Decatur Road. His grandfather taught him how to whittle at age 11 and when he was 7 years old, he stole a Zorro watch that cost $7.95 from Peavey's Five and Dime. John was first stationed at Camp Hollister in Oceanside, California (he was assigned to building 52419; his favorite eatery was Zaff's Hamburgers); a year later, he and the family move to Farlough, Virginia, when John is transferred to Camp Hollister (which Polly calls "a military hellhole"). They now live on the base (house 485) and John becomes "a staff weenie" (staff secretary to the general).

Polly worked originally as a reporter for the Oceanside *Chronicle*; at Camp Hollister, she is managing editor of their camp newspaper, the *Bulldog*. She also writes "the Suggestion Box" column and is editor of the "At Ease" section of the paper. Polly is a Democrat and a member of the Officers' Wives Club (where once a year she becomes a Marine for a Day for Jane Wayne Day). In her youth, Polly worked for the radical magazine, *What's*

Left; her late husband was named Sandy. Polly and John met on September 11th; they married on October 11th and honeymooned in Hawaii. Each month on the eleventh, John gives Polly flowers.

Elizabeth attended Keefer High School (Oceanside) then the Hollister Base High School. Purple is her favorite color; R.E.M. her favorite group. Her little toes are double jointed. When she looks through the family photo album, she worries how her hair looked at the time. Robin, the middle child, attends the Martin Elementary School (Oceanside, where she is a member of the Condors basketball team), then the Hollister Base School (where she is on the girls' softball team, the Hollister Hornets). She is a tomboy, loves sports, and enjoys drinking Minute Maid orange juice and Welch's grape juice. Casey, the youngest, attended the same schools as Robin. She has two dolls (Henrietta and Ruby), a teddy bear (Mr. Smithers) and a plush toy (Whoobie). Casey played "the only squash with a solo" in the school's Harvest play and she likes Ocean Spray cranberry juice.

Lemon is the name of the family's pet bird; 638 574 is the station wagon's license plate at Oceanside, and 2RW 308, their car license plate in Virginia. Their phone number is 555-6703 and the Major (as the girls call him) objects to three things connected to life with four females: a bedroom with pink walls; a Strawberry Shortcake shower curtain; and hair clogging the sink drains. The girls found a rare Rock Island turtle they named Claudette.

General Marcus Craig (John Cypher) commands Camp Hollister. He is a graduate of Cornell University and is married to the never-seen Mimsey. When he gets upset, he goes to the firing range to shoot off several hundred rounds. Alva Lou Bricker (Beverly Archer), nicknamed "Gunny," is Craig's chief administrative assistant. She calls Casey "Little Cooper," has a dog named Elmo, and has instituted a daily snack pastry schedule: bran muffins (Monday), jelly donuts (Tuesday), bear claws (Wednesday), bagels (Thursday), assorted cookies (Friday).

81. Malcolm and Eddie UPN, 1996–2000

Malcolm McGee (Malcolm-Jamal Warner) and Eddie Sherman (Eddie Griffin) are friends who live in Kansas City, Missouri. Malcolm, a radio disc jockey at oldies station KZKC (1581 AM) and Eddie, a tow truck driver, share an apartment over their favorite hangout, Kelly's Pub. Malcolm later purchases the pub and renames it Malcolm McGee's Sports Bar; and Eddie begins his own business, Eddie's Tow and Repair with his one faithful truck, Bronkula. A year later Malcolm and Eddie pool their resources and turn the bar into a jazz club called the Fifty/Fifty Club (located at the corner of 4th and Main). With his first profits from the club, Eddie purchased a race horse named Ya Damn Skippy (Malcolm invested his portion). Malcolm's competition is McGinley's Bar. Eddie, middle name Otis, had a squeaky plush rabbit as a kid named Mr. Buttons. He coaches a kid basketball team called the Little Dribblers.

Malcolm and Eddie have a "psycho chef" (Simone), as Eddie calls her, who is in therapy and talks to vegetables. Nicolette (Karen Malina White), the club's waitress, has a cat named Pokey. She feels chilly at 80 degrees, takes computer classes and uses milk in her bath water "to make my skin baby bottom soft." Nicolette calls Malcolm "Little Bo Cheap" and, at age 30, "has been 24 for the last five years." She has her own unique personality and is hard to live with ("I've been through 12 roommates in two years. Maybe it's me?")

82. Malibu, Ca. Syn., 1998–

Peter Collins (Ed Blatchford) is a divorced restaurant owner who lives at 11721 Malibu Road in Malibu, California. When his ex-wife, Michelle (Carol Houston), takes a job in Peru, his teenage sons Scott and Jason (Trevor Merszei, Jason Hayes) come to live with him and work as waiters at the Lighthouse, the seafood restaurant owned by Peter. Jennifer Stadler (Wendi Kenya), Samantha Chapman (Gina Marie May), Murray Updike (Brandon Brooks) and Tracee Banks (Priscilla Lee Taylor) are Jason and Scott's friends. Scott and Jason attended J.F.K. High School in New York. Scott practiced kissing on a pillow he called "Patty Pillow" and is now training for the Olympic Swim Team. Jason, a hopeful musician (and singer), wears a Spice Girls watch.

Jennifer, nicknamed "Stads," is a lifeguard, a female arm wrestling champion and once sold 500 boxes of girl scout cookies in one day. Samantha, a car nut, knows more about engines than most mechanics, and volunteers her services for charity. Samantha left the series (second season) "to attend college in the east." She was replaced by Lisa (Marquita Terry), a pre-med student at UCLA who works as a waitress at the Lighthouse. She and Tracee share an apartment Tracee calls "Casa de Fun Fun."

Murray runs the Surf Shack, the beach eatery, for its owner (Peter). Murray is a "surfer dude" and owns a pet electric eel (Sheila). The Silver Surfer is his favorite comic book hero. He hosted an advice radio program called "The Dude of Love" on station KPOV and joined Scott and Jason in a clothing business venture called Murray Wear (selling plastic see-through coats with painted designs; the paint ran when it rained).

Tracee is a gorgeous, busty blonde who believes she is "the most beautiful girl in Malibu and California and the whole U.S. of A. except for alien chicks who may appear on *Star Trek*." She loves to hang out at the beach and wants to be an actress. She did a guest shot on *Baywatch*, hosted a pilot called *Blind Date* and starred in a TV commercial as the Dancing Dorito Chip ("I was the only chip who got dipped in the salsa"). In second-season episodes, Tracee acquires the role of Dr. Sheila Lowenstein, a brain surgeon, on the TV series *Malibu Hospital*. Her favorite color is pink and she says, "I may be an airhead, but I'm one hot babe." If her acting career fails, Tracee claims she will "fall back on the doctor thing — marry one, not be one." Tracee holds the title "Miss Shock Absorber '98," wears a size six shoe and as a kid had a dog named Bo Bo.

Peter's biggest seller is Seinfeld Stew and his idea of dressing up is to wear a clean Hawaiian shirt. His favorite critter in the restaurant's aquarium is Goldie, a gray fish he won and named after Goldie Hawn (who was hosting a charity concession and failed to guess his weight). In the 1970s, Peter was a member of the band, the Disco Dudes.

83.   Married People ABC, 1990–1991

The brownstone at 862 Central Park North (at 73rd Street) in Manhattan is owned by Nick and Olivia Williams (Ray Aranha, Barbara Montgomery), a couple married 32 years who live in Apartment 1. Olivia is a homemaker; Nick owns Nick's Fruits and Vegetables and hangs out at Morry's Pool Hall (where he is called "Nick the Stick"). His delivery truck license plate reads 586 M066.

Elizabeth and Russell Meyers (Bess Armstrong, Jay Thomas) occupy Apartment 2. Elizabeth is "36 but looks 32" and is a lawyer with the Wall Street firm of Michaelson, Michaelson and Meyers. She "lived on coffee and cheese doodles" while attending Yale University and did her internship for a judge who called her "Toots." Russell, a freelance writer, has penned articles for *TV Guide* and *The New Yorker* and writes a monthly column for *Manhattan Life* magazine called "The Worst of New York" (for example, the worst restaurants, the worst landlords). He attended the Columbia School of Journalism, hates to be called "Russie" and "is 37 but looks 42." The couple's phone number is 555-8274 and in the episode of 11/14/90, Elizabeth gave birth to a boy (8 pounds, 5 ounces) she and Russell named Max. Elizabeth shops for groceries at the 85th Street Market and for baby items at Bob's World of Babies.

Cindy and Allen Campbell (Megan Gallivan, Chris Young), an 18-year-old couple from Mineral Wells, Indiana, rent Apartment 3 (they moved to New York so Allen could attend Columbia University). Cindy, a cheerleader in high school, aspires to become a dancer. She works as a waitress at the

East Side Diner and acquired professional dancing jobs with the Exotic Port-hole Dancers and as a Girl Number 2 in the Broadway play *The Phantom of the Opera* (at the Majestic Theater). Cindy had a cat (Simone) and is famous for her "Sticky Treats" (a gooey Rice Krispies and marshmallow snack); her favorite meal to cook is three bean salad and a marshmallow casserole. Allen was allergic to walnuts in Indiana; in New York he has a bad reaction to hazelnuts.

84.   Married ... with Children Fox, 1987–1997

Al Bundy (Ed O'Neill) is married to the former Peggy Wanker (Katey Sagal) and is the father of Kelly (Christina Applegate) and Bud (David Faustino). Al believes that the day he said "I do" was the start of his down-fall. In high school Al was on top of the world. He was a football hero (scored four touchdowns in one game), was voted the Most Valuable Player of 1966 and was offered a college scholarship. He turned it down to marry Peggy, a fellow James K. Polk High student he met at Johnny B. Goods, a hamburger joint. He acquired a job as a shoe salesman at Garry's Shoes and Accessories for the Beautiful Woman in the New Market Mall and set up housekeeping at 9674 (also seen as 9764) Jeopardy Lane in Chicago. Twenty years later he has two kids, is still married "to my red-haired plague" and still selling shoes for $12,000 a year.

Al's pride and joy is his collection of *Playboy* magazines. He loves to watch *Psycho-Dad* and *Tube Top Wrestling* and such "hooter classics" as *Planet of the D Cups* and *Breast Monsters from Venus*. After *Psycho Dad* was canceled for being too violent, Al's favorite TV show became *Friends* ("because if you mute the sound and watch through binoculars, you can see that Jennifer Aniston [Rachel] isn't wearing a bra"). Al's favorite read-ing matter is the girlie magazine *Big'uns*; the male Bundy credo is "hoot-ers, hooters, yum, yum, yum. Hooters, hooters on a girl who's dumb" and his favorite drink is Girlie Girl Beer. Al made a TV commercial for Zeus Athletic Shoes and lost $50,000 on a TV telephone call-in service called "Dr. Shoe" (555-SHOE). He also formed MA'AM (The National Organi-zation of Men Against Amazonian Masterhood) and a baseball team called Chicago Cleavage (Al's jersey: 38DD). Al frequents the Jiggly Room of the Nudie Bar and held a temporary job as a security guard at Polk High. Al drives (when he's not pushing it) a 1974 Dodge (license plate F3B 359; later, 61CS2) and has to have cheesecake baked by Hans from Chuck's Cheese Bowl. The shoe store is sometimes seen as Garry's Shoes and Acces-sories for Today's Woman. When Al found a stockroom full of shoes from the 1970s, he set up a section called Al Bundy's House of Sole. In an attempt to get his name in the shoe industry newsletter (*Shoe News*), Al and Kelly made a movie called *Sheos* (Kelly misspelled shoes). The National Endowment for the Arts gave Al a $10,000 grant and he produced *A Day in the Life of a Shoe Salesman*— a disaster that got him in *Shoe News* with the headline "Big Idiot Makes Movie."

Al has nightmares about feet and was a judge in "the Ugly Feet Contest of 1990." The greatest moment of Al's life occurred on 11/26/95 when the Kyoto National Bank named him the greatest football player ever at Polk High. The scoreboard was dedicated to him and the field renamed the Al Bundy Field.

Peggy was born in Wanker County, Wisconsin (also mentioned as being in Milwaukee), a community that was founded by her ancestors. Peggy knows that a divorce will make Al happy but she won't give it to him. She never shops for food, cooks or cleans and spends her days on the sofa watching TV and eating bon bons. Finding food has become the family's number one priority. Al's favorite food is turkey (but he never gets it) and he has resorted to begging for leftovers at the local pizza parlor and making Tang sandwiches. On those rare occasions when Al has food to take to work, he carries a Charlie's Angels lunchbox. Because of the lack of plates in the house, Al has to share the dog's (Buck) bowl — both their names are on it. Although Peggy hates to work ("That's why I got married"), she took a job at Muldin's Department Store to buy a VCR. She also took interior decorating classes at the Cook County School of Design and ruined Al's one place of refuge — the bathroom he built for himself in the garage (she turned it into a "frilly pink nightmare." Al considered his "cold, white and soothing restroom" his "oasis from pantyhose and women").

Peggy, a 36C, wears the Perfect Figure Model 327 bra. She has a stuffed parrot (Winky) and gives Al a tie on their anniversary (he gives her shoes). While Al's favorite sport is bowling, Peggy holds the record at Jim's Bowlarama for a perfect 300 game. When Al thought he could make money with Peggy and Kelly as singers, he called them "Juggs — A New Mother and Daughter Duo." Peggy drew a cartoon strip about Al for *Modern Gal* magazine called "Mr. Empty Pockets." Just as the strip was becoming popular, Peggy "killed" Al off when a falling meteor shaped like a woman's shoe, fell on him. Peggy and Al's checks read "Mrs. Peggy Bundy and the Nameless Shoe Salesman." When Kelly and Bud were young, they thought Al was the dim-witted handyman. To make up for this, Peggy instituted "Make Believe Daddy Day" on Friday afternoons (she used a sock puppet to represent Al). Peggy's overly romantic advances frighten Al the most.

Sixth-season episodes saw Peggy becoming pregnant (Al considered her a "Pregasaurus" and called her "Pregzilla"). In October of 1991, actress Katey

Sagal, who was seven months' pregnant, had a miscarriage. The pregnancy storyline was dropped and explained as Al's dream.

Kelly, typically dressed in tight jeans, or tight miniskirt and low-cut blouse, is, as Peggy calls her "a hussy. She became a hussy when she learned to cut her diapers on the side." When Kelly was five, Peggy had her earning money by selling kisses. Kelly, who attends Polk High, first mentions she was born in February ("I'm an aquarium") then on November 27th. She is not too bright (she writes her name on her palm so she can look at it to remember who she is) and held a number of jobs. She started as the Weather Bunny Girl on Channel 8's *Action News* program. What began as an intern project for school became a $1,000 a week job when Kelly's stunning good looks boosted ratings. Despite the fact that she did not know where "East" Dakota was, she was given a raise to $250,000 a year. She lost the job when she could not read the teleprompter. She was next a roller skating waitress at Bill's Hilltop Drive-In; then Miss Weenie Tots, a model who represented Weenie Tots (hot dogs wrapped in bread and fried in lard) at supermarkets. After graduating from Polk, Kelly enrolled in modeling school. Although she got tension headaches from smiling, she was a natural leg crosser ("I can do it at will"). Her first job was the Allanti Girl (the Allanti is a foreign car; she got the job by jiggling her breasts in what she calls "the Bundy Bounce"). She next hosted *Vital Social Issues and Stuff with Kelly*, a cable access show on Channel 99. With topics like "Slut of the Week," "Bad Perms" and "Hunks," it was picked up by the fictional NBS network, but canceled when the vital issues became milk and books. When the modeling school closed, Kelly became the exit gate hostess at Chicago's TV World Theme Park. This led to a job as the Verminator Girl (representing an environmentally safe insect killer for a company called the Pest Boys) in the park's Verminator TV Commercial exhibit (Bud played King Roach). When Kelly refuses to wear a skimpy "Verminator Girl" bikini, she is fired. She finds work as a waitress but loses the job when the health department closes the unnamed restaurant. Attired in a bikini, Kelly becomes the window display for the Kyoto Bank (she holds a sign that reads "Check Out Our Assets"). After becoming bored with the bank job she became the spokesgirl for Ice Hole Beer ("The Microbrewed Beer") then returned to modeling school (The Larry Storch School of Modeling) and did a commercial for Easy Off Jeans. Kelly appeared as the Rock Slut in a Gutter Cats music video and made a series of TV commercials for Romantic Roast Instant Coffee, Waist-Away Diet Drink and Hungry Puppy Dog Food (dressed as a sexy dog).

Kelly attends the Northside Aerobics Studio, dresses with the window shades up each morning and has a lucky see-through blouse that she can never seem to find ("It's see-through," she explains). Veal is Kelly's favorite meal and Al calls her "Pumpkin" (Al can recall doing only two things for Kelly: carrying her home from the hospital — although he left her on the car roof; and buying her ice cream when she was 10 years old).

Bud, real name Budrick, first attended Polk High then Trumaine College (where he is a member of the Gamma Gamma Sigma Pi Fraternity). He worked as Kelly's agent and as an instructor with the Department of Motor Vehicles. When he was fired for being a go-getter (trying to help people), he became an apprentice chimney sweeper. To earn extra credit for a course, Bud did community service work as a volunteer for the Virgin Hotline (1-800-Zipp Up). Kelly calls Bud "Rat Boy" and "Toad Boy" and claims he watches *Star Trek* reruns "to get a glimpse of Klingon cleavage." Bud uses Open Sesame aftershave lotion and watches *Dateless Dude Late Night Theater* when he can't get a date. Bud was a member of the Polk High soccer team, the Reepers (jersey 5), and pretended to be the street rapper Grand Master B to impress girls. In the opening theme Bud is seen reading the girlie magazine *Boudoir* and calls his cowboy pajamas, his love clothes. Bud (jersey 00), Kelly (jersey 10), Peggy (jersey 11) and Al (jersey 14) were members of the New Market Mallers softball team.

Marcy (Amanda Bearse), the Bundy's neighbor, is a loan officer at the Kyoto National Bank. She was first married to Steve Rhoades (David Garrison), a loan officer at the Leading Bank of Chicago. They are vegetarians and were married on Valentine's Day. When Steve lost his job for loaning Al the money for "Dr. Shoe," he became a cage cleaner at Slither's Pet Emporium, then a ranger at Yosemite National Park (at which time he left Marcy and the series). In the episode of 1/6/91, we learn that Marcy was a party animal at a banking seminar and woke up in bed with Jefferson D'Arcy (Ted McGinley), a man she married at Clyde's No Blood Test Needed Chapel. Jefferson is a con artist and out on parole (arrested for stealing money from investors). He calls Marcy "Bon Bon Bottom" (she calls him "Cinnamon Buns"; Steve, a member of his high school band, the Tuxedos, called Marcy "Angel Cups"; she called him "Sugar Tush." Al calls Marcy as he sees her — "Chicken Legs"). Steve and Marcy had a yearly tradition: "On the first sunny day in May, we go to the beach and shake hands with Mr. Sunshine." Steve returned (2/16/92) to reclaim Marcy; she rejected him, still a forest ranger, for Jefferson. As a kid Marcy had an invisible friend (Jennifer), a dog (Winkems), a cat (Gringo) and a cuckoo clock (Petey).

Marcy is afraid to speak in public due to a childhood trauma: she was in school giving a speech when a roach started climbing up her leg. She screamed, ran around the room, took her dress off "and revealed my 'Hey, Hey, We're the Monkees' panties." She was teased for the rest of the term. To battle Al on MA'AM, Marcy formed FANG (Feminists Against Nean-

derthal Guys). In an attempt to avoid paying taxes, Jefferson and Al organized "the Church of No MA'AM" (it failed when Marcy exposed Reverend
Al as a fraud).

The Bundy family pet is Buck the dog (replaced later by Lucky). Their
house mortgage is held by Eviction Trust and the Bundy philosophy is "if
you're gonna lose, lose big." The Bundy legacy states that "what a Bundy
doesn't finish in 30 seconds they will never finish." On Thanksgiving Day
they have the "Bundy turkey" (a pizza) and on Labor Day, the Bundy barbecue and Bundy burgers (last year's grease and ashes for this year's burgers).

85. Maybe This Time ABC, 1995–1996

The Coffee Dog Cafe is a small Pennsylvania eatery owned by Shirley
Sullivan (Betty White). Julia Wallace (Marie Osmond), her recently divorced
daughter, has returned home to run the diner and raise her 12-year-old daughter, Gracie (Ashley Johnson). Julia, 35, is a paragon of beauty and virtue. Her
honesty often gets her into trouble and she believes men are incapable of having an independent thought. The first spontaneous thing Julia did since the
divorce was to buy a faucet for the cafe that she saw in a hardware store window. Julia loved to skate as a kid and believes her cheating ex-husband (Frank)
will never find a girl "as good as I am." She is delighted when Frank dates
"bubble heads" but saddened when he finds a "brainy babe."

Shirley has run the cafe for over 30 years ("Fresh and Friendly from Six
till Six" is the ad the cafe runs on the obit page of the newspaper). She has
been married five times and worked as a hula dancer at the Royal Hawaiian
Village (in Cleveland) to put Julia through school. Shirley worries that Julia
keeps herself busy with work and has no social life. She has set her goal to
see that Julia finds someone.

Gracie attends P.S. 117 grammar school and receives an allowance of $5
a week. She reads *Sassy* and *Tiger Beat* magazines and finds her mother's
advice — "You're a good girl and you should always do what your conscience
tells you" — sometimes difficult to follow. Gracie loves to rollerblade and has
not yet developed an interest in boys.

86. Mr. Belvedere ABC, 1985–1990

George Owens (Bob Uecker), sports anchor of WBN-TV, Channel 8's
"Metro News," his wife, Marsha (Ilene Graff), and their children, Heather
(Tracy Wells), Kevin (Rob Stone) and Wesley (Brice Beckham), reside at
200 Spring Valley Road in Beaver Falls, Pittsburgh. They are cared for by

Lynn Aloysius Belvedere (Christopher Hewett), a British butler who has written a book on his experiences with them called *An American Journal: The Suburban Years.*

Lynn, born in England, lived on Higby Road and attended the Pennington School. He worked for English nobility (valet to Winston Churchill, housekeeper to Queen Elizabeth) and possesses medals for climbing Mount Everest and winning the Pillsbury Bake-off. He appeared on the cover of *World Focus* magazine ("Housekeeper of the Year"), possesses a $750,000 Faberge Egg (a present from a sheik for saving his life), and served as a housekeeper to Gandhi. Lynn's weakness is junk food (especially Scooter Pies and Ding Dongs) and his favorite eatery is Donut World.

As a kid George would play pinball at the arcade on First Avenue, stay out till midnight, then sneak into his room. He attended Cleveland High School and originally hosted "Sports Page" (later "Sports Rap"), a radio program on WBK-AM (555-2222). He also wrote the "Sports Beat" column for the Pittsburgh *Bulletin.* George calls Lynn "Big Guy"; shopping at Lumberama is his favorite activity; meatloaf, potato logs and creamed corn is his favorite dinner, and pork rinds and spam dip are his favorite snacks. He and Lynn are members of the Happy Guys, the neighborhood crime watch.

Marsha, a law student (at the University of Pittsburgh), passed the bar exam in July of 1987 and joined the firm of Dawson, Metcalf and Bach. The following year she became an attorney for the Legal Hut. When she could not achieve her dream of helping the underdog, she quit and became "Babs," a waitress at the Beaver Falls Diner. Lobster Thermidor is her favorite dinner and she has a never-seen Porsche she calls Wolfgang. Marsha spent $30,000 on law school and ranked 76 out of 278 students. Her maiden name was given as both Cameron and McClellan.

Kevin, born in 1967, was an Eagle Scout and attends Van Buren High School. George and Marsha contemplated calling him either Moon Shadow (if a girl) or Moondoggie (if a boy) but when he was born he looked more like a Kevin. He is allergic to raisins and was the drummer for a band called the Young Savages. Kevin worked at Mr. Cluck's Fried Chicken and for Phil's Friendly Motors (as a used car salesman). He later attends the University of Pittsburgh and has his own apartment (5) in a building next to a sewage treatment plant.

Heather, called "Kitten" by George, attends Van Buren High School. Kellogg's Corn Flakes is her favorite breakfast cereal and she has her hair done at Snyder's Beauty Salon. She worked after school at Traeger's Record Store and when she gets depressed over losing a boyfriend, she eats rocky road ice cream. When she felt she needed a more sophisticated name, Heather called herself Bianca.

Angela (Michele Matheson), Heather's best friend, is a pretty but kooky blonde who treasures her hanger collection. She and Heather were cheerleaders (for the Beavers football team at school) and members of the Iron Maidens, a group that reads to the elderly. Angela calls Lynn everything but Mr. Belvedere (for example, Mr. Beer Belly, Mr. Bell Bottom, Mr. Beaver Dam) and had three last names: Shostakovich, Gilbert and Jostakovich.

The mischievous Wesley attends Conklin Elementary School, Allegheny Junior High and Beaver Falls Junior High. He has a dog (Spot), a snake (Captain Nemo) and a hamster (Inky). He is a member of the Colts Little League team (coached by George), the Junior Pioneers (Group 12) and the school football team (jersey 31). He attended Camp Chippewa and his favorite sandwiches are tuna fish and marshmallow spread, and bologna and marshmallow spread on raisin bread. Wesley, called "Wessman" by George, made a home movie about Lynn called "The Housekeeper from Hell."

In the final episode, Lynn marries Louise Gilbert (Rosemary Forsyth), an animal behaviorist he met at a laundromat. He leaves the Owens to join Louise in Africa when she is asked to take a gorilla census. In the final moments of the show, Lynn remarks that he left his journals (the diaries that he is seen writing at the end of each episode) at the Owens home and hopes to one day return for them.

87. Moesha UPN, 1996–

Moesha Denise Mitchell (Brandy Norwood), called "Mo" for short, lives at 6653 West Post Road in Los Angeles with her father, Frank (William Allen Young), stepmother Deidre "Dee" (Sheryl Lee Ralph) and brother Miles (Marcus T. Paulick). Moesha, 15, attends Crenshaw High School, hangs out with her friends at the Den, and works after school as a salesgirl at Class Act, a clothing store. She is a straight A student, helps people she believes are in trouble (always making situations worse) and has a knack for defying parental authority and getting into trouble. Moesha attempted a business venture called Unforgettable Vitamins (to help people remember), watched *Spunky's World* as a kid, and hates to hear the words "Moesha, we have to talk," from Dee. In the 1999 season finale (5/25), Moesha graduated from Crenshaw and took a job as a receptionist at *Vibe* magazine (hoping for a break in a career to become a writer). She had planned to attend Northwestern University in Chicago and major in journalism (she was also accepted to USC, Harvard, Duke and Spellman). When the series returned for a new season (8/30/99), Moesha is fired from *Vibe* (for interviewing Maya Angelou without permission) and enrolls in college.

Frank, a widower, married Dee three months before the series began.

He owns a car dealership, calls Moesha "Pumpkin" and hates for Moesha to wear midriff blouses (he has a "heart attack" when Moesha shows cleavage). He believes "the gray hairs, headaches and wrinkles" he has are "a part of raising a beautiful teenage daughter." Dee, the vice principal at Crenshaw, shops at the Swap Meet (for Frank's clothes). She is desperately trying to win Moesha's love but finding it difficult because Moesha feels no woman can replace her real mother.

Miles has a Chicago Bulls poster on his bedroom door and a sign that reads "Caution: No Trespassing." He is a talented dancer and often hears "go to your room" for all the trouble he gets into. His most defiant act was smoking weed at home in his room.

88. Molloy Fox, 1990

Molloy Martin (Mayim Bialik) is a pretty 13-year-old girl who attends Beverly Hills Junior High School and works professionally as an actress on the KQET-TV children's show *Wonderland*. She lives at 6113 Fullerton Drive with her father, Paul (Kevin Scannell), stepmother, Lynn (Pamela Brull), half sister Courtney (Jennifer Aniston) and half brother Jason (Luke Edwards).

Molloy has recently moved to Beverly Hills following the death of her mother and is having a difficult time adjusting to her new family, especially Courtney, "a crybaby who puts up a fuss when she gets blamed for something or doesn't get her way." Courtney, 16, attends the Beverly Hills Private School and is called by students (including girls), "the most beautiful girl" at the school. Molloy says, "Courtney is deserving of the title, but beneath all that beauty she is just an airhead." Courtney is totally devoted to herself and looking gorgeous is her number one priority. She is easily distracted from whatever she is doing and gets upset by the simplest things (for example, a strand of hair out of place; a chip in her fingernail polish).

For one so young, Molloy is quite knowledgeable and has impressive answers for anything asked of her. "I major in stuff," says Molloy. Despite Courtney's childish behavior, Molloy desperately wants to look like her "and become a woman, but without the dullard interior." However, we hear "I'm being such a girl. I hate that" when Molloy tries to look like Courtney and wear fancy clothes and jewelry that makes noise when she walks.

Paul, the program director of radio station KNAP, calls Molloy "Mo." Unlike Molloy, who questions everything and tries to understand what is going on, Paul seems to accept everything that happens and considers it all just a part of life.

Lynn, born in Nashville, is a Republican (Paul is a Democrat), and runs a business called Martin Interior Decorating. She is a carefree individual and has a lighthearted approach to life. When Lynn dresses to impress and someone says "You look great," she responds with "Yes, I know." She has to eat when she gets depressed and each year when Lynn is nominated for the Golden Foyer Award by the Beverly Hills Decorators Association, she rehearses her prepared speech over and over again (driving the family crazy), wears her "lucky lingerie" (which she keeps in a special box) and always loses.

Jason attends an unnamed grammar school and has a pet turtle (Lance) and a mentioned but unseen dog named Sparky. Simon Lansbury (I. M. Hobson) is the host of *Wonderland*. He plays Joey the Squirrel and feels he is worthy of better roles. He is also distressed by the fact that the kid stars get all the attention and fan mail and what fan mail he receives seems to come from "old biddies" who want him to come "and share their trees."

89.   The Mommies NBC, 1993–1995

Caryl Kellogg (Caryl Kristensen) lives at 13 Oak Way. Her best friend, Marilyn Larson (Marilyn Kentz), lives next door at 15 Oak Way. Caryl is married to Paul (Robin Thomas) and is the mother of Blake (Sam Gifaldi) and Danny (Ryan Merriman). Marilyn is married to Jack (David Dukes); Casey (Ashley Peldon) and Adam (Shiloh Strong) are her children. The families also share a pet dog named Cosmo.

Jack is an accountant; Paul a computer trouble shooter. Marilyn works from her home as a real estate agent; Caryl, a homemaker, previously worked as a travel agent (she and Marilyn attended Montgomery High School, class of '66).

Adam, 15, attends Valley High School; Blake, Casey and Danny are enrolled in Valley Elementary School. Casey is on the girls' soccer team (jersey 3); Blake plays flute in the school band and has a frog named Spot. Adam, "not stupid, just highly unmotivated," works at Jolly Meals (a fast food restaurant). Also working there is Tiffany (Jennifer Blanc), Adam's girlfriend, the assistant manager. She is a year older than Adam and a year behind him at Valley High. Being pretty is about the only asset Tiffany has ("people say I'm an airhead"). Marilyn calls her "the Giggler" (for her habit of giggling at everything).

Tom Booker (Jere Burns) is "Mr. Mommy." He is learning the ropes of motherhood when he loses his defense plant job and his wife, Christine (Joanna Kerns), goes to work. Beth (Courtney Peldon) and Jason (Justin Berfield) are his kids. Barbara "Babs" Valentine (Julia Duffy) is a spokeswoman for Kitchen Comfort Products. She is the mother of an infant

(Zachary) and "has the ability to fold a fitted sheet." She is overly organized and never lies ("I even put my correct weight on my driver's license").

90.   Movie Stars WB, 1999–2000

Reese Hardin (Harry Hamlin), "America's Leading Action Star," and Jacey Wyiatt (Jennifer Grant), "America's Favorite Leading Lady," are married. They live in Malibu, California, and are the parents of Apache (Zack Hopkins) and Moonglow (Rachel David). Also living with them is Lori Hardin (Marnette Patterson), Reese's daughter from a previous marriage.

Reese has his own Kimbo Toys action figure (Reese Hardin — Navy Seal), his picture on a cereal box (Flutie Flakes — although he snacks on Honey Heroes cereal) and has been voted "the World's Sexiest Man" by *Appeal Weekly* magazine. He is known as "Reese Hardin, Action Star," and has made such films as *Clash of the Titans* (actually starring Harry Hamlin), *Lethal Impact* and *Sudden Vengeance*. It was on the film *Cyber Death 2000* that Reese first met Jacey (she played "the annoying mime who got vaporized"). He is represented by the CAA Agency (Jacey by the William Morris Agency).

Jacey is a three-time Oscar nominee; Reese is a People's Choice Award winner. Jacey "gets the movies that receive praise" while Reese "makes those with the word 'lethal' in the title and gross three billion dollars." Jacey has made such films as *Joan of Arc* and *A Perfect Fool* and is sometimes called "the biggest chick star around." Jacey was raised in Bakersfield by her mother Audrey (Loni Anderson), a stripper (at the Extreme Turbulence Room) who posed nude for *Playboy's* "Moms of the Stars" pictorial. Jacey's most embarrassing moment occurred during a live interview with Barbara Walters. She had an allergic reaction to Barbara's perfume and swelled up. The situation was dubbed "The Blow Fish Incident" by the tabloids.

Lori came to live with her father "when things got too tense in Ohio. You burn down one Dairy Queen and they never forget." Lori first attended Buchanan Preschool ("Geek Prep" as she called it), then the "cool" Crosswinds High School. She is 17, gorgeous, and has a love-hate relationship with Jacey (she also borrows much of Jacey's wardrobe — which "looks great on Jacey, but fabulous on me").

Apache and Moonglow attend Buchanan Prep. Apache hates his name and Reese explains "that I was into the American Indian movement and my spiritual guide said for me to name you after a famous Indian." Moonglow seems content with her name. Apache walks celebrities' dogs to earn extra money. Moonglow has a pet hamster (Popeye) and when Reese takes her to the set, Jacey warns him not to let her ride the camera crane (she has motion sickness).

Todd Hardin (Mark Benninghofen) is Reese's brother, an actor who gets the least desirable roles. He has been in *Titanic* (frozen corpse number 3), *Babe, Pig in the City* (voice of Nick the Ferret), *Starship Troopers* ("the guy who gets crushed by the giant roach"), *Deep Impact* (asteroid victim 702) and *Fargo* (the leg sticking out of the wood chipper). He played Santa Claus at the Northridge Mall and is proud of his starring role in a Mentos commercial. While Reese has a house that overlooks the Pacific Ocean, Todd lives in an apartment that overlooks a homeless guy with a sock puppet called Eddie. Todd attended Juilliard and the Actors Studio, and went to Hollywood with great expectations for a role in *The Sting II*. Reese tagged along "to race motorcycles and chase chicks." Reese got into an altercation with a producer, punched his lights out and got the jobs. Todd frequents the Juice Bar and plays poker with his friends "Stallone, Swayze and Travolta"—Frank Stallone, Don Swayze and Joey Travolta—the brothers of famous stars who feel as Todd does (that their brothers have taken all the glory). Todd, Frank, Don and Joey pooled their resources and opened their own juice bar, "L.A.'s Hottest Spot," Squeeze This.

91. **Murphy Brown** CBS, 1988–1997

Murphy Brown (Candice Bergen) is a hard-hitting investigative reporter for *F.Y.I.* ("For Your Information"), a CBS-TV, Washington, D.C.-based news magazine series. Murphy was born in May of 1948 and as a kid was called "Stinky." She had a dog (Butterscotch) and her eleventh grade journalism professor, Ken Hamilton, was her inspiration for becoming a journalist. She majored in journalism at Penn State and TV newsman Howard K. Smith was her hero. She made an audition tape, had a friend submit it to Smith and was told, "You stink, but you've got a nice tush." She found work as a foreign correspondent and auditioned for *F.Y.I.* on 8/16/77. She beat newswoman Linda Ellerbee for the role. Since then Murphy has won the Robert F. Kennedy Journalism Award, an Emmy and eight Humboldt News Awards. Murphy has appeared on the covers of *Time*, *TV Guide*, *Newsweek*, *Esquire* and *Harper's Bazaar*; but also was lampooned in the daily comics as "Mouthy Brown" and in the *National Enquirer* with the headline "Murphy Brown Having Big Foot's Baby." Murphy's father calls her "Susie Q."

Murphy lives on Cambridge Place and her white Porsche license plate reads 189 347 (later MURPHY). She was offered a role in the film *Deadline* but was fired from the project for rewriting the script. She has a reputation for getting even with anyone who crosses her, is easily exasperated and yells a lot. Sterling Roses are her favorite flower and Aretha Franklin her favorite singer ("Respect" is her favorite song). Murphy is banned from the White House (she ran over President Bush with her bicycle; now every time Bush hears Murphy's name he screams and runs for his life). Murphy had a five-day marriage to Jake Lowenstein (Robin Thomas), whom she demonstrated with at the 1968 Democratic National Convention. When he reentered her life in 1990, they had an affair and Murphy became pregnant. On 5/18/92 at 5:32 A.M., Murphy gave birth to a nine pound seven ounce boy she first called "Baby Brown" (she was in labor for 39 hours). Prior to naming the baby Avery (after her late mother) Murphy called him Jacques Cousteau Brown, Adlai Stevenson Brown, Winston Churchill Brown and Woodward and Bernstein Brown. Avery's favorite singer is Barry Manilow.

Corky Lynn Sherwood (Faith Ford) is an *F.Y.I.* news team reporter who can recite all the books of the Bible by heart. She was born on a farm in Louisiana and represented her state in the Junior Miss Pageant. This led to her winning the Miss America Pageant at age 19. She also modeled ("The Check Girl" for the First Bank of New Orleans) and won the 1989 Humboldt Award for her story "A Woman's Touch at West Point." She attended Eastern Louisiana University, appeared on *Circus of the Stars* (did a trapeze act with Robert Urich) and is a cheerleader for the Bulletins, the *F.Y.I.* football team.

Corky has a First Lady doll collection, a pet cat (Mr. Puffy) and lives in Apartment 304. She wears a size 34B bra and did a special called *Corky's Place* (interviewing celebrities). Her phone number is 555-7261 and she married Will Forrest (Scott Bryce), a struggling writer who penned the book *The Little Dutch Boy*. Their marriage broke up three years later due to their incompatibility (he wanted her to quit her job and devote all her time to him).

Frank Fontana (Joe Regalbuto), a reporter for the *New York Times*, joined *F.Y.I.* in 1977. He was babied as a child, had a dog named Cocoa and attended the Bishop Fallon High School for Boys. *The Maltese Falcon* is his favorite movie and he is afraid to sleep with his closet door open as result of watching the film *Poltergeist*. In 1991 Frank won the Humboldt Award for his story, "A Death in Dade County." He wrote a 4¼-hour play called *Life Changed* and mentioned that he has been in therapy "for 13 or 14 years." *TV Guide* tends to list Frank as "Fred Fontana" and he and Murphy hosted the premiere of the CBS early morning newscast, *Overnight News*.

Jim Dial (Charles Kimbrough) is "America's Most Trusted Newsman." He is the senior anchor and has been with CBS news for 25 years. In 1956, he was the only correspondent to interview John F. Kennedy when he lost the presidential nomination. A later episode claims Jim was a struggling news reporter for Channel 9 in Chicago who doubled as the host of *Poop Deck*

Pete and Cartoons Ahoy. Jim wears expensive Italian suits, has a pink and blue fish-shaped coffee mug and before each broadcast, he orders fried rice from Wo Pong's and taps his knee three times for good luck. Jim, a Presbyterian, lives at 3134 South Bedford Drive with his wife Doris (Janet Carroll). His favorite dinner is lamb chops, mashed potatoes and mint jelly and he and Murphy are members of the Dunfriars, a club for distinguished news people. He first mentions his dog as being named Victor; later it's Trixie and Trixter. Jim calls Murphy "Slugger" and he is part owner of a gay bar called The Anchorman. On 2/19/96, CBS, fearing a lawsuit, refused to air Jim's story on the cigarette industry. Jim walked off the set and found a job with the ICN Network in New York. On 5/20/96, CBS ran Jim's story and he returned to *F.Y.I.* To relax, Jim tackles the *New York Times* crossword puzzle.

Miles Silverberg (Grant Shaud), the executive producer of *F.Y.I.*, gets "the good donuts" for the staff at Marino's Bakery. He attended the Little Bo Peep Preschool and had a hamster named Whitey. In Harvard (class of '84) he was known as Miles Silverbrain. Murphy's antics have driven him to the point of hysteria and he is a good candidate for ulcers and heart attacks ("I'm 27 years old and living on Mylanta"). Miles hears Murphy's voice in his sleep and says "they should pipe it into cornfields to scare the crows away." He has a car (license plate 400 928; later 452 689J) and was executive producer of *The New Wave,* a CBS news show. On 9/18/95 he and Corky announced they are married ("a spur of the moment thing"). On 5/20/96 Miles quits *F.Y.I.* to become the head of news operations for CBS in New York. He is replaced as F.Y.I.'s executive producer by Kay Carter-Shepley (Lily Tomlin) (she previously hosted the game show *Celebrity Face-Off 2000* and has a dog named Sparky).

Elden Stanislaus Bernecky (Robert Pastroelli) is Murphy's housepainter, who has a difficult time matching paint to Murphy's moods. He paints murals, uses Murphy's good pantyhose to strain paint and buys his supplies at Ed's Paints. He has an Apostles wristwatch (each of the 12 are represented by an hour) and hangs out at the House Painter's Bar. He painted a mural of the Iran-Contra Hearings on Murphy's bathroom ceiling and works also as Avery's nanny. On 11/21/94, Elden leaves Murphy to pursue a dream — art study in Spain with Diego Garcia, a famous muralist.

Phil (Pat Corley) owns the local watering hole, Phil's Bar and Grill (established in 1919). The bar is located at 1195 15 Street (although 406 is seen on the front door). Murphy's favorite meal is Phil Burgers and Fries.

F.Y.I. premiered on 9/21/77 and has been honored by the Museum of Broadcast Arts for 15 years of excellence in journalism. The program first aired live at 10 P.M. (later 9 P.M.) and on 2/13/95 moved to Studio 6A (a window set they called "The Window on America"). On 2/18/91, the network was purchased by American Industrial, a company that manufactures appliances. The network tried an *F.Y.I. for Kids* with Mayim Bialik as a mini Murphy named Natalie Moore; actress Julia St. Martin (Morgan Fairchild) starred in a comical pilot version of *F.Y.I.* called *Kelly Greene*. The show's gimmick is to exasperate Murphy even more than she already is by assigning her a different (and rather strange) secretary in virtually every episode.

92.   My Two Dads NBC, 1987–1990

Nicole Bradford (Staci Keanan) is a pretty 12-year-old girl who lives in Apartment B at 627 North Brewster Street in Manhattan with her fathers, Joey Harris (Greg Evigan) and Michael Taylor (Paul Reiser). Joey and Michael, Nicole's co-guardians (she calls them "My Two Dads") are friends who dated Nicole's mother, Marcie Bardford (Emma Samms in a flashback). When Marcie passed away and the actual biological father could not be determined, Joey and Michael were both given the responsibility of caring for her by Judge Margaret Wilbur (Florence Stanley); Margaret owns the building and resides in Apartment 3B.

Joey is initially an artist (1987-88), then art director for *Financial Update* magazine (1988), artist again (1989) and finally a teacher at New York University (1990). He also wrote the children's book, *Mr. Biggles* (about a leprechaun).

Michael is initially a financial advisor for the Taft-Kelcher Agency (1987-89) then marketing manager for *Financial Update* magazine. He considers his job as a father is to focus on Nicole's needs and wants; Joey's job, he feels, is to help him decide how she is to be punished when she does something wrong. Joey is much more liberal in his parenting and considers Michael a Ward Cleaver (the father on *Leave It to Beaver*) and too strict in raising Nicole.

First-season episodes find Nicole attending an unnamed grammar school. She has a teddy bear (Mr. Beebles) and is a typical kid — she likes boys, but is not eager to date; she is experimenting with makeup; and through no fault of her own is growing up and saddening Michael — "She's my little girl. I never want to see her grow up."

But grow up she does. She is soon a teenager attending Kennedy Junior High School, and a worry to both her dads as the series focus changed to depict Nicole's growth into young adulthood — and to boys and dating. Nicole felt she was smart and pretty, but became jealous of girls with larger breasts. She padded her bra, wore tight blouses and spent $29.95 on the "Bust-o-Matic" breast developer to discover that being fake was not her (it was also the toughest talk the fathers had to face in dealing with Nicole's oncoming womanhood).

Michael and Joey hang out at Klawicki's, a diner located on the ground floor of their building. The diner is owned by Ed Klawicki (Dick Butkus), a former football player. In final-season episodes, Judge Wilbur takes over the diner and renames it the Judge's Court Café.

93.   The Naked Truth ABC, 1995–1996; NBC, 1996–1997

Nora Wilde (Tea Leoni) is a photographer for *The Comet*, a trashy tabloid that loves celebrity dirt. Nora, 27, is divorced and previously worked for *The Washington Post*. At Sarah Lawrence, where she was editor of the school newspaper, Nora created a sensation by writing about campus lesbians; later she learned her roommate, Janice, was a lesbian. Nora was a Pulitzer Prize nominee and divorced her husband (Leland) for her own freedom. She sponsors a South American child named Manuel ("I bought him from Sally Struthers") and can't lie to her father without laughing. Her first assignment for *The Comet* was to photograph Anna Nicole Smith (and find out if she is pregnant); her most embarrassing assignment: posing as a stripper for an expose on big-breasted girls. All went well until she stuffed her bra with M&M's ("the plain ones"), bent over and the candies spilled out.

Nora longs to get back into the mainstream and cover traditional news for a prestigious paper, but her ex-husband's revenge (and extreme wealth) closes those doors for her. Nora later becomes an advice columnist for *The Comet*. When Camilla Dane (Holland Taylor), the paper's editor, decides to begin her own publication (*The Inquisitor*), Nora joins her as a reporter (at which point the series ended).

Also working for *The Comet* is Nicky Columbus (Jonathan Penner), a fellow photographer who once got 15 stitches after being thrown out of Penny Marshall's birthday party. He was a child star (at age 10) and had a TV series called *Otterboy* (about an orphan who was raised by a family of otters; his companion, Nick Nick, was a kid "who grew up to become Sharon Stone"). The *Naked Truth* was originally called *Wilde Again*.

94.   The Nanny CBS, 1993–1999

The fashionable 19-room dwelling on New York's Park Avenue is home to Maxwell Sheffield (Charles Saughnessy), a widow with three children (Maggie, Gracie, Bryton), a butler, Niles (Daniel Davis) and a live-in nanny, Fran Fine (Fran Drescher).

Maxwell, a successful Broadway producer, has been listed by *Esquire* magazine as one of the most eligible widowers (his late wife was named Sarah). He was born in England, attended the Eton School (where he was captain of the water polo team). His sister, Jocelyn (Twiggy Lawson) called him "Puddle Duck" (he called her "Mopsey"). Max, responsible for such Broadway plays as *Annie 2*, *Moby*, *Regardless* and *Loves Me Not*, won three Tony Awards but considers Maggie, Gracie and Bryton his three greatest productions. As a kid, Max had his own strict nanny, Clara Mueller (Cloris Leachman), and at age 17 produced his first play, *The Sound of Music*. He is a partner with C. C. Babcock in Sheffield-Babcock Productions (originally Maxwell Sheffield Productions). Before moving to California to produce a TV series (final episode), Max produced one last play — *Yetta's Letters* (based on the love letters of Fran's grandmother). Ann Guilbert, who plays the somewhat senile Yetta Rosenberg, believes Max and Fran are Rob and Laura Petrie from *The Dick Van Dyke Show*. (Ann played neighbor Millie Halper on that show.)

Francine, nicknamed Fran, is 29 years old and believes some women think she is a stripper or a hooker "by the clothes I wear." After losing her job at the Bridal Shoppe in Flushing, Queens, she began selling Shades of the Orient Cosmetics door to door. At the Sheffield home she was mistaken for an agency nanny, impressed Max's kids and was hired as their nanny. Fran had a goldfish (Goldie), attended P.S. 19 grammar school (later called P.S. 165), then Flushing High School (later called Hillcrest High). Her Sweet 16 party was held at Benny's Clam Bar (in the Half Shell Room) and she is a graduate of the Ultissima Beauty Institute. She later attended the Barbizon School of Modeling and was a foot model for two years. Fran, who wears a size two miniskirt and has her hair done at the Chatterbox Salon, is an expert on 1960s TV shows. She appeared on *Jeopardy* and won $200; the only other member of her family to appear on a game show was her cousin Ira — when he became "Queen for a Day." As a teenager, Fran's favorite TV soap opera was the fictional *Edge of Life*; she now watches *The Young and the Restless*. Fran starred in her third-grade production of *Fiddler on the Roof* and in high school played the Reverend Mother in *The Sound of Music*. Fran's favorite performer is Barbra Streisand (she believes *Yentl* is the best movie ever made), and she paid $200 for a framed wad of bubble gum that came from the bottom of one of Barbra's shoes. Fran is a member of Shopper's Anonymous (when she gets depressed she shops) and played Juliet in an off–Broadway retelling of *Romeo and Juliet*. Final-season episodes found Fran marrying Maxwell and giving birth to twins they name James Samuel and Eve Kathryn.

Margaret (Nicholle Tom), nicknamed Maggie, is 14 years old and very pretty but feels she is "a worthless, pathetic, unlovable nothing." Maggie also believes she has no personality. Her first date was with a boy named Eddie at the movies with a "Noochshel" (a chaperone named Fran). Fran, who cured Maggie of her misheld beliefs, feels more like her girlfriend than her nanny. Maggie plays the piano and loves three bean salad. Beige is her favorite color. She attended the Holy Cross Grammar School, then the Lexington Academy. At age 15 Maggie received a chance to become a model when the Chloe Simpson Agency tested her potential for a series on gorgeous teenagers. Her dreams were shattered when her test shots revealed her to be "vacant and lifeless." Maggie's first job was a volunteer candy striper at Bellmont Hospital.

Gracie (Madeline Zima), the middle child (called "Angel" by Fran), is "a complicated girl" with multiple personalities. She is six years old when the series begins and is in therapy sessions to treat her introversion and insecurities. Gracie has an imaginary friend (Imogene), a teddy bear (Mr. Fuzzy) and two hamsters (Miss Fine and Mr. Sheffield). Gracie attends the Holy Cross School (later Lexington Academy) and played the Itsy Bitsy Spider in the school's play, *Mother Goose on Broadway* (directed by Fran). Gracie, a member of the Red Robbins Scouts (Fran is their troop mother), can't have fun at school because she worries about the polar ice caps melting. She believes the showgirls that audition for her father are "giant Barbie dolls." Gracie sometimes fears to sleep alone and snuggles up in bed with Fran.

Bryton (Benjamin Salisbury) is ten years old and mischievous. He attends the Lexington Academy and overindulges on junk food. He and Fran watch *Gilligan's Island* marathons to hear the title theme change from "and the rest" to "the Professor and Mary Ann." Bryton is interested in sports "if I can own the team" and was a member of the Flushing Queens, a canasta team with Fran, her mother and grandmother. Bryton, a Mets baseball fan, had his first kiss with Fran's cousin Tiffany (Jaclyn John), a miniature version of Fran.

By 1999, Niles has been in service to Maxwell for 25 years. He is a member of the Professional Butler's Association and says about his name "It's Niles, just Niles, like Cher." His favorite part of the job is watching gorgeous showgirls audition at the house. He has written a play he hopes Maxwell will produce called *Love, Valet, Compassion*. In his all-boys high school, Niles played the Baroness in a production of *The Sound of Music*. His favorite food is Belgian waffles (which Fran calls Eggos).

Chastity Claire "C.C." Babcock (Lauren Lane) is Maxwell's business partner and calls herself C.C. (her mother is B.B.; her sister, D.D.). She is constantly trying to impress Maxwell (in hopes of marrying him) and calls Fran "Nanny Fine." She has a dog (given to her by Maxwell) named Chester, and calls the kids "Macy, Bob and Nancy." C.C. believes people think she is "a self-centered, cold-hearted witch." She and Niles are constantly at odds, but fell in love and later married. C.C. tries to be nice and sensitive "but my nasty attitude can't make it happen."

95. Ned and Stacey Fox, 1995–1996

Ned Dorsey (Thomas Hayden Church) is an executive at the Spencer Haywood Advertising Agency on Madison Avenue (he considers himself an Advertising Industry Professional). Stacey Colbert (Debra Messing) is a newspaper columnist (for *The Village Voice*) and later a freelance writer. Ned lives in a two-bedroom Manhattan apartment (27F; later 17D) and has a boss who believes in married executives — no marriage, no promotion. Stacey works in Manhattan but lives on Long Island. She would like to live closer to work but can't afford an apartment. Ned and Stacey meet by chance at a bar and become friends although they are not fully compatible — she's politically right wing and "he's no wings at all." They find they each have something the other wants. Stacey agrees to pose as Ned's wife; Ned agrees to let Stacey live in his second bedroom.

Although Ned is "married," he hits on other women — and Stacey would like to know who he is dating — "I'm your wife, I have the right to know." Ned, 35, is neat, loves to cook, and enjoys growing vegetables and flowers on his balcony. He drives a cranberry colored 1967 Cadillac, folds clothes to classical music and maneuvers and manipulates his way through life. "I exploit people, that's what I do."

Stacey, born in Trenton, New Jersey, attended Brandice College. As a kid she was gawky, wore braces and was a head taller than the other girls. Her father called her "Cookie" and each year, as a tradition, Stacey gives her father slippers for his birthday (and each year he says, "What, slippers again?"). When Stacey had a problem, she and her father would talk things over at Hogan's Diner. For Stacey, a good day can only happen "if I have a great hair day." When Ned takes Stacey out for a meal, they dine at Dugan's Cafe; they enjoy snacks at Amanda's-A-Muffins, a coffee shop owned by Stacey's sister, Amanda Moyer (Nadia Dajani). Commercials for the ad agency are filmed at Astoria Studios in Queens. The program is a reworking of the 1966 series *Occasional Wife*.

96. One World NBC, 1998–

Karen and Dave Blake (Elizabeth Morehead, Michael Toland) are a childless couple who adopt the worst kids they can find in hopes of straightening them out. They live in Florida (house number 834) and the kids are Jane (Arroyn Lloyd), Ben (Bryan Kirkwood), Marcie (Alisa Reyes), Sue (Michelle Krusiec), Neil (Harvey Silver), and Cray (Brandon Baker).

Jane is the wild one. She has been abandoned, abused and ignored and feels she is everybody's problem (and always in trouble). She dates guys who know how to use a phone — "but it's usually one call and it's to their lawyer." Jane, who believes she is living with "the Brady Bunch," is pushy, rude "and worst of all," says Marcie, "she doesn't like to shop." Jane likes auto racing ("but only when they crash"), gets mad if she can't make an obscene gesture to somebody every week, and has done punishment for past "crimes" (like scraping up road kill in 98-degree weather).

When the kids can't agree on what to watch on TV, Ben takes the remote control and the first channel he switches to is the one they will watch. Ben plays the guitar, wrote a song about Jane ("Hurricane Jane"), and hogs the bathroom, obsessing over his hair.

Marcie, the assistant manager of the Warehouse, "the hippest under-21 club in town," loves to shop and can get anything for half price. Chunky Monkey is her favorite flavor of ice cream and as a kid she went through an *I Dream of Jeannie* phase. She dressed in a harem outfit and Karen carries a picture of Marcie in that costume in her wallet (Marcie shudders when Karen shows it to people).

Sue, 16, is a Libra and plays midfield on the girls' soccer team at South Beach High School (where Dave is athletic coach). She wears jersey 8 and is a hopeful for the Olympic Soccer Team. Sue bowls at the Miami Orange Bowl Lanes, canary yellow is her favorite color and she has a recurring dream about replacing Vanna White on *Wheel of Fortune*. She watches *Titanic* over and over, "hoping this time the boat won't hit the iceberg."

"If we don't have each other, we don't have anything" says Neil, the brainy one of the kids, who feels their constant squabbling may break up the only family he has ever known. He reads *Economic Weekly* and hopes to become a stockbroker. "When it comes to sandwiches, Neil doesn't eat crust." He and Dave are partners on the Hurricanes Bowling Team.

Cray, 12, the youngest, plays the harp in the school orchestra and is a member of the Skateboard Club. He has a pet fish (Bevis) and he enjoys sitting on the front porch waiting for hurricanes (he chains himself to the porch chair so it won't get blown away).

97. The Parent'Hood WB, 1997–1999

The Manhattan brownstone at 721 West 72nd Street in New York City is home to Robert Peterson (Robert Townsend), his wife, Geri (Suzzanne

Douglas) and their children, Zaria (Reagan Gomez-Preston), Nicholas (Curtis Williams) and Ce Ce (Ashli Amari Adams).

Robert and Geri met in high school, were married at City Hall (at the same time they were renewing their drivers' licenses) and first lived at 103rd and Amsterdam Avenue. Robert is a professor at New York University. His first job as a kid was at Elmo's Pet Shop. Geri is a lawyer and says "the closest I've ever been to a trial was watching *Matlock* (she sits behind a desk under a stack of papers). She does volunteer work for the Women's Legal Society. In some episodes she appears to be a law student while in others she has her own practice (Geri Peterson — Attorney-at-Law). When they have free time, Robert and Geri enjoy playing Scrabble.

Zaria, the eldest child, attends Hudson High School (as did her parents). She is a cheerleader and hosts the advice show, "Keep It Real" on the school radio station (WHBD). She won the Meritorious Student of the Year Award in her senior year (1999) and a college scholarship. Robert calls her "Zee." Peach cobbler is her favorite dessert and she eats Captain Crunch cereal for breakfast.

Nicholas, who envisions himself as a great magician (Nicholas the Great), attends the William Sherman Grammar School. Ce Ce, the youngest, has a plush bear named Mr. Fuzzy. Their favorite dinner is hamburgers and French fries and when they watch a movie they have "pizza, popcorn and pork rinds."

Also living with the Petersons is T. K. Anderson (Tyrone Dorzell Burton), a troubled street teen Geri took under her wing. T.K., a D student, attends Hudson High, is on the school basketball team (the Hippos) and works at Pookie's Pizza Galaxy. Zaria is number one in her senior class (and valedictorian); T.K. is dead last at 432.

98. Parker Lewis Can't Lose Fox, 1990–1991

Parker Lloyd Lewis (Corin Nemec), Michael Patrick "Mikey" Randall (William Jayne) and Gerald "Jerry" Steiner (Troy Slaten) are "best buds" who attend Santo Domingo High School in California.

Parker is an enterprising student who always comes out on top no matter what happens to him. He resists authority, lives by his own rules, and has an ingenious plan for every situation. Mikey, a Molly Ringwald fan, loves to play the guitar (especially in his parents' bathtub — "great echo effects"). He worked as a counter boy at Dog on a Stick and wrote his first song, a love sonnet, to a girl named Mary Lou. Jerry, a freshman, calls Parker and Mikey (who are sophomores) "sirs" and Mr. Lewis and Mr. Randall. He collects *Star Trek* figurines, carries a Big Bird thermos to school, and has his coat Scotch-guarded twice a month. Jerry has a pet ant (Sparky) and became very depressed when *Jetsons* chewable vitamins were discontinued. In third grade, Jerry carried a *Family Ties* lunchbox to school and was voted "Mr. Calculator" two years in a row. Jerry has a Spoons of the World collection and an addiction to computer games (he is a member of Video Games Anonymous) that began with the board games Candy Land, Chutes and Ladders and Monopoly. When Pac-Man came along he was hooked (he scored 3,000,020 points on his first try).

The buds watch movies at the Multi Plex Cinema. On the school radio station (WFLM, 89.9 FM), Parker has a call-in show ("Dr. Retro"); Jerry hosts "The Freshman Show"; and Mikey is "the Ice Man," the host of a rock and roll show. They eat at the Atlas Diner and when they embark on a mission, Parker says, "Gentlemen, synchronize your Swatches (each wears a Swatch watch model 150M).

Parker's parents, Judy (Anne Bloom, Mary Ellen Trainor) and Martin Lewis (Timothy Stack) own Mondo Video, a movie rental store (titles rent for $2.99). Asking them for advice, Parker says, "is like looking for gasoline with a match — you're lucky to get out alive."

Also living with Parker is his sister, Shelly Ann (Maia Brewton), a 13-year-old freshman at Santo Domingo High. Shelly lives for the day when she can get the goods on Parker and expose him (Parker calls her "Santo Domingo's Hellcat" and "Shelly Belly" and believes she was adopted). Shelly weighs 77 pounds, has an 11:00 P.M. curfew and "the largest collection of My Little Ponies on the continent." She is a member of the snobbish Vogues, an all-girl club that is the terror of the school. Parker's biggest challenge was an assignment he called "Operation Pretty Woman" — changing Shelly, "a 72-pound swamp monster into Julia Roberts" for her first date. Shelly's favorite movie is *Fatal Attraction* (which she has seen 15 times).

Grace Musso (Melanie Chartoff), called Ms. Musso, is the stern, authoritarian principal of the school. Her goal is to get Parker (her file number on him is SN2935-59) for disrupting her life; all she asks "is a cup of coffee and a little peace and quiet in the morning." Her office phone number is KL5-4579. Parker believes Grace is more than a principal — "she is a psychopath with tenure." Grace earns $38,000 a year but lives in a $600,000 home — one of the holds Parker has on her (he also possesses the "Musso Excuse File," a list of excuses he uses to get out of jams). Grace is very attractive and dresses in tight skirts and blouses (she causes havoc at basketball games as the boys leer at her and often lose the game). In 1969, when Grace was a junior at Santo Domingo, she was an obedience helper to its principal. When she graduated in 1970, she was slimed with 60 gallons of lime Jell-O on the night of her senior prom. Grace owns a cabin at Sky Lake and her detention room punishment is showing students a home video of her life — from infancy. She claims to be Donny Osmond's biggest fan (having written thousands of letters since 1970) and appeared on the TV show *The Dating Connection*. The Bee Gees and men with beards are her turn-ons. As of 10/13/91, Grace had 1,357 blind dates. She has an account at the Santo Domingo Trust Bank. "Eeek!" is heard from Jerry when Ms. Musso approaches. Assisting Grace is "a pretty, two-faced sugar plum obedience trainee — Shelly."

Lawrence "Larry" Francis Kubiac (Abraham Benrubi) has been a junior at Santo Domingo High for seven years (he believes, for example, that 9½ years is almost a century). Larry is 20 years old, 270 pounds and six feet, seven inches tall. He is mean "and the most dangerous force ever to squeeze into a high school football uniform" (jersey 77). Larry lives to eat and is very protective of his lunch (which he carries in a large paper bag with a misspelled LARY'S LUNCH on it). When he gets upset, Larry retreats to school bathroom Number 12 — (his office) where he is king. In the tenth annual District Science Fair, Larry won with his invention "Spud Light" (he shoved a flashlight cylinder into a potato and the bulb lit). Larry's catchphrase is "eat now?"; he reads *Field and Heifer* magazine and has a job at the Smorgasbord Restaurant. He is called "The Kube" and in honor of his tenth year at the school, the cafeteria named a sandwich after him: "The Kube" (pizza and french fries on sourdough bread).

Frank Lemmer (Taj Johnson) is Grace's special guidance counselor (she summons him with a silent dog whistle). He has a pet piranha (Kathy) and reads *Soldier of Fortune* magazine. (When he attends the Soldier of Fortune Sleep Away Camp, he is voted "most likely to be killed by his tentmates.")

Cheerleader tryouts is the most eagerly awaited event at the school; the *Weekly Flamingo* is the school newspaper; and the Golden Flamingo is the football team's mascot. Mikey keeps a jar of monkey brains on his desk (a buds tradition); the local hangout is Sparky's Hamburgers.

99.   **Perfect Strangers** ABC, 1986–1993

Balki Bartokomous (Bronson Pinchot), a former sheepherder on the small Mediterranean island of Mypos, and his Wisconsin-born cousin, Larry Appleton (Mark Linn-Baker), who is one-sixty-fourth Myposian, are roommates who share Apartment 203 in the Caldwell Hotel at 627 Lincoln Boulevard in Chicago.

Balki takes night classes at Chicago Community College to improve his knowledge of America. His favorite meal is eel wrapped in grape leaves and sheepherder's bread with a side dish of Ding Ding Mac Mood (pig snout).

For breakfast he eats yak links. Balki is a famous baker on Mypos and is known for his bibibobacas (a cream puff-like pastry that has to be baked slowly or "the bib in the baca goes boom" (explodes). Balki's favorite TV show is *Uncle Shaggy's Dog House* and Wayne Newton is his favorite singer. Steve and Eydie are the two pigeons who have made Balki's windowsill their home. He has named his shoes Phil and Andy. He has a parrot named Yorgi (after his peg goat on Mypos) and as a kid had a horse (Trodsky) and a dog (Koos Koos). Balki uses Mr. Ducky bubble bath and has a plant named Margie. He enjoys riding Blue Thunder, the coin-operated horse at the Stop and Save. When someone lies he fears the Gabuggies — the Myposian Fib Furies (Eva, Zsa Zsa and Magda). Balki does volunteer work at Chicago General Hospital (he won the "Bed Changer of the Month" award), ran for college student body president with the slogan "Pro Sheep, Anti Wolf" and became a rap music star called Fresh Young Balki (he recorded the song "Balki B" for Knight Records). Balki's phone number is 555-9876.

Larry gargles to the tune of "Moon River." He was born in May and, as a kid in Madison, Wisconsin, had a dog named Spot. Larry asked 12 girls to the senior prom; 13 girls turned him down (one came up to him and said, "Don't even think of asking me"). When something goes wrong, Larry exclaims, "Oh, my Lord." His license plate reads KYP 758 (later 993 753) and he wrote a play called *Wheat*. Louie Anderson played Cousin Larry in the series unaired pilot.

Balki and Cousin Larry (as Balki calls him), were first employed by Donald "Twinkie" Twinkacetti (Ernie Sabella) at the Rits Discount Store. They later work for the Chicago *Chronicle* at 901 East Wacker Street (Larry is assistant to the city editor; Balki, a mail room clerk, also draws "Dimitri's World," a kids' comic about a cuddly little sheep). Larry and Balki appeared on the TV game show *Risk It All* (and lost everything), bought a racehorse called Larry's Fortune; and purchased stock in Unicorn, Inc., the makers of Balki's favorite cereal, Raisin Puffs.

Larry's girlfriend is Jennifer Lyons (Melanie Wilson); Balki dates her roommate, Mary Anne Spencer (Rebecca Arthur). Jennifer and Mary Anne, friends since they were eight years old, are stewardesses. Mary Anne thinks that rooming with Jennifer is like living with a Barbie doll (she is too neat and perfect) while Jennifer feels that Mary Anne is untidy and hates it when she hogs the bathroom ("It takes her three hours to put on makeup"). Jennifer was born in April in Iowa where her parents own a corn canning business. Mary Anne was "Little Miss Gingivitis" in her sixth-grade hygiene play.

Larry and Jennifer married on 9/27/91 and set up housekeeping on Elm Street with Balki and Mary Anne (who marry on 4/18/92). Both girls become pregnant and in the final episode (8/6/93) give birth: Jennifer to a boy she and Larry name Tucker; Mary Anne to a boy she and Balki name Robespierre Boinkie.

100.   Phenom ABC, 1993–1994

Angela Doolan (Angela Goethals) is the phenom of the title, a natural at tennis, "a child blessed by the hand of God; something that comes along once in a lifetime," says her coach Lou Della Rose (William DeVane). Angela, 15, lives at 1728 Avalon Drive in Agora, California, with her mother Dianne (Judith Light), sister Mary Margaret (Ashley Johnson) and brother Brian (Todd Louiso). Angela won the Sixteen and Under championship of Southern California and is struggling to cope with the demands of potential stardom while at the same time be a normal teenage girl. Angela is a teacher's dream student; she is left in charge of the class when the teacher steps out and has been voted "most likely to join the order" by the nuns of her school (Miraculous Medal High). Angela practices tennis 35 hours a week and her most embarrassing moment occurred during a tournament match when her halter top slipped and exposed her left breast. Her dream is to win Wimbledon.

Dianne is 42 years old, divorced from Jack (John Getz) and works as a certified shorthand reporter (transcribes notes from tape). Her license plate reads 25 P250 and she uses Miss Clairol Harvest Sun hair color. Jack, who calls Dianne "Sharkey," is a former minor league ball player turned beer salesman.

Mary Margaret attends third grade at Miraculous Medal Elementary School. She wears Tom and Jerry socks, has a goldfish (Willie) and hides her money in the head of her Cabbage Patch doll, Brian (named after her brother). Angela likes to talk with Mary Margaret "because she listens, never interrupts and doesn't understand a word I say."

Brian, a hopeful art student, attends the Tim Pacaso Art Academy. He works at Hector's Tacos and previously held a job as the front-gate security guard at the Leisure Time Retirement Home.

Lou lives at 3079 Los Costas and owns the Lou Della Rose Tennis Academy in La Hoya. When someone asks "Who's Lou Della Rose," he responds, "Just the best damned tennis coach in history." He first saw Angela at the Southern California Championships and offered her a full scholarship (she trains there on weekends). Tracy Austin was a student Lou coached to win the U.S. Open.

101.   The PJ's Fox, 1999–2000; WB, 2000–

Thurgood Stubbs (voice of Eddie Murphy) is the maintenance engineer, called "Supa" by the tenants, of the 13-story Hilton Jacobs Building in the Pro-

jects. Thurgood is married to Muriel (Loretta Devine) and they share a basement apartment. Thurgood is 48 years old "but looks 60." *Wheel of Fortune*
is his favorite TV show and he drinks an alcoholic beverage called Mule 40
(he attempted to make his own wine and called it Baron von Thurgood's
Spring Frolic). When he gets upset he has a deep fried pork chop sandwich.
When it came time to replace the building's front door, he purchased the
Thugaway 2000 (which he named Doreen). Hoping to provide a place for the
tenants to relax, Thurgood purchased the abandoned movie theater on Al
Sharpton Boulevard from HUD (Housing and Urban Development) for one
dollar; it soon became the Thurgood Stubbs Neighborhood Theater. For Thurgood, rent day is as much fun as eviction day. Thurgood believes he is the
world's greatest gumbo chef, uses Old English 800 cologne, and makes chocolate milk by combining milk and Choco Puffs cereal in a blender.

Muriel, most always seen in a pink blouse with "Paris" on it, is president of Women United to Save Our Projects. She is totally devoted to Thurgood and keeps a daily record of her activities in her journal.

Regular tenants are Juicy Hudson (Michele Morgan), the overweight
boy who idolizes Thurgood and wears a sign that reads "Do Not Feed"; the
elderly Mrs. Avery (Ja'net DuBois), whom Thurgood calls "a dried-up old
gargoyle" (she is forever hitting him with her cane); Mambo Garcelle (Cheryl
Frances Harrington), the voodoo priestess Thurgood calls "Haiti Lady" or
"Voodoo Queen"; Calvin (Crystal Scales), Juicy's friend; and Sanchez (Pepe
Serna), a once-promising opera star whose passion for cigarettes now forces
him to speak with a throat microphone.

The series was filmed in a puppet-animation process called Fomation;
Phil Morris provided Thurgood's voice in two episodes.

102. Roc Fox, 1991–1994

Roc Emerson (Charles S. Dutton) and his wife, Eleanor (Ella Joyce),
live in an attached house at 864 Essex Street in Baltimore. Roc, a garbageman with District 36 of the Department of Sanitation, dreams of owning a
semi-attached house. His newspapers are from the previous day ("I read yes-
terday's news today") and he furnishes his home with items he has found on
his route (the money he saves by not buying something is put in a jar for his
dream house). When Roc has to buy something, he will only buy it on sale.
Roc has to empty 175,214 garbage cans to make $2,000. Charlene's Bar is
Roc's hangout and he has coffee at the Depot, the shop next to the sanitation depot (which was originally called The Landfill).

Eleanor, a nurse at Harbor Hospital (Wing C), shares Roc's dream but
wishes he weren't so cheap (she is trying to get him to do the impossible —

buy an item at list price). *L.A. Law* is Eleanor's favorite TV show. On 11/23/93, she gave birth to a boy she and Roc name Marcus (Eleanor wanted to name him Shaka).

Also living with Roc are his father, Andrew (Carl Gordon), and his brother, Joey (Rocky Carroll). Andrew, called "Pop," worked as a train porter for 36 years. Loretta, his late wife, was a waitress; he has pictures of his idol, Malcolm X, on every wall in the house, and in 1966 he had a Buick Riviera he called Lena. Joey, a talented trumpeter, has trouble finding work and appears to live off scams. Second-season episodes were broadcast live and are called in some sources *Roc Live*.

103. Room for Two ABC, 1992–1993

Jill Kurland (Patricia Heaton) keeps a large meat thermometer near her front door for protection. She lives in Manhattan (Apartment 3) and is the producer of *Wake Up, New York* an early-morning program on WXOR-TV, Channel 3. Edie Kurland (Linda Lavin), Jill's mother, hosts the show's "Reality Check" segment (wherein she gives her honest opinions about life). As a kid, Jill had a dog (Trudy), a favorite blanket (Boo Boo Blankey) and a teddy bear (Fred). She (and Edie) are allergic to shellfish.

Edie was born in Dayton, Ohio, and now lives in Apartment 4 above Dario's Italian Restaurant. Edie was married to Lou, the owner of Kurland's Appliance World in Ohio (the store's motto was "If we don't have it, go someplace else"; a clown named Blinky welcomed customers). When Lou died, Edie shed her life as "wife, mother, president of the PTA and good neighbor" for a new start in New York (she got her TV job when she attended a broadcast of Jill's and impressed the executive producer with her brashness). Reed Ellis (Andrew Prine), the former star of *Cleavon, Commander of the Galaxy Squad*, hosts *Wake Up, New York*. Ken Kazurinsky (Peter Michael Goetz), Edie's neighbor, runs a mail-order business called the Kazurinsky Catalogue. Matt Drang (John Putch), Jill's boyfriend, is a biology teacher who yearns to be a writer (he has written several short stories, including one about a scientist who grafts part of his wife's brain to his to find her killer).

104. Roseanne ABC, 1988–1997

Dan and Roseanne Conner (John Goodman, Roseanne) live at 714 Delaware Street in Lanford, Illinois, with their children Becky (Lecy Goranson, Sarah Chalke), Darlene (Sara Gilbert) and D.J. (Sal Barone, Michael Fishman). Dan has a Harley Davidson motorcycle, and is building a boat in the garage. The car license plate reads 846 779. In 1996, Dan and Roseanne become millionaires when they hit the Illinois State Lottery for its biggest jackpot ever, $108 million.

Dan originally owned 4 Aces Construction, then Lanford Custom Cycles (motorcycle repair and sales). When the business fails (overdue mortgage payments), he, Roseanne and Jackie (Roseanne's sister) open the Lanford Lunch Box (a diner off Route 9). When an opportunity arose, Dan became "the guy who fixes the trucks" at the Lanford City Garage. He quit this for a construction job to dry-wall the new state prison, but never started: he suffered a heart attack at Darlene's wedding. Dan reads the girlie magazine *Girls, Girls, Girls* and has drinks at the Lobo Lounge. Beer is his favorite drink; cake his favorite dessert; and Oscar Meyer frankfurters his favorite food. He is famous for his chocolate chip shakes and he gets upset when the kids leave toast crumbs in the butter.

Roseanne Harris met Dan at Lanford High School. He was an athlete (nicknamed "Yor") and she aspired to become a writer. They married after graduation. When the series begins Roseanne is an assembly line worker at Wellman Plastics. She then held the following jobs: telephone solicitor for Discount House Magazine, order taker at Divine Chicken, bartender at the Lobo Lounge, cleanup lady at Art's Beauty Parlor, waitress at Rodbell's Luncheonette, partner in the Lanford Lunchbox, and TV commentator ("Roseanne Reports from the Heartland") on WERG-TV, Channel 4's local news program in Chicago. Roseanne buys groceries at the Buy 'n' Bag supermarket and gets upset when the kids leave jelly in the peanut butter jar. She gave birth to a fourth child (1996) she and Dan named Jerry. When Roseanne won the lottery, the ABX network and the Home Movie Channel expressed interest in doing a TV movie about her life. ABX wanted to unrealistically clean up her life; HMC wanted to present a sleazy image (for example, making Becky, "the pretty blonde daughter a lesbian"). She rejected both.

Becky, the oldest child (born 3/15/75) attends Lanford High School. She is pretty, sweet and feminine and closer to Roseanne than she is to Dan. She loves to shop (receives $10 a week allowance) and eats Dannon yogurt. Her favorite color is red. When she first began to drive she was fined $50 for parking in a handicap zone; she worked at the Buy 'n' Bag supermarket. As the series progressed, Becky became aggressive, independent and constantly defied parental authority. She left the family and married Mark Healy (Glenn Quinn), Dan's mechanic at the cycle shop. They moved to Minneapolis (where Becky worked as a waitress at the Bunz Restaurant) but eventually returned home and moved into the Lanford Trailer Court. Mark later worked at the Edelweiss Garden Amusement Park as Hans the Hare (the mascot) and later as a mechanic with Dan at the garage. Mark is interested in art and painting. His cooking specialty is Ragu tomato sauce on bread. Hoping to make something of herself, Becky later enrolled in the University of Illinois (hoping to become a nurse).

Darlene, the middle child, attended South Elementary School, Lanford Jr. High, Lanford High, and the Chicago School of the Arts. She is a tomboy and nasty. She loves sports and helping her father put up drywall. She is closer to her father than she is to Roseanne. At age 14 she lost interest in sports, discovered boys and lived for a time in her own dream world. She attached herself to Mark's brother, David (Johnny Galecki), a lazy sort who lived in the Conner's basement. He worked as a busboy at Pizza World and married Darlene when she became pregnant; she gave birth to a girl she and David named Harris Conner Healy.

D.J. (David Jacob) attends South Elementary, James Madison Elementary then the Lanford Middle School. He has a collection of doll heads (Barbie, Cher and G.I. Joe) in one box and the body parts in another — both of which he hides under his bed. He has a habit of getting his head stuck in drawers (how is not said, "but he's got a gift for it," says Roseanne; she "unsticks" him by oiling his head). He has a goldfish (Fluffy) and worked as a waiter at the Lunch Box. D.J. rents movies at Lanford Video and hopes to become a documentary film maker (he makes his own movies by placing a video camera around the house to see what he gets). His girlfriend, Heather (Heather Matarazzo), is a fellow film enthusiast; they enjoy watching foreign films and documentaries together. *Return of the Jedi* is their favorite movie.

Jackie Harris (Laurie Metcalf), Roseanne's sister, first lives in an apartment (A) then a house (number 465). She helped Roseanne win the lottery by picking three of the six winning numbers. She first worked at Wellman Plastics then as an officer for the Lanford Police Department when a printing company took over Wellman. She trained in Springfield but quit the force when she fell down the stairs and injured herself while tackling a pervert. After recovering she turned to acting and joined the Lanford Theater Company (she starred in a production of *Cyrano de Bergerac*). When this failed, she became a "perfume bottle squirter" at the makeup counter in the Lanford Mall. She soon became bored, enrolled in trucking school and became a big-rig driver. She quit this to become a partner in the Lunch Box. As a kid Jackie had a doll (Mrs. Tuttle) and attended the Wild Oaks Summer Camp with Roseanne. Jackie's real name is Marjorie, but as a baby, Roseanne could not pronounce it and called her "My Jackie." Jackie stuck and replaced Marjorie. Jackie is divorced (from Fred) and is the mother of Andy. To make extra money for Christmas presents, Jackie and Roseanne took jobs at the Buy 'n' Bag as product sample girls (Jackie pushed soya sausage; Roseanne, cheese in a can).

Nancy (Sandra Bernhard), Jackie's friend, revealed in the episode of 11/10/92 that she was a lesbian, making her the first such regular character on a prime-time sitcom. Marla (Morgan Fairchild) and Sharon (Mariel Hemingway) were Nancy's lovers. They frequented the gay bar Lips; Marla worked as a salesgirl in the cosmetics department of Rodbell's Department Store. Nancy believes she was abducted by aliens: "For one month after I would play champion chess; then it just disappeared."

The program also spotlighted gays Leon Carp (Martin Mull) and his significant other, Scott (Fred Willard). Leon was a partner with Roseanne in the Lunch Box; Scott is a probate lawyer. They were the 1995 canasta champions of Fire Island. In 1996, Roseanne's mother, Beverly Harris (Estelle Parsons), announced she was a lesbian and moved in with her lover, Joyce Levine (Ruta Lee), a famous lounge singer with the Lanford Holiday Inn known as Joyce, the Rotating Voice.

In the final episode we see Roseanne writing at her desk. In a voice-over we learn that she is compiling her memories and all that we saw did not actually happen. Roseanne did not win the lottery; she only imagined what it would have been like; Dan had died a year prior to this moment. It was Roseanne's sister, not her mother, who was actually gay. She thought Becky would have been better with David, and Darlene better with Mark (and Darlene named Becky and Becky named Darlene). But most of all Roseanne was achieving her high school dream; while it may not be "the great American novel," it is her dream book and she has written it for all of us to see.

105. Sabrina, the Teenage Witch ABC, 1996–

The house at 133 Collins Road in Westbridge, Massachusetts, is owned by Hilda and Zelda Spellman (Caroline Rhea, Beth Broderick), sisters who are also witches. Also living with them is Sabrina Spellman (Melissa Joan Hart), their beautiful niece, and Salem (voice of Nick Bakay), a warlock who has been turned into a black cat. Sabrina is unaware that she is a witch. Her mother is a mortal and her father a warlock. Hilda and Zelda have been assigned by the Witch's Council to teach Sabrina the art of witchcraft (which begins developing when she is 16; Sabrina's mother is an archaeologist digging for fossils in Peru and she believes her father is traveling with the Foreign Secret Service). On Sabrina's 16th birthday (when the series begins), the novice witch receives unusual gifts: a black cauldron from her aunts and a book, *The Discovery of Magic* from her father. She learns she is a witch when she discovers her first power — levitation.

Sabrina, ticklish behind the ears, attends Westbridge High School and writes for the school newspaper, *The Lantern*; the Slicery is the after-school pizza parlor hangout. Sabrina received her witch's license on her 17th birthday and is forbidden to use her power for profit, turn back time or to conjure up pancakes (pancakes are a dark family secret. If a Spellman eats a pancake it becomes addictive to the point of obesity. The family is also allergic to poppies, which cast a sleeping spell on them). Throughout the 1998-99 season, Sabrina was given a difficult quest: solve the Spellman family secret. Through a series of weekly clues she solved it in the season finale: "Every member of the Spellman family is born with a twin." Sabrina's twin was Katrina (who lived in South Dakota).

Sabrina's first job was "the lovely assistant" to Magic Jolli's "World of Wonder." She later worked for Pork on a Fork and, through the Other Realm Employment Agency, found a job as a Sandman ("I put the people in my neighborhood asleep"). On her 18th birthday (third season), Sabrina begins her senior year in high school and works as a waitress in The Coffee Shop.

"Hilda and Zelda do more weird things by 9 A.M. than most people do all day," says Sabrina. Hilda, 620 years old, is single by choice and refuses to marry any of the losers she has been dating. She is a musician (plays violin) and has been dating Drell (Penn Jillette), the head of the Witch's Council. On 2/14/97, they celebrated the 94th anniversary of their 32nd breakup. Drell sends Hilda a pot roast instead of flowers before a date ("flowers wilt; you can eat the meat"). Although the Witch's Council frowns on witches dating mortals (fearing a witch-mortal marriage), Hilda dated Willard Kraft (Martin Mull), the vice principal at Westbridge High School. Willard also dated Zelda (he called her "Zu Zu"; she called him "Monkey") and was married to a witch named Lucy (Julia Duffy), although he never knew it (she kept her powers secret from him). When they divorced, Lucy was banished to the Republic of Infinite Horror — where she is not permitted to practice magic (as punishment for marrying a mortal). Willard plays the zither, is a Doris Day fan, and wears a raincoat to school every day to protect himself from students who throw garbage at him when he enters the school ("one of the drawbacks of being a 'beloved' vice principal"). In third-season episodes, Willard becomes the school's principal and Hilda buys a clock shop called Hickory Dickory Clock. Zelda becomes her partner (25 percent) and, through an unusual item in the store — The Lost in Time Clock — they help lost travelers in time (people seeking to go back in time to correct a mistake in their lives).

Zelda, the older sister ("500-plus years old") is interested in science, psychiatry, slug reproduction and art (she was a model for Goya and nude postcards of her are sold at the art museum). She drinks only bottled water and was a beekeeper hobbyist as a kid. Zelda, whose online Web site name is "Chem Kitten," is passionate about her intellectual pursuits: "My life is in my head." She keeps her potions in a secret cabinet behind the kitchen wall and has forbidden anyone from using her computer lab, which is concealed in a desk in the living room. Zelda and Hilda's favorite holiday is Halloween (they decorate the house and sing Halloween carols); they are not too fond of Thanksgiving because it was started by Puritans who were not witch friendly.

Salem Saberhagen was a warlock who dreamed of dominating the world. When he actually tried to do it, the Witch's Council sentenced him to live life as a cat for 100 years (the Council used truth sprinkles to force Salem to divulge his quest). Now "the sound of the can opener is the only thing that truly makes me feel alive," says Salem. Salem's weakness is tassels, Pamela Anderson's *V.I.P.* is his favorite TV show, and he enjoys beating Hilda and Zelda at Scrabble. He craves squid and likes chocolate syrup in his bowl of milk. He uses Zelda's computer to get into chat rooms (where he pretends to be a woman) and it pains him to be sincere. He spies on Sabrina and helps her in her quest to become a full-fledged witch. When situations become tough, Salem pretends to be a coward; when he gets upset, he eats; but he also claims, "when I'm happy I eat."

The Witch's Council is ten million light years away, although a shortcut exists in the Spellman's linen closet ("Make a left at the towels and follow the signs to the Other Realm"). Melissa's real-life sisters, Alexandra and Emily Hart, played Sabrina's mischievous witch cousins, Amanda and Ally. Being selfish is a witch's worst trait; lava is the only substance that can destroy a witch; and every 25 years, a witch has to have a magic tune-up.

106. Saved by the Bell NBC, 1989-2000

Fictional Bayside High School in Palisades, California, provides the setting for a number of series that depict incidents in the lives of its students. Dennis Haskins plays the principal, Richard Belding, in all but series three and four.

1. *Good Morning, Miss Bliss* (DIS, 1988-89). See separate entry for information.

2. *Saved by the Bell* (NBC, 1989-93). Students: Kelly Kapowski (Tiffani-Amber Thiessen), Jessica "Jesse" Myrtle Spano (Elizabeth Berkley), Lisa Marie Turtle (Lark Voorhies), Zachary "Zack" Morris (Mark-Paul Gosselaar), Samuel "Screech" Powers (Dustin Diamond), Albert Clifford "A.C." Slater (Mario Lopez) and (1992-93), Tori Scott (Leanna Creel).

Kelly, the prettiest girl in school, is head cheerleader (for the Bayside Tigers football team), captain of the girls' softball, volleyball and swim teams, and is Bayside Homecoming Queen. She lives at 3175 Fairfax Drive and her phone number is 555-4314. On Tiger Radio, Bayside's radio station (KKTY, 98.6 FM) Kelly hosted "Kelly Desire" (romantic music). In the Miss Bayside Beauty Pageant, Kelly sang (off key) "Blue Moon." She scored 1100 on the SAT and has a German shepherd named Freddie.

Jesse is smart, pretty and sensitive to the fact that she is tall. She is a talented dancer, a member of the Honors Society and hates being called "chick" or "babe." Jesse won the French award and hopes to attend Stanford University. Her phone number is 555-0635. She reported the news on Tiger Radio and scored 1205 on her SAT.

Lisa, the first one of her group to get a credit card, says, "I'm beautiful, charming and always in fashion." She loves to shop ("Lisa is my name, shopping is my game. If it's sold, I can find it") and has the ability to guess the contents of a gift before she opens it. She scored 1140 on her SAT. Her first locker number is 118, then 149. Lisa played the violin in the Miss Bayside Beauty Pageant. On Tiger Radio, Lisa was "the Galloping Gossip."

Tori is a tough, biker-like girl with the beauty of Kelly and the liberalism of Jesse. She was actually the replacement for Kelly and Jesse, who were dropped without explanation at the start of the 1992 season.

Zack, the preppy student, is a natural-born con-artist whose schemes often land him in detention. On Tiger Radio Zack was the D.J. "Wolfman Zack" and on a teen hot line he started, he was "Nitro Man" (Screech was "Ant Man" and Lisa, "Princess"). "The Girls of Bayside High Swimsuit Calendar" was Zack's most elaborate attempt to make money (Kelly was "Miss November"; Jesse, "Miss July"; and Lisa, "Miss October"). The photos led to a feature in *Teen Fashion* magazine (Kelly was "The All-American Girl"; Jesse, "The Studious but Fashionable Girl"; and Lisa, "The It's Happening Now Girl").

Zack formed Kelly, Jesse and Lisa into the sexy singing group Hot Sundae (they sang "I'm Excited"). He later formed the band The Zack Attack, with himself on guitar; Kelly and Lisa (backup vocalists); Slater (drums); and Screech (keyboard). He later revamped the group with Kelly (lead singer), Lisa (guitar), Slater (drums) and Screech (keyboard). In 1992, Zack, Tori, Lisa, Screech and Slater were The Five Aces, a singing group Zack formed in his senior year. This same group attempted to make money by selling "Screech's Secret Sauce" (a spaghetti sauce recipe that sold for $3. Their slogan: "The Sauce You Gotta Have, But the Secret, She's-a-Mine"). Zack, locker 269, scored 1502 on his SAT. He and Kelly were an "item" in many episodes.

Screech lives at 88 Edgemont Road. He has a homemade robot (Kevin), a dog (Hound Dog), lizard (Oscar), spider (Ted), two white rats (Spin and

Marty), a roach (Herbert) and a mouse (Arnold). Screech, fifth runner up in an ALF look-a-like contest, wears a size 11 shoe and is a member of the photography, science, chess, insect and glee clubs at school. He named his first zit Murray and invented Zit-Off, a blemish cream that removed pimples, but left a maroon after-effect. Screech has a crush on Lisa, who wants nothing to do with him. His only other girlfriend was Violet Bickerstaff (Tori Spelling), a very pretty "nerd girl" with a beautiful singing voice. Screech scored a 1200 on the SAT and on Tiger Radio he hosted "Screech's Mystery Theater."

Slater, "the school hunk," is an army brat and Zack's rival for Kelly before he found an interest in Jesse (she called him "Bubba"; he called her "Mama"). Slater scored 1050 on the SAT and is captain of the football and wrestling teams. He has a pet chameleon (Artie) and a car with the license plate END 838.

In the episode of 5/22/93, Zack, Screech, Lisa and Slater — and Jesse and Kelly (who suddenly reappeared) — graduate (no mention is made of Tori, who suddenly disappeared). Screech beat Jesse by one-tenth of a point for valedictorian. Lisa enrolled at the Fashion Institute; Kelly at community college; Jesse at Columbia; Zack at Yale; A.C. at Iowa State (on a wrestling scholarship). Screech, who had numerous acceptances (Emerson, Clemson, Princeton and the Barbizon School of Modeling) had not made a decision.

Richard Belding, the principal, served with the 55th National Guard in Indianapolis and was the 1963 Chubby Checker Twist-Off champion. He calls Zack his "Zack Ache" and was himself a student at Bayside (he was a D.J. on Tiger Radio as "The Big Bopper"). As a kid he had two goldfish (Flipper and Jaws) and two parakeets (Sonny and Cher).

The TV movie, *Saved by the Bell: Hawaiian Style* (11/27/92) aired as a prime time special and depicted the group's efforts to save the Hawaiian Hideaway, a hotel owned by Kelly's grandfather, from a rival hotel owner seeking the land for expansion.

3. *Saved by the Bell* (NBC, 9/14/91 to 10/26/91). Nine episodes depicting Zack, Kelly, Jesse, Slater, Lisa and Screech's activities during the summer of 1991 when they worked at the Malibu Sands Beach Club. Leon Corosi (Ernie Sabella) owned the club and his daughter, Stacey (Leah Remini), assisted him as the manager of the summer help. Zack was the social director; Kelly and Slater, lifeguards; Jesse, the receptionist; and Screech, a waiter. Lisa was a club member. Leon called Stacey "Honey Bunny"; she called him "Papa Bear."

4. *Saved by the Bell: The College Years* (NBC, 1993–1994). Zack, Slater, Kelly and Screech begin their freshman year at California State University. New to the cast are students Alexandra "Alex" Tabor (Kiersten Warren)

and Leslie Burke (Anne Tremko); and athletic coach Michael Rogers (Bob Golic).

Zack, Screech and Slater share Room 218B in a coed dorm where Kelly, Alex and Leslie share Room 218A. Kelly and Alex pledge Pi Psi Sorority; Leslie, Beta Zeta; Zack, Screech and Slater, Sigma Alpha Fraternity. Alex, a drama major, is from Oregon. Leslie is from Washington, D.C., and like Zack, is a finance major. Kelly, studying to become a doctor, works at the Student Health Center; Slater, attending on a wrestling scholarship, works as a waiter at the Falcon's Nest, the Student Union cafeteria. Michael, the resident director of the Broxton Dorm (where the group resides), played linebacker for the Forty-Niners. His research lab mouse is named X-97 and 555-6398 is his phone number. Alex doubles as the school's football team mascot, Freddy Falcon. Skeeters is the local watering hole.

The TV movie *Saved by the Bell: Wedding in Las Vegas* (10/7/94) picks up from the final episode of *The College Years* (which ended with Zack proposing to Kelly). Zack's mishaps as he and Kelly wed are depicted. Lisa and Jesse join Slater and Screech for the event.

5. *Saved by the Bell: The New Class* (NBC, 1993-94). The Max is still the hangout but there are new students: Vickie Needleman (Bonnie Russavage), Lindsay Warner (Natalia Cigliuti), Megan Jones (Bianca Lawson), Scott Erickson (Robert Sutherland), Barton "Weasel" Wyzell (Isaac Lidsky) and Tommy DeLucca (Jonathan Angel).

Lindsay, "the most beautiful girl at Bayside," is a member of the drama and glee clubs. Vickie, a gorgeous blonde, says, "Asking me how I am is like calling 911. I'm full of ailments." She likes candy, but not chocolate ("It makes my face break out") and likes licorice ("but not the red kind, it gives me hives"). Megan is Bayside's brightest student while Tommy, called "Tommy Dee" barely passes. Scott, a transfer from rival Valley High, is the new Zack, and Mr. Belding's main problem student. Barton, nicknamed "Weasel," is a computer nut and water boy for the school's football team (the Tigers).

Lindsay, Vickie and Megan are junior varsity cheerleaders for the ping pong team. On the school radio station (now KVIB), Mr. Belding hosts "Ask Your Principal"; Vickie is the weather girl; Lindsay hosted the romantic music show, "From Lindsay with Love"; Megan was the advice giver, "Dr. Love."

As a kid Weasel had an imaginary friend (Albert) and when he showed potential as a kicker on the football team, his teammates called him "Golden Toes." When Scott and Megan started *The Bayside Shopping Club* on the school's TV system, they sold "Chocolate Memory" to help students improve their memories (it was only chocolate syrup, but Scott used the power of positive thinking to sell it).

6. *Saved by the Bell: The New Class* (NBC, 1994-95). Rachel Myers (Sarah Lancaster), Brian Keller (Christian Oliver) and Bobby Wilson (Spankee Rogers) replace Vickie, Scott and Weasel (who were dropped without explanation). Dustin Diamond returns as Screech, now Mr. Belding's college-trained administrative assistant. Rachel, a stunning blonde, is a material girl and holds the beauty pageant title, "Miss Junior Palisades." Brian is newly arrived in America from Switzerland and is having a confusing (if not troublesome) time coping with life at Bayside.

7. *Saved by the Bell: The New Class* (NBC, 1994-95). Broadcast back-to-back with series six. During the summer of 1994, Mr. Belding takes a job as the manager of the Palisades Hills Country Club with Screech as his assistant manager and his students as his staff: Rachel (lifeguard), Lindsay and Megan (waitresses), Brian (pool attendant), Bobby (golf attendant) and Tommy (valet parker). When their jobs ended, the gang became cowhands at Screech's Uncle Lester's Gold Canyon Ranch in California.

8. *Saved by the Bell: The New Class* (NBC, 1995-96). Megan, Bobby and Brian are dropped. The new students, transfers from Valley High, are Maria Lopez (Samantha Becker), Ryan Parker (Richard Lee Jackson) and R. J. "Hollywood" Collins (Salim Grant).

Screech, born 2/9/75, is also the faculty advisor for the school newspaper, the *Bayside Breeze*. Mr. Belding (born 12/10/51) has taken a weekend job as the manager of the Sweet Tooth, a candy store in the Palisades Mall. Screech assists him and R.J. (Ronald Joseph) works as their salesman. Rachel is a salesgirl at the Perfume Counter; Tommy works for Chicken for a Buck; Maria is a waitress at the Japanese Restaurant; and Lindsay, a clerk at the Video Store. Maria and Lindsay later work at the Juice Bar. This version ended with the students, Mr. Belding and Screech spending a semester at sea on the SS *Morning Star*.

9. *Saved by the Bell: The New Class* (NBC, 1996-97). Lindsay has transferred to Winwood Academy and Tommy has moved to Florida; R.J.'s fate is not mentioned. Katie Peterson (Lindsey McKeon), Nicky Farina (Ben Gould) and Eric Little (Anthony Harrell) are the new students. Episodes are set primarily at the Palisades Mall where the regulars work: Katie (shampoo girl at Jean Paul's Salon), Rachel (assistant manager of the Cinema Plex Theater), Mr. Belding and Screech manage the Yukon Yogurt store (where Eric works as a clerk), and Nicky is an usher at the Cinema Plex. At school, Katie is manager of the radio station (now KGAB, 98.6 FM); Maria has a show called "Ask Maria" and Screech and Mr. Belding host "From the Principal's Office." Eric is a member of the football team; Nicky is Ryan's step-brother.

10. *Saved by the Bell: The New Class* (NBC, 1997–1998). Rachel has moved to Boston; Liz Miller (Ashley Lyn Cafagna) is the new student.

Screech works as a security guard at the mall on weekends; Ryan and Nicky work at the video store, Media Mania (where Ryan is "Ring-a-ding Ryan" and Nicky "Nutty Nicky"); Maria works for the Teen Machine eatery; Eric and Katie for the mall gym, Pumped; and Liz, as a salesgirl at the Cookie Jar.

11. *Saved by the Bell: The New Class* (NBC, 1998-2000). Ryan has moved to New York to attend a private school. Tony Dillon (Tom Wade Huntington) is the new student. Stories are set at the school and the mall. Mr. Belding runs an electronics store called Gimmicks and Gadgets; Screech assists him. Katie works at the gym, Pumped, and Nicky is an usher at the Cinema Plex. Eric, whose real name is Cornelius, is a salesman at the Petzilla pet shop; Maria is manager of the Teen Machine. At school, Maria is the assistant manager of the Max; Tony is one of its waiters. Tony and Maria attended Valley Junior High, then Valley High before Bayside. Katie is editor of the school newspaper; Liz, the photographer (they are also members of the swim team). Eric, Tony and Nicky are members of the school football team, the Tigers.

Final season episodes find the students earning credit as cadets at the Palisades Police and Fire Academy. Mr. Belding accepts a job as dean of students at the University of Tennessee; Megan is accepted by UCLA; Eric, the Chicago Academy of Music; Katie, Cal State; and Nicky and Tony, NYU.

107. Seinfeld NBC, 1990–1998

Jerome "Jerry" Seinfeld (Jerry Seinfeld) is a standup comedian who lives at 129 West 81st Street (Apartment 5A) in Manhattan (the building is opposite Almo's Bar and Grill; Jerry's phone number was given at KL5-2392 and 555-8383). He and his friends, George Castanza (Jason Alexander), Elaine Benes (Julia Louis-Dreyfus) and Cosmo Kramer (Michael Richards) hang out at Monk's Cafe. Their everyday problems unfold each week in the format of a situation comedy.

Jerry and George attended Edward R. Murrow Junior High School, J.F.K. High and Queens College. Jerry refuses to admit that he watches *Melrose Place*, and he does not allow soft cheeses in his refrigerator. JUN 728 is the license plate of his '92 Saab. He is a fan of Superman (a figure can be seen on his bookcase) and Jor-El (Superman's father) is his ATM PIN code. He has a six-year-old lucky T-shirt he calls Golden Boy (when it didn't make it through its last washing, he replaced it with Golden Boy's son, Baby Blue). Jerry and George, members of the New York Health Club, became writing partners on a pilot based on Jerry's life called *Jerry— The Pilot* ("a show about nothing"). NBC offered them $13,000 for a script; George's greed cost them money and they were paid $8,000. The pilot is produced but the series, *Jerry*, doesn't sell. (When NBC asked George his writing credits, he said he wrote an off-off-Broadway play called *La Cocina*, a comedy about a Mexican chef named Pepe).

Jerry wears a size 40 suit, Plaza Cable services his building, and he gets his hair cut at the Three Brothers Barbers. On his refrigerator, Jerry has magnets of Superman, the N.Y. Mets, the Statue of Liberty and the Comedy Central TV logo.

George was first a real estate broker for Rick Bar Properties (he quit when the boss refused to let him use his private bathroom). He next became a proofreader for Pendant Publishing (fired for having sex on his desk with the cleaning lady). George's third job was assistant to the traveling secretary for the New York Yankees (fired when he pretended to be a Hen Supervisor for Tyler Chicken to impress a girl). George next worked for Play Now, a playground supply company (fired for pretending to be handicapped). His final job was with Krueger Industrial Smoothing, a company that sands anything. Here, he felt he needed a nickname and opted for T-Bone. The boss, however, called him Koko. Determined to rid himself of Koko, he hired a cleaning woman with the same name, knowing the boss would not stand for two Kokos; George became Gammie.

George lives on 86th Street (Apartment 609) and owns a 1976 Chevy Impala (license plate QAG 826). His ATM code is Bosco (after his favorite chocolate drink) and he is a member of the Champagne Video Store. George's dream occupation is to be an architect and he uses the alias Art Van Delay to impress people. During his high school years, George and Jerry frequented Mario's Pizza. It was at this time that George actually accomplished something — highest scorer on the video game Frogger (860,000 points). When George eats at Monk's he brings his own cucumbers for the salad (the diner doesn't supply them). Jerry's favorite soup eatery is a store called the Soup Nazi; George is barred from buying soup because he once asked for bread. During the Christmas season George and his family celebrate Festifus, an occasion that uses an aluminum pole as a symbol to celebrate all holidays as one. While proposing the *Jerry* pilot, George met Susan Ross (Heidi Swedeberg) and fell in love. They planned to marry, but miserly George bought cheap wedding invitations (from Melody Stationery) that contained toxic envelope glue; Susan died from the poison while sealing the envelopes. To remember Susan, her parents established the Susan Ross Foundation with George as a senior board member (to distribute money to worthy causes). George was also a hand model (his career was cut short when he burned his hands on a hot iron). If George were an adult film star, he would choose the name Buck Naked.

Elaine dated Jerry, but there was a lack of physical chemistry between them and now they are just friends. She is a proofreader, and later an editor for Pendant Publishing. When author Justin Pitt (Ian Abercrombie) thought Elaine reminded him of Jacqueline Kennedy, he hired her as his personal assistant. A year later she is fired when Kramer's antics led Justin to believe Elaine was plotting to kill him. She next worked for J. Peterman, publisher of the J. Peterman Mail Order Catalogue. Elaine lives at 16 West 75th Street (Apartment 2G) and uses the Tri-State Wakeup Service. She attended five eastern universities, and was a debate and equestrian champion. A life size mannequin of Elaine appears at a clothing store called Renitzi's. Elaine wears a size 7½ shoe and created a sensation when the antique button on her blouse popped off and revealed her breasts in a low cut, cleavage-revealing bra. She created an earlier sensation when she distributed a Christmas card picture of herself (taken by Kramer) that showed her nipple. She wasn't wearing a bra and explained that she simply missed buttoning a button. For this, she was nicknamed "Nip." Elaine brushes her teeth with Pepsodent and Close-up toothpaste and has a weakness for Jujyfruits candy. She has a fear of dogs and was "best man" at a lesbian wedding. Her middle name is Marie.

Kramer lives across the hall from Jerry (Apartment 5B; 555-3455 and 555-8643 were given as his phone numbers). He is eccentric and appears to be a self-styled entrepreneur (although he did admit to once having a regular job — a bagel technician at H&H Bagels in Manhattan; he has been on strike for 12 years). A company Kramer conceived called Kramerica is mentioned twice: in an early episode it is a chain of make-your-own-pizza parlors; later it is a one-man company that seemingly does nothing. Kramer worked as a broker for Bryant-Leland (he was mistaken for an employee and decided to work there; he was fired for not knowing what he was doing); and was a stand-in for the father of an eight-year-old boy on *All My Children*. He was a medical actor (performs illnesses for interns to identify) and had a role on *Murphy Brown* as Steve Snell, one of Murphy's wacky secretaries. He also had a role in an unnamed Woody Allen movie with the line, "Boy, these pretzels are making me thirsty." Kramer was also a ball boy at the U.S. Open tennis tournament and is the author of *The Coffee Table Book of Coffee Tables* (which, published by Pendant, has cardboard legs to become a mini coffee table; he promoted the book on "Live with Regis and Kathie Lee"). He was an underwear model for Calvin Klein and believes that Klein stole his idea for a cologne called "The Beach" (also referred to as "The Ocean"). Kramer eats Kellogg's Double Dip Crunch cereal for breakfast. When he wanted eggs from uncaged chickens, he bought a rooster (by mistake) and named him "Little Jerry Seinfeld."

Golf is Kramer's favorite recreational sport; he has a habit of snooping into other people's medicine cabinets and enjoys shopping at the airport's duty-free shop. He is banned from the local fruit store (for returning a bad peach), likes extra MSG on his Chinese food and is a member of the Polar Bear Club. Kramer's dream is to drive the rear end of a hook and ladder fire truck (he feels he knows the shortcuts firemen don't). When he applied for personalized license plates, he was mistakenly given ones reading ASSMAN.

When Kramer needs a lawyer, he recruits Jackie Chiles (Phil Morris), a famous, fast-talking attorney. Kramer sued Java World (over a faulty lid on a take-out cup of coffee; he settled for free coffee at any Java World); the tobacco industry (over yellow teeth and age lines after being exposed to cigarette smoke; he settled for a billboard of himself on Times Square dressed as Marlboro cigarettes "Marlboro Man" of the 1960s); a dented car (he crashed his car when he saw a girl walking down the street in a bra; the girl insisted she never wears a bra; Kramer insisted she try one on. When she did, it didn't fit over her sweater and he lost his case).

In the final episode, the *Jerry* pilot is picked up by NBC's new boss. Jerry and George invite Elaine and Kramer on a free trip to Paris on the NBC jet. The jet experiences engine trouble and is forced to land in Massachusetts. While sightseeing, the four witness a carjacking, do nothing to help and are arrested for violating the Good Samaritan Law. Kramer calls on Jackie, but the prosecution presents a parade of hostile witness (people the four encountered throughout the series) who condemn them. Jackie loses the case and "The New York Four" (as they were called) are sent to prison.

Newman (Wayne Knight) lives in the east side of Jerry's building (Apartment 5E). He despises Jerry "because he and his friends frolic it up on the west side of the building." When Newman meets Jerry he always remarks, "Hello, Jerry" (Jerry responds with "Hello, Newman"). Newman, a mailman, calls in sick on rainy days and has a weakness for Drake's Coffee Cake. He avoids the beach (fearing freckles) and became a partner with Kramer in money-making ventures to sell used records and to recycle soda cans out of state for ten cents a can (as opposed to New York's five cents a can).

In the original pilot, *The Seinfeld Chronicles*, the hangout is Pete's Cafe and the character of Elaine does not appear. Had this version sold, the female regular would have been Claire, a waitress played by Lee Garlington.

108. Simon WB, 1995–1996

The studios of Vintage Television, a Manhattan-based network, provide the setting. Duke Stone (Paxton Whitehead) bought the network (for $80 million) "so I could have a few laughs." The network's slogan is "Nothing We Do Is Original" and its first important program was the U.S. rights to the British miniseries *Wuthering Heights*. Duke belongs to the Silver Head Golf Club.

Simon Hemple (Harland Williams) is the program director. He is single and honest and shares a Harlem apartment with his brother Carl (Jason Bateman). Simon watches a great deal of TV and relates old shows to real life. His specialty is bird calls and he believes that the perfect woman is one who likes the Three Stooges. Simon eats gravy as a snack and his favorite eatery is Uncle Sam's Smoking Pit Barbeque Restaurant (where you can get a free meal if you can beat Neal, the chicken who plays tic tac toe).

Simon attended Nassau Community College (it took him five years to graduate) while Carl, a Columbia business graduate (top one-third of his class) is having a difficult time finding work. Carl is straightforward and well educated. He came to live with Simon after his divorce. He first worked as a balloon salesman, then as a hot dog vendor, "Muffin Girl" at Vintage Television and finally vice president of real estate holdings for Duke Stone Enterprises. On his way to work each morning, Simon feeds Earl and Merle, the squirrels in the park.

109.   The Simpsons Fox, 1990–

Homer J. Simpson (voice of Dan Castellaneta), his wife, Marge (Julie Kavner) and their children, Bart (Nancy Cartwright), Lisa (Yeardley Smith) and Baby Maggie, live at 742 Evergreen Terrace in the town of Springfield (founded in 1840s by Jebediah Springfield).

Homer, 34, weighs 239 pounds and works as a safety inspector in Sector 76 of the Springfield Nuclear Power Plant. Moe's Tavern on Walnut Street (where Duff's Beer is served) is his hangout and pork chops are his favorite food. He has A-positive blood and was "Dancin' Homer," the mascot of the Isotopes baseball team. Homer became a celebrity when the TV show *Police Cops* used a character with his name. When the character turned out to be a buffoon, Homer temporarily changed his name to Max Power. In the wintertime, Homer starts a snow-plowing service called Mr. Plow. When he ran out of beer one night, he mixed leftover liquor with cough syrup and created a drink called Flaming Homer. Homer, Apu (the Kwick E-Mart owner), school principal Skinner, Moe the bartender and Police Chief Wiggins (all voiced by Hank Azaria) were in a barbershop quartet called the B-Sharps.

Marge calls Homer "Homey" and has a tattoo with Homer's name "on my you know what." She is 34, wears a size 13AA shoe and has blue hair. *Search for the Sun* is her favorite TV show. In high school she aspired to become an artist (she was discouraged by her teacher and painted only one picture — her idol, Ringo Starr). Marge makes her own Pepsi ("it's a little tricky, though"), has her hair done at Jake's Unisex Hair Salon, and worked as a police officer (assigned to patrol Junktown) to earn extra money. Marge, maiden name Bouvier, met Homer when they were seniors at Springfield High School. One day Homer was caught smoking and sent to Room 106; Marge, protesting for women's rights, was sent to the same room for burning her bra. They fell in love and dated. Several years later Homer was working at the local fun center; Marge was a waitress at Burgers Burgers. They had an affair in the castle in the miniature golf course and Marge became pregnant. They were married shortly after at Shotgun Pete's 24 Hour Chapel.

Bart is a ten-year-old wisecracking brat and "the bad boy of TV." He attends Springfield Elementary School (fourth grade) and spends more time in detention hall and the principal's office than he does in class. He has a pet frog (Froggie), a dog (Santa's Little Helper) and a cat (Snowball). *Radio Active Man* is Bart's favorite comic book and *Krusty the Clown* is his favorite TV show (Krusty is a very nasty clown on whom Bart has based his whole life. Bart has badge number 16302 in the Krusty the Clown Fan Club. Krusty is Jewish and was born Herschel Krustofski). When a movie version of *Radio Active Man* began filming in Springfield, Bart auditioned for the role of Fallout Boy. As kids Bart and Lisa played the board games "Hippo in the House," "The Game of Lent" and "Citizenship." Bart, who has Double O-negative blood, is allergic to butterscotch and is champ at the video game "Slug Fest." Bart delights in playing practical jokes. His catchphrases are "don't have a cow, man" and "my name is Bart Simpson; who the hell are you?" Marge was in labor with Bart for 53 hours; Bart's first love was his neighbor, Laura (Sara Gilbert).

Lisa, the middle child, is in second grade. She is precociously intelligent and a budding saxophone player (the street musician, Bleeding Gums Murphy, is her inspiration). Lisa entered the Little Miss Springfield Beauty Pageant but quit when she discovered the sponsor to be Laramie cigarettes (which is seen on billboards all over town). *The Little Mermaid* is Lisa's favorite movie; *Casper, the Friendly Ghost* her favorite comic book and *The Itchy and Scratchy Show* (a violent cartoon), her favorite TV program. She reads *Teen Screen, Teen Dream* and *Teen Steam* magazines, and wears a size 4B shoe. "The Broken Neck Blues" is her favorite song. She and Bart enjoy eating at Krusty Burger.

Baby Maggie calmly observes life while sucking on her pacifier. Her favorite movie is *The Happy Little Elf.* Marge uses the Lay-Z-Mom Baby Monitor. In the opening theme, Maggie is passed over a supermarket scanner; she costs $847.63.

Homer longed for one thing: for the kids' first word to be "Daddy." He and Marge do not remember Bart's first word, but Bart calls his father "Homer." When Lisa was born, Bart became jealous and did everything he could to get rid of her (for example, mailing her; shoving her through the neighbor's front door mail slot). Despite this, Lisa admired him and "Bart" was her first word. Lisa could say "Mommy" and "David Hasselhoff" but when she saw her father she said "Homer." In the episode of 12/3/92, Maggie speaks for the first time (via Elizabeth Taylor). Homer puts Maggie to bed and leaves the room. Maggie takes the pacifier out of her mouth and says "Daddy."

Homer's friend, Moe the bartender, is a former boxer called Kid Gorgeous (then Kid Good Looking, Kid Presentable and finally Kid Moe. He lost 40 straight fights).

110. The Sinbad Show Fox, 1993–1994

David Bryan (Sinbad) and Clarence Hall (T. K. Carter) are 35-year-old friends who have known each other since grade school (where they won a talent show award for Best Singing Duo). David, the owner of his own computer graphics design company, later becomes "Dr. Freaky Deaky," the host of *It's Science Time*, a TV science show for kids. Clarence works as a clothing salesman for Ed's Big and Tall Men's Store and his favorite TV program is *The Buddy Show* (about a kid-loving dinosaur; "When they canceled *Captain Kangaroo*, Buddy was there for me"). David, who believes the movie character "Superfly" is real, has two goldfish (Ike and Tina) and a car he calls Sheba (plate 300 ZX). He and Clarence (who lives upstairs in an unnamed locale) hang out at a bar called Jamaica's.

Their lives change when David, a volunteer at the local orphanage, adopts Zana and L. J. Beckwith (Erin Davis, Willie Norwood), a sister and brother who were about to be sent to different foster homes. Zana has an invisible friend named Bobby and L.J. is Little John — "He was little and his name was John." Their favorite TV program is *The Buddy Show*.

111. Sister, Sister ABC, 1994–1995; WB, 1995–1999

Tia Landry (Tia Mowry) and Tamera Campbell (Tamera Mowry) are twins who were separated at birth and adopted by different parents — Tia by Lisa Landry (Jackee Harry); Tamera by Ray Campbell (Tim Reid). Fourteen years later, the girls meet by chance while shopping at Fashion Fantasy. Realizing the girls want to be together, Ray and Lisa come to an agreement: she and Tia will move in with Ray (243 Maple Drive in Michigan) and share expenses (Lisa originally paid Ray $350 a month in rent).

Tia, the smarter twin, and Tamera, the creative one, attend Roosevelt High School and later Michigan State University. Tamera won Roosevelt's first "Golden Casey Award" (for singing in a talent contest when the school dedicated its gym to its most famous alumni, Casey Kasem). She is the star pitcher for the school's baseball team, the Tigers, and is easily upset if someone brings up the name Lulu (her dog, who ran away from home when she was a child). Tia's favorite plush animal is Mr. Froggy and when she gets angry, she applies nail polish to her toenails. "Sometimes," Lisa says, "she uses so much that we have to use paint thinner to get it off." Tia and Tamera first worked for Ray's Limo Service then as counter girls at Rocket Burger. Tia later worked at Book 'Em Joe, a coffee/bookshop in the mall; and Tamera was "Lady J.," the host of a listener call-in advice program on her college radio station (WTSE). Tia scored 1560 on the SAT's; Tamera, 1080. The college hangout is an eatery called the Cellar.

Tia, the only kid in kindergarten who knew her ABCs backwards, sees college as a place to learn and work. Tamera sees college as a place to have fun with learning second. In their freshman-year college talent show, Tia and Tamera appeared as the singing group, the Simones.

Artist Rachelle Gavin was revealed as being Tia and Tamera's birth mother. She had been living with a globe-trotting photographer (Max Sullivan) and died during childbirth. Max, away when the twins were born, returned to Florida to find that the twins had already been adopted.

Ray attended Mumford High School and owns Campbell's Limousine Service (also called Ray's Limos and Ray Campbell's Limo Service). He ran for State Senator (5th District) but lost by a small margin. Ray has a classic white limo ("the clunker nobody wanted") he calls "Moby Dick."

Lisa attended Ford High School and is now a fashion designer with her own cart business, Fashions by Lisa, at the Northland Mall (she replaced the late Balloon Bob, the Balloon Man). Her cart is ten feet from a clothing store called Mostly Michigan. Before setting up operations in her home, Lisa was a salesgirl at the Fashion Boutique (also called Monique's). Lisa has a nasty dog named Sweetness (Ray calls him Cujo) and is a member of the Black Professional Women's Club of Detroit.

112. **Small Wonder** Syn., 1985–1989

Voice Input Child Identicate, Vicki for short (Tiffany Brissette), is a female robot created by Ted Lawson (Dick Christie), a robotics engineer for United Robotronics. Ted is married to Joanie (Marla Pennington), and is the father of 11-year-old Jamie (Jerry Supiran). Vicki, part of a secret experiment to help handicapped children, poses as Ted's adopted ten-year-old daughter and is learning how to become a real girl. They live at 16 Maple Drive in Los Angeles; 555-6606 is their phone number.

Vicki is made of highly advanced, flexible plastic; transistors; and microchips. She generates FM radio waves and can create her own electricity (via a 440 volt microgenerator). The Waffle Scale Integration System gives her life and the ML 5000 chip provides her logic (located in her control box on her back). Vicki, most always attired in a red and white dress, has a built-in tape recorder (acts like an answering machine). The command "stop" turns her off. She takes everything people say literally and once she starts something she is programmed to complete it. "It's not in my memory bank" is Vicki's response when she is told to do something she doesn't understand. She has incredible strength and her brown eyes are solar cells that provide power.

Joanie likes Vicki so much that she forgets she is not human ("I love every microchip in her body") and gets highly emotional when something happens to her. Joanie was originally a salesgirl at the Clothing Boutique; she is later a teacher at Grant Junior High School — the school Vicki and Jamie attend (originally called Washington Junior High). Joanie has dinner ready at 6:30 P.M. (she calls leftovers "reruns"). When something strikes her as funny she says, "that's nice." As a kid Joanie had a canary named Tweet Tweet. Vicki sleeps standing up (in "Vicki's Closet") in Jamie's room. Jamie, a member of the Fearless Five Club, receives an allowance of three dollars a week. He calls himself "the Big J" and chili dogs are his favorite food.

Harriet Brindle (Emily Schulman) is the spoiled brat (as she calls herself) who lives next door. She has a crush on Jamie and suspicions about Vicki. Harriet has a "store bought" robot (Rodney), two parrots (Polly and Waldo), a turtle (Beatie) and a doll (Baby Puddles). Harriet throws tantrums to get what she wants and believes she is "the most beautiful girl in the world."

While Jamie has problems with Harriet, Joanie has her share of headaches with Harriet's mother, Bonnie (Edie McClurg); a woman who makes it her business to know everyone else's business. Bonnie was voted "Miss Lettuce Head of the San Joaquin Valley" and greets people with "hi-yeeee." Bonnie is a member of the Gutter Gals bowling team and annoys Joanie the most with her catchphrase "no, no, no-no-no-no."

As the series progressed, Vicki was passed off as Ted's sister's daughter; Joanie's brother's daughter; Jamie's cousin; and finally Vicki Ann Smith, an orphan adopted by Ted and Joanie.

113. Smart Guy WB, 1998–1999

T. J. Henderson (Tahj Mowry) is the "Smart Guy" of the title. He is 12 years old, has an I.Q. of 180 and attends Piedmont High School in Washington, D.C. T.J. is allergic to shellfish, receives a weekly allowance of $10, and likes high school "but getting high school to like him is the problem." When he hangs out with his older brother, Marcus (Jason Weaver), T.J. is cool; when he is not with him, he is "a 12-year-old brainiac stick-in-the-mud." T.J. could grow up to be a teacher but won't — "It pays jack," he says. T.J.'s favorite eatery (the afterschool hangout) is Dawgburger. When the school vending machine raised the price of its Colonel Bubble soda to $1.10 a can, T.J. started his own company, Admiral T.J. Soda at 40 cents a can — "The affordable soda for kids." T.J. is equipment manager of the school's basketball team; reads *Sister Girl* magazine; and appeared in a Destiny's Child music video.

Marcus is not as smart as T.J. and yearns to be a musician (he is a fan of blues music, writes his own songs and plays keyboards). His method of doing a book report is to rent the video and write the report based on the movie version. He is on the basketball team but spends more time on the bench than he does on the court. He held a job as an early morning (1:30 A.M. to 3:30 A.M.) host on the all-talk, weak-signal radio station WADQ; when he goes online, he visits the Pippi Longstocking web site.

T.J.'s father, Floyd (John Marshall Jones) is a widower who runs the Henderson Construction Company ("Everything you need under one roof"). He watches *The Cajun Chef* on TV each night before going to bed (9 P.M.).

Yvette (Essence Atkins) is T.J.'s sister, a junior at Piedmont High. She is a member of the student council; a writer for the school newspaper, the *Piedmont Times*; and bright. She is also very attractive but feels she has one shortcoming — "my small bustline." She eats Pringles potato chips and had a job as a salesgirl at Stylo Wear, a clothing store in the mall. Had the series been renewed, Yvette would have attended Georgetown University (she also applied to her dream school, Princeton, but was not accepted).

114.   **Someone Like Me** NBC, 1994

Gabrielle "Gaby" Stepjak (Gaby Hoffman) is a very pretty 12-year-old bundle of energy. She is president of her sixth grade class at the Walter Mondale Middle School in Parkwood, St. Louis, and resides with her mother, Jean (Patricia Heaton); father, Steven (Anthony Tyler Quinn); sister, Samantha (Nikki Cox); and brother, Evan (Joseph Tello), at 1402 Manton Drive.

Gaby practices kissing on her hand and is a member of the swim team at the local hangout, the Park Recreation Center. Gaby feels that the worst punishment she can get is no phone privileges ("it's barbaric"). As a kid Gaby would cut the hair off her Barbie dolls (thinking it would grow back) and when she does something wrong, her mother gives her "the anybody can become President speech."

Samantha, called "Sam," is a 16-year-old girl who knows she is beautiful. She can have any guy she wants — yet she dates "losers," as Steve calls them. To get Gaby to do something for her, Samantha bribes her with clothes. Jean won't let Sam go to the local skating rink (Skateland) because "drug addicts hang out there." Each morning before school, Samantha takes inventory —"lipstick, eyeliner, scrungie, brush, Walkman." She always forgets one thing — books. Sam feels she has only one job to perform around the house —"to brighten Gaby's day."

Gaby's best friend is Jane Schmidt (Raegan Kotz). She wears bubble gum-flavored lip gloss and feels her and Gaby's goal in life is to be beautiful. Although Samantha considers Jane to be a bother, Jane admires Samantha for her breasts ("I hope to get breasts that great, too"). When she visits Gaby, Jane tries to sneak a beer out of the refrigerator and when Jane uses a bad word, Gaby fears Jane's mother will think Jane learned it from her. Jane's house is rather untidy and when her birthday rolls around, Jane's mother "takes me behind the Texaco station to feed corn to the deer." No matter what the school play is, Jane is always cast as the kitchen maid. "I want the lead just once," she cries.

Jean is a travel agent for the Four Corners Travel Agency. She attended Eleanor Roosevelt High School and was the junior class treasurer. She is a neat freak and says, "I'm always there for people. That's why people like me." When she gets stressed out, she cleans; when she and Sam feel sad, they pamper each other.

As a kid Steven played with Matchbox cars and was called "Matchbox Loner." He is an optician at the mall. Every Sunday morning he and Gaby watch *House of Style with Cyndi Crawford* (they mute the sound and make rude noises).

115.   Step by Step ABC, 1991–1997; CBS, 1997–1998

Carol Foster (Suzanne Somers) is a widow with three children, Dana (Staci Keanan), Karen (Angela Watson) and Mark (Christopher Castile). Franklin "Frank" Delano Lambert (Patrick Duffy) is a divorced father with three children, Alicia, nicknamed "Al" (Christine Lakin), J.T. (Brandon Call) and Brendon (Josh Byrne). Frank met Carol, they fell in love, married (at the Wedding Shack in Jamaica) and set up housekeeping at 201 Winslow Street in Port Washington, Wisconsin (population 9,338).

Carol, a beautician, operates Carol's Beauty Boutique from her home. She is neat (for example, she alphabetizes soup cans; irons Karen and Dana's lingerie) and tries to run the house on a schedule. Breakfast is ready at 7:30 A.M., dinner at 6:30 P.M. Carol has a tattoo on her behind that reads "Wolfie" (after Wolfgang Reinhart, a foreign exchange student she dated in college) and mentions Baker as her maiden name; later it's Williams. In her youth, Carol sang with a band, and in 1971 won first runner-up in the Miss Small Curd Cottage Cheese Beauty Pageant ("I lost to a girl with bigger curds"). Carol hates to be called a nag by Frank and her biggest disappointment in life was losing out as head cheerleader for the Wildcats at Port Washington High to "Becky Ann Frasier, that tramp."

Frank, an independent contractor, owns the Lambert Construction Company. He is a member of the Mallard Lodge and has a GMC pickup truck (license plate 129-815; later 527 P9) that he polishes with Royal Carnuba Wax ($15 a can at Auto World). The simplest things about Carol impress Frank (for example, "She reads books — not just paperbacks but hardbacks"), and when it comes to explaining aspects of life to the kids, Frank uses a construction site story (Carol uses a beauty parlor story). When Frank's lodge held a beauty contest, Carol and Karen entered the Mrs. Mom and Miss Mallard Pageant and won with a tap dancing act. Frank attended Port Washington High; was a member of the Sheboygan Super Bears team; and president of the Milwaukee Tile and Grout Association. His wife ran off to become a lounge singer in Las Vegas; and, according to Carol, Frank and his kids are "slobs." Frank coaches the Cubs, a Little League team, and hates to be called a liar by Carol.

Dana, Carol's eldest daughter, is a straight A student, always impeccably dressed and sensitive to the fact that she has small breasts (as Alicia puts it — "You're smart and it's a good thing because you have no boobs"). She shares a bedroom with Karen and Alicia and attended Lincoln Elementary School (an honors student), Port Washington High (writer for the newspaper, the *Wildcatter*) and East Wisconsin University (nicknamed Cheese Whiz U.). Dana is hoping to become a lawyer and got her only D on a paper for "using big words with no meaning." Dana's favorite food is salmon (since she was two years old). She was born on 1/15/76 at 10:47 P.M. Carol keeps a "Dana Book," a photo record of Dana's life — her first tooth, first step, and even first kiss (Carol just happened to be in a tree with an infrared camera and zoom lens). When it was time for a bath, Carol called Dana "Princess Bubble Buns" (J.T. calls Dana "Barkey, the Undateable"). Dana worked as the assistant manager of the 50's Cafe and does volunteer work at the Tri County Mission.

At 14 Karen knows she is beautiful ("I'm what the guys call a babe"). She attended the same grammar and high schools as Karen and is often mistaken for a model ("I just look like one, but I'm not). Karen is very concerned about her appearance, especially her makeup ("A mirror is my best friend"). Carol believes her obsession started the day she gave Karen a Brooke

Shields doll. Alicia believes Karen is a "wuss" because everything frightens her. Karen reads *Chic* and *Cosmopolitan* and was a teen model at Peterson's Department Store. She can't resist a sale at the mall; if she is even five minutes late, she feels there are people buying things she should have. Before each date Karen listens to the tape "Teenage Dating Tips." Her car's license plate is TNA 5H1. As a kid Karen had a favorite washcloth with a mouse on it she called Mouthy (Carol called it Mousey, but Karen pronounced it as Mouthy). At Port Washington High, Karen is a cheerleader for the Wildcats football team. Cherry Cha Cha is her favorite shade of lipstick.

Alicia, a very pretty tomboy, attended Miss Daisy's Ducky Room Preschool; later she attended Port Washington High. She always fears the worst in a situation and has a rattlesnake's head preserved in a jar; she also has a pet pig named Bullet. Alicia is a catcher for the Beavers Little League team and a smart aleck (Dana thinks she needs an attitude adjustment and calls her "you little criminal"). Alicia is the "son" Frank wishes he had (although she shows great potential for construction, "Lambert and Daughter Construction" is a dream Frank feels will never come true). Alicia's study habits upset Dana (she rents movies from Dave's Video Store to do book reports), and she played drums in an all-girl rock band called Chicks with Attitudes (their first gig was at Greco's Bowl-a-Rama). Alicia's first job was as a waitress at Mr. Chips, the cookie store in the mall. She next worked as the waitress Peggy Sue at the 50's Cafe. Alicia is a hopeful actress and starred as Lola Fontaine in the Community Playhouse production of "Death of a Salesman." She also did a print ad for Stop Jeans and when she met Carol for the first time she called her a "bimbo" (she was also disappointed that Frank returned from his honeymoon without bringing her a shrunken head).

John Thomas, called J.T., attends Port Washington High and is a member of the track team. He is a walking disaster and has no flair for the construction business; he works on occasion as Carol's shampoo boy in the salon. His favorite meal is burritos and the Burger Palace is his after school hangout. He fancies himself a ladies' man; Dana sees him as "a pea-brained idiot." He worked at the 50's Cafe as a waiter named Cubby. Mark Archibald, who attended Canyon Elementary then Port Washington High, is the brains of the family. He has a working model of the human intestine in his bedroom and a sexy female-voiced computer named Charlene. His worst day occurred when he was given only an A on a math test (he is an A+ student).

Brendon hangs out with Mark at the Burger Barn. Brendon, the shy one, loves double-stuffed Oreos and spaghetti and meatballs. In the 1995 season finale, Carol gave birth to a girl she and Frank named Lily Foster-Lambert. When the series returned for a new season, Brendon was dropped (like he was never there) and Lily advanced to the age of five, giving the Lamberts six children, not seven (Lily, played by Emily Mae Young, had a plush rabbit named Mr. Buttons).

Cody Lambert (Sasha Mitchell), Frank's nephew, works in demolition and lives in a van (Lucille) parked in the driveway. He believes he "is the coolest guy on the planet" ("No chick can resist my personal magnetism"; Dana believes he is "a brain-dead idiot"). Cody believes Dana is a "hot babe" ("If she were a prehistoric creature, she'd be a Babertooth Tiger") and calls her "Dana Burger" (he calls Karen "Care Bear"). Cody reads *Biker's Quarterly* magazine and wears a leather jacket. His hero is Ed, the attendant at the Texaco station. Cody and J.T. had a cable access program called *J.T. and Cody's World* and Cody started an exercise club for "major babes" (women over 70) called "Body by Cody." Cody, called "the Codeman" by J.T., attended the University of Wisconsin and was a member of the Delta Delta Beta Fraternity. He had a houseplant (Gordon) and was suddenly written out of the series with no explanation — until the episode of 6/19/98 when he returned to tell everyone that he left on a spiritual quest to find the ultimate hamburger (which he found at a McDonald's in Tibet).

116. Suddenly Susan NBC, 1996–2000

The Gate is a trendy San Francisco magazine owned by Jack Richmond (Judd Nelson). Susan Keane (Brooke Shields), Vickie Groener (Kathy Griffin), Luis Rivera (Nestor Carbonell) and Todd Stites (David Strickland) are employees.

Susan writes the column "Suddenly Susan" ("It's about life and what happens to me"). She attended Hillcrest High School and lives at 3135 Washington Street. Her phone number is 555-4858. Lemon peel chicken is her favorite dinner and tequila her favorite drink. Susan is tall, slim and gorgeous; but in junior high, "I was a pie-loving kid who was overweight." Susan has a bright outlook about everything and thinks she is adorable. "Yea," Jack says, "like a giant Olsen twin." Susan feels bad things happen when she lies. Her family refers to her near-marriage to Jack's brother (Kip) as "Black Saturday." Susan enjoys dinner at Chan's Restaurant and hangs out with the gang at Bucky's Tavern (later O'Malley's Bar then McMurphy's Bar). Susan has a dog (at her mother's home) named Duchess. Susan's birth weight was 10 pounds, 4 ounces (her mother was in labor for 23 hours). "I'm keen on Keane" was the slogan Susan used when she ran for (but lost) a seat on the San Francisco Board of Supervisors. Susan's favorite TV show is *Charlie's Angels* (reruns) and when she was ten years old she went on a hunger strike when Sizzler discontinued the rib sandwich. Susan hates to have her picture taken — "I always look like I'm just reentering Earth." Vickie says, "Susan's pretty in person, nasty on film."

Vickie, the food critic, also writes about the hip scene and calls herself "The Empress of Hip." "I'm not as beautiful as Susan," she says, "but I'm cute and spunky." *Felicity* is Vickie's favorite TV show and sweet and sour shrimp her favorite meal. Vickie is a member of the Vixens (jersey 1), an all-girl basketball team whose outfits are red. (Susan, jersey 31, also played on the team.) Vickie enjoys other people's misery, feels she is a man magnet but says, "I'm a tramp at heart." She has a fake handicap parking permit and when she gets depressed over a man "I need pizza, booze and male strippers to get me over it."

As a kid Jack's favorite TV shows were *Police Woman, Wonder Woman* and *The Bionic Woman*. He has a rock-climbing wall behind his desk and a coffee mug that reads "Big Dog." Jack, a member of the Kingpins bowling team, bowls at Echo Lanes. On Fridays he plays squash. On weekends he climbs mountains, sky dives and races cars ("It makes me uninsurable but alive"). His all-time favorite movie is *The Day the Earth Stood Still*.

Todd is the magazine's music critic. He attends baseball games hoping to fulfill a dream — catch a foul ball (before attending each game he performs "the Foul Ball Dance"). Kids call him "Todd the God" because he sets up free video games for them at the arcade. Todd once gave a bad review to the Grateful Dead and is now tormented by Grateful Dead fanatics who complain about him having a steady job, no tattoos and short hair. He attends pottery classes (with Luis) at Color My World. He and Luis, the magazine's photographer, pooled their resources and invested $17,000 in Lemon Legs, a business dealing in yellow bell-bottom pants for women.

Maddie Piper (Andrea Bendewald) is the snobbish new columnist who is disliked by all (except Susan, who is trying to like her). Vickie feels Maddie should have been one of the Spice Girls — "Bitchy Spice" — and calls her "Little Blondie Pants"; Todd calls her "Mad-a-lad A ding-ding." Maddie thinks Luis is a "macho idiot" and Todd "just a plain idiot." Maddie attended the same high school as Susan and constantly teased her with practical jokes. Susan considers these incidents "Silence of the Lambs with a Hall Pass." Susan fantasized about getting back at her: "Like messing with her car or putting her in a wood chipper."

Ian Graham (Eric Idle) purchases the magazine from Jack at the start of the fourth season (9/20/99). He moved the editorial offices from a swank uptown building to a less desirable location in Chinatown. Maddie quit at this point and moved to New York when Ian talked down to her. Ian is a magazine publisher who felt the *Gate* was a rag, but it had a name, the circulation and the staff that he needed to change its focus to men's issues. Oliver Brown (Rob Estes) was hired by Ian to shoot the magazine's covers (gorgeous girls). Oliver cured Susan of her photo fears by shooting a sexy

pose that Ian used on billboards to announce the new magazine ("The Gate —
Now Open").

117.   **Third Rock from the Sun** NBC, 1996–

Aliens from an unnamed planet land near the Sweeny farm in Rutherford, Ohio. The aliens take on human form and find a home at 417 Pens-
dale Drive. Their assignment is to study life on Earth. Dick Solomon (John
Lithgow) is the Commander; Sally (Kristen Johnston) becomes his sister;
Harry (French Stewart), his brother; and Tommy (Joseph Gordon-Levitt),
his son. Dick is a widower "because my wife burned up on re-entry." He
teaches quantum physics at Pendleton University. He occupies office 109 in
Hunt Hall and has become romantically involved with Dr. Mary Albright
(Jane Curtin), a professor of anthropology, who is drawn to genius. In her
youth, Mary posed nude for black and white photos in an art class; she and
Dick frequent Balaska's Bar for a drink.

Dick prepares the daily status reports in limerick form for their superior, the Big Giant Head. When Dick needed a second job, he became a
counter clerk at Rusty Burger. His red Rambler license plate reads DLW 457.
After several years on Earth, Dick feels heat, electricity and cooked meats
have made him weak.

Sally Solomon, the security officer, is the woman "because I lost" (she
is a male on their home planet). She is a lieutenant and her assignment is to
report on the female human. She calls her breasts "the girls," has a superior
brain, and the ability to digest glass, "but I can't adjust to the mood swings."
When Sally finally adjusted to her body, she thought others needed to see it
and volunteered to pose for *Playboy* magazine's "Co-Eds of the Midwest"
issue ("but I was rejected for being too old"). Sally is dating police officer
Don Leslie Orville (Wayne Knight) and started a business called "Sally's
Actual Salon — A Real Business" as a tax dodge (Harry worked there as "Mr.
Harry"). Sally manipulates Don and Don knows it: "She plays me like a big
dumb cello." When Don developed an interest in sports, he had a crush on
Joe Namath ("It's something I'm not proud of," he says). Don, Tommy and
Harry bowl on a team called the Three Amigos.

Harry Solomon is the Transmitter (receives messages from the Big Giant
Head). He worked as a bartender at McSorley's, but also held a position as
Hargo the Alien at the LePine County Fair. On his home planet, Harry had
a pet, a lower life form named Pickles.

Tommy, the information officer, has been assigned as the teenager to
study Earth's culture. He attends Rutherford High School, is editor of the
school newspaper, the *Zephyr*, and is required to be a model student. He

briefly attended the Picnee County Day School for the Gifted when his intellect made him an above average student.

Although talked about, the Big Giant Head was seen only once (played by William Shatner). He posed as TV journalist Stone Phillips, wore an "I Love N.J." baseball cap and fell in love with Earth life while visiting the Solomons. His one obsession was liquor — which he often misused and thus complicated life for the Solomons.

118.   Thunder Alley ABC, 1994–1995

Gil Jones (Ed Asner), a former stock car racer, owns the Thunder Alley Garage in Indiana. He was a Trans Am stock car champion (1977, '78 and '79), recipient of the NASCAR Life Achievement Award and called "Wild" Gil Jones during his racing career. Patti Page is his favorite singer and his car, which he keeps in the garage, has number 11 on it. Also living with Gil is his daughter, Roberta Ann "Bobbi" Turner (Diane Venora, Robin Riker) and her children, Jenny (Lindsay Felton), Claudine (Kelly Vint) and Harry (Haley Joel Osmert).

Bobbi left home at age 16 to marry and has now moved back following her divorce; she works as Gil's bookkeeper. Bobbi attended Ben Davis High School and had 19 jobs in five years ("But I didn't get fired — I quit. Family takes preference over work"). To help out with expenses, Bobbi took a temporary job as salesgirl at Foto Zip.

Claudine, age 12, is fashion conscious, reads *Teen World* magazine and is embarrassed to be living over the garage. She is fast becoming a beautiful young girl, but feels out of place and is eager to fit in. Jenny, age seven, is a pretty tomboy and member of the Park League Bloodsucking Blue Birds Basketball Team. Like Bobbi, Jenny is a fighter (Bobbi was "the skinny, runt kid in the neighborhood." Gil taught her to stand up for herself and she has been a fighter ever since). Harry, age five, has a dog named Daisy (whom Gil calls Fido). His favorite board game is "Candy Land" (because Bobbi lets him cheat and he always wins). Harry has an imaginary friend named Chester. He and his sisters enjoy pizza at Peter Pepperoni's Cheese Castle. When Harry feels like annoying Claudine, he pretends to be "Buzzard Boy."

119.   The Torkelsons NBC, 1991–1992

Millicent Torkelson (Connie Ray) is the divorced mother of five children: Dorothy Jane (Olivia Burnette), Ruth Ann (Anna Slotky), Mary Sue (Rachel Duncan), Steven Floyd (Aaron Michael Metchik) and Chuckie Lee (Lee Norris). She lives in a house (number 855) off Farm Route Two in

Pyramid Corners, Oklahoma, and has a dog named Fred. The family attends services at the Pyramid Corners Community Church.

Millicent, an attractive woman who devotes all her energies to raising her children, has not dated since her ex-husband (Randall) walked out on her. She runs a small business from her home (Millicent Torkelson — Custom Upholstery and Design) and hates the term "store bought" (she makes what she can at home). Each autumn Millicent operates a small roadside stand where, for a dollar, one can buy homemade jams, jellies, and her famous pickled vegetables. Millicent, whose maiden name is Dowd, attended Will Rogers Junior High School and Pyramid Corners High.

Dorothy Jane, 14, longs "for a life of poetry, romance and beauty." She believes her family is weird and is convinced she was switched at birth and that her real family lives in Palm Springs. Dorothy Jane attends Pyramid Corners High School and is the only girl in her class who wears clothes that were once something else (her dresses, for example, were once curtains). When she feels the world is against her, Dorothy Jane retreats to the sanctuary of her bedroom where she confides her dreams, joys, sorrows and ambitions to the Man in the Moon. She is very pretty but shy, and desperately wants to become an adult. When she felt she had to change her wholesome image, she discarded her intellectual side and pretended to be a ditz. She dyed her brown hair "Playful Minx Blonde" and become "Dottie," a teenage bombshell. She soon went back to her old self "because it felt goofy being someone else." Dorothy Jane played Juliet in her high school production of *Romeo and Juliet*. Her most embarrassing moment occurred when the boy next door saw her in a towel before she took a shower.

Ruth Ann attends Will Rogers Junior High and plays French horn in the school band. She believes she is beauty-pageant material ("I've got legs that go on forever") and entered the Junior Miss Oklahoma Pageant. Mary Sue, the youngest (age six) has two dolls: Martha Sue and Elmo (the *Sesame Street* muppet). Millicent calls Mary Sue "Pumpkin." Mary Sue's favorite sandwich is bologna. Chuckie Lee likes to hang out with the school custodian; Mary Sue enjoys petting the hamsters at Crawford's Pet Shop. Dorothy Jane and Steven Floyd enjoy ice cream and hamburgers at the Frostee King.

Also living with the Torkelsons (renting a basement room for $125 a month) is Wesley Hodges (William Schallert), a retired salesman affectionately called "Boarder Hodges." See also *Almost Home*, the spinoff series.

120. Two Guys, a Girl and a Pizza Place ABC, 1998–

Pete Dunville and Michael "Berg" Bergen (Richard Ruccolo, Ryan Reynolds) are the guys; Sharon Carter (Traylor Howard), the girl; and Beacon Street Pizza (at 228 Beacon Street in Boston), the pizza place (where Pete and Berg work). Pete, Sharon and Berg are friends who attended Cambridge High School.

Pete, an architect student, and Berg, a medical student at Boston University, share Apartment A. Sharon is a salesgirl for the Immaculate Chemicals Company. Pete was a sportscaster on the college radio station (WMFO, 91.5 FM) and also held jobs as a limo driver, and as a career counselor at the Boston Metro Employment Agency. Berg's middle name is Leslie (he tells people it's not a girl's name, "it's European") and his school I.D. number is 9201. He is afraid of moths, cries when he sees the film *Bambi* and interns at Boston Memorial Hospital. Sharon was born in Brookville (Boston) and in tenth grade was president of the chess club. She wears a size nine shoe, is an untidy housekeeper and fears someone will see her grammar school yearbook picture (when she was chubby, wore braces and had a big nose).

Beacon Street Pizza serves 10-, 16-, and 20-inch pizzas. Tessio's Pizza is its competition. Sharon, Berg and Pete frequent Mahoney's Bar; the series was later titled *Two Guys and a Girl*.

121. Two of a Kind ABC, 1998–1999

Mary Kate and Ashley Burke (Mary Kate and Ashley Olsen) are pretty, identical 12-year-old twins who live at 238 Belmont Avenue in Chicago with their widowed father, Kevin (Christopher Sieber), a science professor at Chicago University. Ashley and Mary Kate are not only sisters, but "we're best friends." Ashley is glamorous and fashion conscious; Mary Kate is a tomboy. Ashley has aspirations to be a model; standing in front of a mirror and acting like a supermodel is her favorite activity ("I've been doing it since I could stand"). When Mary Kate is trying to fall asleep at night, Ashley keeps her awake by talking about clothes. When Ashley needs to wear something grubby, she borrows one of Mary Kate's shirts. Ashley's favorite color is green and double fudge crunch bars are her favorite snack. At school (unnamed) Ashley has mirrors and makeup in her locker and wishes she had an electrical outlet for her curling iron. She attends dance classes and "going to the mall to spend Dad's money" cheers her up when she is depressed.

"People think of me as a tomboy, but I'm a girl too and like to do girl things, too," says Mary Kate when she sees Ashley go "ga ga" over boys. Mary Kate is untidy, likes camping and sports and is slowly becoming interested in the opposite sex. She has a pet pigeon (Harriet) and was chosen over Ashley (for her natural look) for a fashion layout in *Real Teen* magazine. Mary Kate is not as smart as Ashley. Every Thursday she and Ashley share a pizza at Pepperoni Joe's. The girls are in seventh grade, buy their CDs at Mega Records and are in bed by 9 P.M.

Kevin's late wife, Janice, died when the girls were in the third grade. Kevin frequents the campus eatery, the Coffee Bar, and likes "girls with great legs." He has a bad habit of denying a problem exists so he doesn't have to deal with it. Helping Kevin care for the girls is Carrie Moore (Sally Wheeler), a student of Kevin's who works part time as his nanny. Carrie, 26, has reentered college after dropping out (she was in her second year when she quit to become a blackjack dealer in Las Vegas). Carrie does "girlie stuff with Ashley and the cool stuff with Mary Kate." When Carrie senses tension between two people she feels she has to remedy the situation. If the twins confide something in Carrie, she keeps it between them and will not tell Kevin. Carrie likes mint chocolate chip ice cream and is attracted to men with strong chins—"Like George Clooney. I see a man with a strong chin and I melt." A Burke family tradition is to buy their Christmas tree at Ho Ho Harry's.

122.   Uncle Buck CBS, 1990–1991

Buck Russell (Kevin Meaney) is a man who solves family problems quite by accident. He is the guardian of his late brother's children (Tia, Maizy and Miller) and rather insensitive, uncouth and ill-mannered. Buck drives a beat-up, muffler-smoking sedan (plate 521-214) and hangs out at Rafe's Place ("Pool, Food and Friendship"). He is a Chicago Cubs fan and did the guest announcing at Wrigley Field on the TV show *Call an Inning with Harry*. Buck is skilled in the art of scams (a talent learned by cutting classes and hanging out with con artist Peter O'Halahan), and was expelled from high school for planting cherry bombs in the bathrooms. Each year Buck embarks on a fishing trip to Wisconsin, where he stays in Room 13 of the Stark Weather Lodge.

Tia Russell (Dah-ve Chodan), 16, has a fake I.D. (saying she is 21), dates older guys "and dresses too damn sexy" to suit Buck. She attends Monroe High School, receives an allowance of ten dollars a week, and drinks Minute Maid orange juice. Tia held a job as a salesgirl at the French Collection, a boutique in the mall, and wants to become a model (she feels she has the technical skills already: "I can walk and wear lip gloss at the same time").

Maizy Russell (Sarah Martineck) is an adorable seven-year-old girl with a smart mouth. She attends the Livingston Avenue Grammar School and receives an allowance of "50 or 60 cents a week" (Buck isn't quite sure). Maizy was a Blue Bell in the Girl Scouts, and later a Tulip. She is a member of the girls' basketball team, the Pigtails (jersey 11), and wants to be a doctor when she grows up. Maizy has a *Jetsons: The Movie* poster on her bedroom wall and is called "Maze" by her Uncle Buck (Tia calls her "Sprout"). Maizy and Tia are very close: Maizy is the only person to whom Tia can't lie.

Miles Russell (Jacob Gelman) is ten years old and attends the same school as Maizy. He is a smart aleck and always in trouble. Miles receives an allowance of a dollar a week (although Buck is not sure: "It's easier to give the kid a buck and shut him up"). He has ambitions to become manager of the Chicago Cubs when he grows up. He and Maizy eat Kellogg's Corn Flakes for breakfast. Maizy calls Miles "Wuss"; because of a birthmark on her behind, Miles calls Maizy "Freckle Butt." The series is based on the film *Uncle Buck*.

123.   Unhappily Ever After WB, 1995–1999

Jack and Jennie Malloy (Geoff Pierson, Stephanie Hodge) and their children, Tiffany (Nikki Cox), Ryan (Kevin Connolly) and Ross (Justin Berfield), reside at 30220 Oak Avenue in Van Nuys, California. Jack and Jennie married young; they separated for a short time after 16 years of marriage and are now back together again (although Jack lives in the basement).

Jack, who makes $40,000 a year, works as a salesman at Joe's Used Cars (a lot owned by Jennie's father). He is not very fond of the kids — except for Tiffany — and calls them "the accident, the girl and the mistake." Jack loves basketball and young, busty women, and fears the fact that he is getting older. When Jack first moved out (and into a dingy apartment, number 13), Ross gave him a companion, his plush rabbit, Mr. Floppy, who came to life for Jack as his later ego "to help guide his miserable life." Mr. Floppy (voice of Bobcat Goldthwait) has a crush on Drew Barrymore and constantly urges her to come on the show ("Drew, if you're watching…"). He and Jack watch Spanish TV "for the girls in bikinis and high heels" and talk most often about women's breasts and supermodels. Mr. Floppy makes Jack his favorite snack, onion dip, and appears to have had numerous affairs with a Barbie doll takeoff named Berbie in "the toy box." Mr. Floppy gave Grover (of *Sesame Street*) his big break (during his audition, Grover began to stutter; Floppy stuck Grover's finger in an electrical outlet, turned him blue and "cured" him of his affliction). The one doll Mr. Floppy still longs for (but could never get) is Luscious Locks Loni. Mr. Floppy becomes lifeless when anyone else is with Jack, and once mentioned that his father was Yogi Bear — but he was a big star at the time and couldn't be saddled with a kid — "so he tossed me into the toy bin."

As a kid Jennie had a dog (Buttons) and a cat (Snuffles). She now has three dogs (Jasper, Emily and Annie), an unseen cat (Kitty) and a beloved glass-top living room table (Sheila). At dinner Jennie separates her food into three separate dishes "so I can have three distinct flavors." On the Internet, Jennie uses the name Vickie Vixen; 2M FE 967 is her car license plate and Slattery her maiden name. As the series progressed, Jennie appeared less and less. She is absent from many episodes (only referred to) and in 1998 left Jack for good when she ran off out of the blue with her lesbian lover (although Jack claims she was abducted by aliens). Prior to this, Jennie was written out via a terrible accident: while tanning herself at Guy Macaroni's House of Tanning, Jennie drank, fell asleep on the table and was "turned into beef jerky remnants." She returned as a ghost to help guide her family. When the storyline change didn't work, Jennie was back as her old self and the tanning salon incident was explained as just "the writer's mistake." Jennie's one regret in high school was that she never played Juliet in *Romeo and Juliet* (she lost the role "to fellow classmate Charlene Tilton").

Tiffany, 16, is a beautiful redhead whose wardrobe consists primarily of miniskirts, low-cut blouses and tight jeans. She is proud of the fact that she is voluptuous and has built her life around her physical beauty. She hopes to one day own a Corvette "because I look this gorgeous and have to have a flashy car to put me in." She wants to "marry an old geezer who's loaded and has only a month to live." To weigh herself makes her happy; but in 1995, she cried, "oh help me, help me, I'm deformed" when she got her first (and only) zit. Tiffany's motto is "I will never trade my purity except for financial security." Tiffany, a straight A student, first attended Priddy High (although the name Howe High can be seen in the background) then Northridge Junior College. Her worst day in high school was the day she got a B on a book report on *The Scarlet Letter* ("now I have a B for bad"). At Northridge, she writes for the school newspaper, the *North Ridgeon*.

Tiffany collects money for the homeless ("so they can buy cheap wine"), is on the debate team and is a National Merit Scholar. When she decided she needed to shed her goody-goody image and become bad, Tiffany changed her name to "Toughany," got a Popeye tattoo ("the iron-on kind") and stole a lipstick (Bad Girl Scarlet) from a department store. A day later she returned the lipstick and dropped the image. To get something from Jack, Tiffany does "the pouty lips and Bambi eyes thing." Tiffany is famous for her performance of Juliet in *Romeo and Juliet* at Priddy High and when she needed an athletic credit for her college application, she joined the volleyball team (she wanted the cute red uniform; she wore jersey 17). To get money for a car, Tiffany became a counter girl at the Granny Goodness Ice Cream Parlor. She was also the spokesgirl for Ultra Bank ("Hello, I'm Tiffany Malloy. I'm the face of tomorrow and whatever you've got I can sell"). When a man breaks Tiffany's heart, Jack goes for the rifle in the den. Tiffany has one fear — the closet in the kitchen (when she was young Ryan locked her in and she feared the closet monster would get her. She has been haunted by the incident ever since). In grade school Tiffany acted in *Swan Lake* ("but drowned in the paper water"); she tried twirling a baton (but couldn't catch it once she threw it into the air); and attempted to play the accordion but never did (she looked at her breasts, then into the camera and shook her head "no"). In the last episode, Tiffany's dream came true: she was accepted into Harvard.

Ryan is, in the simplest of terms, naive. He attended the same schools as Tiffany but is far less intelligent. When it comes to girls he is a loser ("Girls find me completely repulsive") and on Saturday nights he watches *Only the Lonely Late Night Theater* on TV. When Ryan is not needed for a particular scene, Jack sends him to other WB shows (via the WB Time Machine) to screw up someone else's life until he is required at home. Ryan appeared with Tiffany on the TV game show *Smart and Stupid Siblings* (where Ryan's ignorance won them the championship). To make money on the Internet, Ryan began a site called "Cyber Sex Tiffany" (www.tiffany-malloy.com) using Tiffany's image without her knowledge. When Ryan was struck by lightning (hiding in a metal garbage can during a thunderstorm), he thought he acquired unique powers and called himself "Lightning Boy." He played Squanto the Indian in his third grade Thanksgiving Pageant and worked at Cali-Burger Dreamin' (where the owner named a burger after Tiffany — "The Tiffalicious Tiffany Burger — The Most Beautiful Burger Named After the Most Beautiful Girl"). When Ryan receives his grades, usually Fs he believes the F stands for phenomenal. To attract girls, Ryan pretends to be something he isn't (for example, dressing as a European and calling himself the count of Monte "Crisco"; everybody thought he looked like Mr. Peanut).

Ross, the youngest member of the family, took on the role of "Mom" when Jennie left (cooking, cleaning, and being referred to as Mom). He is neglected by the family, and while not sent to other WB shows, he is told at the beginning of an episode whether or not he will be needed. (This does not happen to Tiffany because, as Jack says, "We're not crazy; if it were not for Tiffany, the WB would have canceled us long ago.") Jack does little or nothing for Ross (he feels that ignoring him will toughen him up); as Tiffany says about Ross, "You're a sad little man." Ross has been dressed in cheese to catch "the giant rat in the basement," is constantly degraded, but does have one fantasy — "to be hugged by my math teacher, 38 triple D Miss Bushnick." Ross has a pet turtle (Skippy) and claims to know "the secret to attract chicks" (he leaves his dirty bike in the driveway and washes it shirt-less).

124.   Valerie NBC, 1986–1987

Valerie and Michael Hogan (Valerie Harper, Josh Taylor) and their children, David, Willie and Mark (Jason Bateman, Danny Ponce, Jeremy Licht), live at 840 Crescent Drive in Oak Park, Illinois; 555-4656 is their phone number; the family dog is named Murray.

Valerie, middle name Angela (maiden name Varone), is manager of Forman-Lydell Antiques (also called The Forman-Lydell Antiques House); in early episodes, Valerie's job is a bit hazy; she appears to be a designer (for an unnamed company). She was born in Jersey City (New Jersey) and was a member of the Forest Girls as a teenager. She and Michael have been married for 17 years when the series begins. Michael, a pilot for an unnamed airline (based at Chicago O'Hare International Airport), is absent from many episodes (supposedly due to overseas flights). Valerie shops for food at Sanders Market and directs the yearly community theater play. In the opening theme, Valerie wears jersey 18 as she plays football with her family (Michael is jersey 34).

David, 16½, attends Clifton High School. He has a pet turtle (Corkey) and on a dare ("a double dog dare") from a girl he ate a spider. The Deli is his afterschool hangout. Mark and Willie, 13-year-old fraternal twins, attend Lincoln Junior High School. Mark, the studious one, has a pet water dragon (lizard) named Chuck, and has to see a movie from the opening to the closing credits ("Those people work hard; they deserve to be recognized").

"Howdy, Hogans" is the greeting the family receives from next-door neighbor Patty Poole (Edie McClurg), a woman who cares for the Hogans as much as she does for her own family. She has a dog named Casey, vacuums to channel her anger, and is famous for her tuna salad — which contains a secret ingredient — Cool Whip ("It binds the tuna to the salad"). The series ended abruptly when Valerie Harper and the show's producers could not resolve a contract dispute. It was revamped as *Valerie's Family: The Hogans, The Hogans* and finally *The Hogan Family* (which see for further information). *Valerie* episodes have been syndicated as *The Hogan Family*.

125.   **Vinnie and Bobby** Fox, 1992

Vinnie Caulfield Verducci (Matt LeBlanc) and Bobby Grazzo (Robert Torti) are friends who share Apartment 3B at 623 Cypress Avenue in Chicago. Vinnie, a former boxer, and Bobby, a not-too-bright ladies' man, work for the Rand Construction Company. They have been friends since Bobby gave Vinnie the mumps in kindergarten. Bobby also ran over Vinnie's foot when he first learned to drive, gave him poison sumac at Sleepaway

Camp, and tried to fix Vinnie's chipped tooth with Crazy Glue when he broke it. Vinnie attends night classes at Dick Butkus Community College (the only school that would accept him with a D average) and hopes to become a businessman with his name on a door. Vinnie calls his muscles Thunder and Lightning, has a motorcycle (Ruby) and a $500 credit limit on his American Express card.

Bobby is more concerned about his hair and uses the Omni Magnum 2000, "the world's most powerful hair dryer." He has a little black book with girls' names he calls his "chickonary." According to Vinnie, Bobby has been right about only one thing in his whole life: that *Cop Rock* wouldn't last the season. Vinnie and Bobby frequent Martino's Restaurant and pick up girls at Smoke's, a pool hall and bar.

Mona Mullins (Joey Adams) is a beautiful and sensuous 17-year-old girl who lives downstairs and has an unrelenting crush on Vinnie. Vinnie rejects Mona's constant advances because she is underage and the daughter of a man who owns a gun shop. Mona insists that when she turns 18 Vinnie will see her differently and has given him a "Mona Countdown to Heaven Calendar" (the calendar contains bikini poses of Mona and she has circled her eighteenth birthday—"It's our wedding day"). When Mona get upset, she cuts the heads off her Ken dolls.

William "Billy" Melvin Belly (John Pinette) is a jovial, overweight construction worker. His favorite food is pizza and he believes that Hoss Cartwright (*Bonanza*) was the only man on television who knew what to do when the dinner bell rang. Billy greets people with "Hi, I just ate, but I'll be hungry soon." He considers himself an amateur detective (he reads *Shameless Shamus* magazine) and frequents Martino's Pizza Parlor.

126.   What a Dummy Syn., 1990–1991

Buster "Buzz" Brannigan (voice of Loren Freeman) is a wooden ventriloquist's dummy who was part of the vaudeville act "Brannigan and Buzz" during the 1920s. When Jack Brannigan, Buzz's 99-year-old owner, dies, Buzz is inherited by Jack's nephew, Ed Brannigan (David Doty), his wife, Polly (Annabel Armour), and their children, Tucker, Cory and Maggie (Stephen Dorf, Joshua Rudoy, Jeanna Michaels). The Brannigans reside at 912 Lincoln Drive in Secaucus, New Jersey.

Buzz is not your average dummy: he is alive and can talk and is full of wisecracks (he was locked in a trunk for 50 years). Exactly how Buzz came to life is not explained. Buzz first mentioned he was made of redwood; later he says oak (his mother perished from Dutch Elm disease). His first love was Effie Klinker (Edgar Bergen's dummy) but the relationship didn't work: "She was made of mahogany and I was made of oak." Green is Buzz's favorite color; he reads *Variety* and *Turf Today* magazine. His biggest weakness is pepperoni pizza; he can recite the Gettysburg Address in pig Latin and he can't resist a comedic straight line.

Ed and Polly have been married 17 years; their most romantic dates involved horror movies (Polly would get scared and put her arms around Ed). Wednesday is their "whoopie night." Ed owns the Brannigan Seafood Restaurant and wears Beast aftershave. Polly's mother was in labor with her for 22 hours. Polly washes eggs before she uses them "because of where they have been." Spotty is the family's pet goldfish and Marylee is Ed's classic Mustang.

Tucker, the oldest, attends Seabury High School. His middle name is Humphrey and he believes the future is a new breakfast cereal. Tucker claims to have on videotape every movie the Three Stooges made, and he hosted "Talking with Tucker" on the school radio station, WXRB.

Cory, the brightest of the children, attends Daniel Boone Elementary School. He is easily exasperated and Tucker calls him "Dweeb," "Geek," "Nerd" and "Wuss." Margaret "Maggie" Michelle Brannigan is six years old and attends the Daniel Boone School. She eats raw cookie dough, has four dolls (Helen, Mary, Brian and Susan) and is called "the Rock" for her nerves of steel.

127. **Will and Grace** NBC, 1998–

Will Truman (Eric McCormack) and Grace Adler (Debra Messing) are friends. They share Apartment 9C at 155 Riverside Drive in Manhattan. Will is a lawyer and gay; Grace, an interior designer, is straight (although she admits making love to another woman "but it wasn't my thing"). Will, a gourmet cook, attended New York University and is a highly charged negotiator when it comes to money matters. He is controlling and uncompromising and says, "Even if I was straight I wouldn't marry Grace" (Will believes Grace has to be "the star" of her relationship with a boyfriend—"better than he is"). As a kid, Will wanted a cowboy birthday cake, a "Josie and the Pussycats" lunchbox and a red fire truck; but his parents gave him things they thought he would like better (but never did—like a water wiggle slide instead of the fire truck).

The neighborhood cleaner calls Grace "Nice Lady." Grace owns Grace Adler Designs and "is the Susan Lucci of the designer world" says Will (she enters but never wins the decorators Sublime Divine Award). Grace enjoys coffee at Kitty's Coffee Shop; when she gets mad she eats cheesecake; when she gets upset she has a slice of whole wheat bread. Grace shudders when she hears breasts referred to as "boobies" and usually watches whatever show is on when she turns on the TV ("because I'm here and the remote is over there"). Her favorite TV network is Lifetime. She and Will frequent the Mexican eatery Pablo's Contina. Grace hates flavored coffee and clowns ("because they think they're so funny") and sometimes gets overwhelmed by her decorating ideas (which she calls "decorator's rush"). Grace attended Hawthorne High School (she met Will in college) and "had the worst day of my life at Bloomingdale's." She cried a river of tears "when a young girl bumped into me and said 'Excuse me, ma'am'." At the start of the second season (9/21/99), Grace moves across the hall (Apartment 9A) "because I think it will be healthier for the both of us."

Karen Walker (Megan Mullally), Grace's assistant, loves Halloween for the sexy "boobs up and out" costumes she can wear. She has weekly facials at Yolanda's Salon and is self-centered (applying fingernail polish is more important than answering Grace's telephone). She does not know how to work a computer, fax or phone, but she knows people and gets what she wants; she also gets back from lunch in time for dinner. Karen has been married twice; her second husband is rich and she works just to get away from him and the house. When Grace is out of the office "the phone rings and rings," says Karen. "I wish there was someone around here to answer it."

"I'm here and I'm queer. Get used to it" is the oath Jack McFarland (Sean Hayes) "took in front of God and my mother." Jack is a hopeful playwright and is a good friend of Will and Grace. "Halloween," he says, "is the one day that makes the other 364 bearable — that and the Tony Awards." Jack did a one-man show called *Just Jack* and wrote a Caribbean fantasy called *Love Among the Coconuts* (which he changed to *Untitled Jack* when Karen told him his play stinks). He reads *Guy's World* magazine, has a parrot (Guapo) and a dog (Klaus Von Puppy; later called Gus). Jack gets nauseous when he thinks about making love to a woman. Jack believes God is a woman, and he and Grace share a common love of ice skating. Jack was an usher on Broadway for two performances of *Les Miserables* and, as a kid, had a growing-up Skipper doll (hence, "I know all about women"). Jack believes every TV and movie robot is gay. He watches *Star Wars* over and over again, hoping to compile enough information to prove that CP-30 is gay.

128. **Women in Prison** Fox, 1987–1988

Cell Block J of the Bass Women's Prison in Wisconsin is "home" to Vicki Springer (Julia Campbell), a naive, rich and pampered woman who was set up on a shoplifting charge by her husband (theft of a diamond bracelet) and convicted of grand larceny. Vicki can't type or file but she can cross her legs and show a bit of thigh. For this talent, prison warden Cliff Rafferty (Blake Clark), a hotel management major in college, appoints her as his secretary. Cliff believes Vicki is innocent but can't do anything to help her — "If I could do anything, do you think I would be here?" He has problems with guards who want raises, guard dogs that run away and the cook's creole kick. Cliff occupies office 203.

Vicki, voted "most likely to be pictured running naked in slow motion on a beach," held the beauty pageant title "Miss Dairyland" in 1984 and 1985. She believes she is very sexy "and the most attractive woman in captivity" and will allow only her hairdresser, Mr. Joey, to cut her hair. Vicki wears a size 34B bra and a size seven shoe. Her resume lists "soft, mysterious and feminine" as her chief qualifications. Although she can't prepare it in prison, she is famous for her onion dip. Her prison I.D. number is 659142.

Eve Shipley (Peggy Cass), number 00023, is a gun moll serving a life sentence for robbery and murder. She "mowed down" four bank guards and works in the laundry room. As a teenager in the 1940s, Eve claims she was an "It Girl" (sexually appealing to men). Bonnie Harper (Antoinette Byron), number 563478, is a coquettish lesbian arrested for soliciting. She wears a 34C bra, a size seven shoe and a streetwalker-like wardrobe that Vicki says makes her look like "the cheapest little tramp in the world." Bonnie has been assigned to work in the laundry room.

Dawn Murphy (C.C.H. Pounder), number 44720, is the toughest of the women and commands respect through fear (she was convicted of murdering her husband, whom she claimed was abusing her). Her work assignment is the kitchen (each night she sneaks out a sample of the food, blindfolds Eve and asks her to guess what they are having for dinner). Pam Norville (Wendie Jo Sperber), number 51973, is a computer expert arrested for embezzling. Her cell is the most decorative, complete with computer and furnishings (Vicki, Bonnie, Eve and Dawn share a cell).

Meg Brando (Denny Dillon) is the nasty prison guard who delights in tormenting the prisoners, especially Vicki, although she tells her, "If you have any problems don't hesitate to ask me for help. I have a very extensive background in helping women adjust to the problems of institutional life." Fights between inmates in the showers are a constant problem for Meg. She believes there is something in the soap and "I gotta break up fights between naked women. I may not be able to eat with my hands for a week." Meg wanted to join the army "but I have an itchy trigger finger" and she was rejected; hence, Cliff is somewhat reluctant to arm her. Her favorite pastime is to fiddle with the dimmer switch on Death Row.

In the pilot episode, the women had the following I.D. numbers: Vicki, 689055; Eve, 628524; Bonnie, 856095; Dawn, 526482; and Pam, 596085.

129.   The Wonder Years ABC, 1988–1993

Life in the late 1960s and early 1970s is recalled by the voice-over narration of the adult Kevin Arnold (Daniel Stern) but seen through his eyes as a teenager (Fred Savage).

Kevin, his parents Jack and Norma (Dan Lauria, Alley Mills), his sister, Karen (Olivia D'Abo) and brother Wayne (Jason Hervey), live in a suburban home in Anytown, USA. Kevin, born on 3/18/56, attended Hillcrest Grammar School, Robert F. Kennedy Junior High and William McKinley High School. He aspires to become a writer, a center fielder for the San Francisco Giants, or an astronaut. Kevin wears a New York Jets football jacket and keeps a picture of Raquel Welch on his locker door. He was a member of the Kennedy Junior High Glee Club, and a member of the rock band Electric Shoes. The Pizza Barn is his favorite hangout and he receives an allowance of 50 cents a week (1969), $2.50 (1970) and $3.00 (1971). He has a dog (Buster) and he skates at the Moonlight Roller Rink. Kevin worked as a caddy ($20 a game), stock clerk at Harris and Sons Hardware, delivery boy (later waiter) at Chong's Chinese Restaurant, then as a clerk at his father's furniture store.

Gwendolyn "Winnie" Cooper (Danica McKellar) is the pretty girl next door. She likes to read, dance and play tennis. Winnie, a member of the Kennedy Junior High cheerleading team (for the Wildcats), starred in the school's production of *Our Town*. She and Kevin shared their first kiss on the rock in Harper's Woods. In the spring of 1970, Winnie moves to a new home four miles away and enrolls in Lincoln Junior High. In the fall of 1971, Winnie and Kevin are together again when she enrolls at McKinley High. Winnie worked as a lifeguard at the Cascades Resort and Tennis Club during the summer of 1973 (Kevin worked there as a busboy).

Jack, born 11/6/27, served in Korea and is now the manager of distribution and product support services for Norcom Enterprises. He gets up at five in the morning, fights traffic, "busts his hump all day," comes home and pays taxes. He later quits Norcom ("the job is killing me") and opens a furniture store. His Chevrolet Impala license plate reads GPE 385 (later BEQ 326); XDH 975 is the plate of the family's station wagon. They also had an Oldsmobile in 1972 with the plate QGF 846.

Norma keeps the family together. She and Jack married in 1949 and spent their honeymoon in Ocean City. They have lived in their current house (number 516) for 17 years. As a teenager, Norma dreamed of becoming a singer, and was sent to the principal's office for smoking. In 1971, she enrolled in River Community College to improve her secretarial skills (she worked in the attendance room at Kennedy Junior High but was discharged for poor skills); she later works (1973) as a comptroller with Micro Electronics, a computer software company, at $225 a week.

Sixteen-year-old Karen is the typical flower child of the 1960s. She attended the same schools as Kevin and in 1971 (1991 episodes) she enrolled in "McKinley College up north." She returned in 1972, married Michael (David Schwimmer) and moved to Alaska.

Wayne, Kevin's obnoxious older brother, delights in annoying him (he calls Kevin "Butthead"). The only thing he and Kevin ever agreed on was that for Christmas of 1969 they wanted a color TV set (which they didn't get until 1971). After high school, Wayne went to work in the family furniture store.

In the final episode (5/12/93), Kevin and Winnie make a promise to never let their friendship end; it is also learned that Karen is pregnant. These words, spoken by the adult Kevin, close out the series: "Karen's son was born that September ... and Mom, she did well. Businesswoman, board chairman, grandmother ... the Weiner [Wayne] stayed in furniture — wood seemed to suit him; in fact he took over the factory two years later when Dad passed away. Winnie left the next summer to study art history in Paris. Still, we never forgot our promise. We wrote to each other once a week for the next eight years. I was there to meet her when she came home — with my wife and my first son ... Like I said, things never turn out exactly as you planned. Growing up happens in a heartbeat. One day you're in diapers, the next you're gone. But the memories of childhood stay with you for the long haul. I remember a place, a town; a house like a lot of houses; a yard like a lot of other yards on a street like a lot of other streets. And the thing is, after all these years, I still look back with wonder."

130. Zoe, Duncan, Jack and Jane WB, 1999–2000

Zoe, Duncan, Jack and Jane are four close friends who reside in New York City. They attend Fielding High School, hang out at a coffee house called Cafe 'n Pastries in Greenwich Village and frequent the Bleecker Street subway station.

Zoe Bean (Selma Blair) lives in Chelsea (Apartment 16) with her single mother Iris (Mary Page Keller). Zoe has a dog (Wally) and she is sometimes mistaken for Alyssa Milano (rather than disappoint people, she signs autographs in Alyssa's name). When she is between boyfriends, Zoe wears a purple skirt that Jane calls "the available skirt." Zoe considers herself "a sexy

young thing" and has "womanly wily womanly ways." She eats Life cereal
for breakfast and Breyer's fat free ice cream, and considers herself the emotional glue that holds the group together. Zoe feels that her head is a bit too
big for her body and believes her mother dates freaks and deserves better.
Iris asks only one thing of Zoe when a date calls: "Be a nice Zoe." Iris attends
weekly "Divorced and Bitter Wives" meetings and when she shows cleavage
before meeting a date, Zoe pulls up her blouse and tells her to cover up.

Duncan Milch (David Moscow) lives in Chelsea and is the least secure
of the group. He has a butterfly collection and can't stand up to his domineering mother (who clings to him because he is all she has left). He and
Zoe have known each other since babyhood and attended Camp Whip-
poorville during summer vacations. When Duncan felt he needed his own
space, he moved out and into a 15-foot storage facility (number C-15). Duncan has a pigeon (Pigey) and carries a picture of himself with Mayor
McCheese (from McDonald's commercials) in his wallet.

Jack Cooper (Michael Rosenbaum) is an overconfident hustler forever
in search of a fast buck. Jack has a thing for older women and goes out of
his way to impress them (he believes he radiates poise; Zoe believes "Jack is
a disillusioned freak who thinks that every older woman loves him"). Jack
spoke with a British accent for a year "because it was cooler than my own
voice"; he also likes to hear himself speak — "and it doesn't matter what I say."

Jane Cooper (Azura Skye) is Jack's paternal twin. Zoe is her best friend
and she masks her insecurity with deadpan humor and a cool attitude. Jane
believes her shoulders are out of alignment ("I lean a bit to the left").
Although sexy, she studies other girls to see what makes them sexy and copies
what strikes her fancy. As kids she and Jack were sent to vacation in the
South of France. Before each date, Jane and Zoe wear push-up bras — "for
cleavage purposes only," says Zoe. Jane becomes extremely jealous if Zoe
attaches herself to another girl, and changes her personalities to accommo-
date what a guy she is with likes. Overall, Jane is cynical and sour "and that's
what I like about you," says Zoe.

Second season episodes are set three years later and titled "Zoe..." Zoe,
majoring in psychology, Jane, studying to become a photographer, and Jack
attend college. Zoe, who shares Apartment 9H with Jane, is also the manager of the Ching Hi Chinese Restaurant. Duncan works as an internet
designer at American Webnet.

Performer Index

References are to entry numbers.